FIGHT AND FLIGHT

WRITING WALES IN ENGLISH

CREW series of Critical and Scholarly Studies
General Editors: Kirsti Bohata and Daniel G. Williams (*CREW*, Swansea University)

This *CREW* series is dedicated to Emyr Humphreys, a major figure in the literary culture of modern Wales, a founding patron of the *Centre for Research into the English Literature and Language of Wales*. Grateful thanks are due to the late Richard Dynevor for making this series possible.

Other titles in the series
Stephen Knight, *A Hundred Years of Fiction* (978-0-7083-1846-1)
Barbara Prys-Williams, *Twentieth-Century Autobiography* (978-0-7083-1891-1)
Kirsti Bohata, *Postcolonialism Revisited* (978-0-7083-1892-8)
Chris Wigginton, *Modernism from the Margins* (978-0-7083-1927-7)
Linden Peach, *Contemporary Irish and Welsh Women's Fiction* (978-0-7083-1998-7)
Sarah Prescott, *Eighteenth-Century Writing from Wales: Bards and Britons* (978-0-7083-2053-2)
Hywel Dix, *After Raymond Williams: Cultural Materialism and the Break-Up of Britain* (978-0-7083-2153-9)
Matthew Jarvis, *Welsh Environments in Contemporary Welsh Poetry* (978-0-7083-2152-2)
Harri Garrod Roberts, *Embodying Identity: Representations of the Body in Welsh Literature* (978-0-7083-2169-0)
Diane Green, *Emyr Humphreys: A Postcolonial Novelist* (978-0-7083-2217-8)
M. Wynn Thomas, *In the Shadow of the Pulpit: Literature and Nonconformist Wales* (978-0-7083-2225-3)
Linden Peach, *The Fiction of Emyr Humphreys: Contemporary Critical Perspectives* (978-0-7083-2216-1)
Daniel Westover, *R. S. Thomas: A Stylistic Biography* (978-0-7083-2413-4)
Jasmine Donahaye, *Whose People? Wales, Israel, Palestine* (978-0-7083-2483-7)
Judy Kendall, *Edward Thomas: The Origins of His Poetry* (978-0-7083-2403-5)
Damian Walford Davies, *Cartographies of Culture: New Geographies of Welsh Writing in English* (978-0-7083-2476-9)
Daniel G. Williams, *Black Skin, Blue Books: African Americans and Wales 1845–1945* (978-0-7083-1987-1)
Andrew Webb, *Edward Thomas and World Literary Studies: Wales, Anglocentrism and English Literature* (978-0-7083-2622-0)
Alyce von Rothkirch, *J. O. Francis, realist drama and ethics: Culture, place and nation* (978-1-7831-6070-9)
Rhian Barfoot, *Liberating Dylan Thomas: Rescuing a Poet from Psycho-Sexual Servitude* (978-1-7831-6184-3)
Daniel G. Williams, *Wales Unchained: Literature, Politics and Identity in the American Century* (978-1-7831-6212-3)
M. Wynn Thomas, *The Nations of Wales 1890–1914* (978-1-78316-837-8)
Richard McLauchlan, *Saturday's Silence: R. S. Thomas and Paschal Reading* (978-1-7831-6920-7)
Bethan M. Jenkins, *Between Wales and England: Anglophone Welsh Writing of the Eighteenth Century* (978-1-7868-3029-6)

Fight and Flight
Essays on Ron Berry

edited by
Georgia Burdett and Sarah Morse

WRITING WALES IN ENGLISH

UNIVERSITY OF WALES PRESS
2020

© The Contributors, 2020

All rights reserved. No part of this book may be reproduced in any material form (including photocopying or storing it in any medium by electronic means and whether or not transiently or incidentally to some other use of this publication) without the written permission of the copyright owner. Applications for the copyright owner's written permission to reproduce any part of this publication should be addressed to the University of Wales Press, University Registry, King Edward VII Avenue, Cardiff CF10 3NS.

www.uwp.co.uk

British Library CIP Data
A catalogue record for this book is available from the British Library

ISBN   978-1-78683-528-4
eISBN   978-1-78683-529-1

The right of the Contributors to be identified as authors of this work has been asserted in accordance with sections 77 and 79 of the Copyright, Designs and Patents Act 1988.

THE ASSOCIATION FOR
WELSH WRITING IN ENGLISH
CYMDEITHAS LLÊN SAESNEG CYMRU

Typeset in Wales by Eira Fenn Gaunt, Cardiff
Printed by CPI Antony Rowe, Melksham

For Ron
1920–1997
'Boy, inseparable from man in his time, his place'

Ron Berry
Photograph by John Pikoulis

Contents

Series Editors' Preface		ix
Acknowledgements		xi
Abbreviations		xiii
Notes on Contributors		xv
1	Ways Out: Ways In: Ways Back: An introduction *Dai Smith*	1
2	*History Is What You Live:* Ron Berry's Rumination on His Conflicted Life and Times *Barbara Prys-Williams*	13
3	A Man's World: The Short Fiction of Ron Berry *Tony Brown*	29
4	Reading Hector Bebb: Masculinity and Mythic Paradigms in *So Long, Hector Bebb* (1970) *John Perrott Jenkins*	49
5	The Full-Time Amateur: Sport in Ron Berry's South Walian Imagination *Daryl Leeworthy*	69
6	'The Inadequates': Ron Berry and Disability *Georgia Burdett*	91

7	'Green always comes back': Ron Berry's Ecocentric Writing *Sarah Morse*	115
8	Land of My Feathers: Ron Berry and Niall Griffiths on the Wing *Tomos Owen*	141
9	'Word-of-mouth cultures cease in cemeteries' *John Pikoulis*	165

Afterword, by Ron Berry's children	177
Bibliography	181
Index	189

Series Editors' Preface

The aim of this series, since its founding in 2004 by Professor M. Wynn Thomas, is to publish scholarly and critical work by established specialists and younger scholars that reflects the richness and variety of the English-language literature of modern Wales. The studies published so far have amply demonstrated that concepts, models and discourses current in the best contemporary studies can illuminate aspects of Welsh culture, and have also foregrounded the potential of the Welsh example to draw attention to themes that are often neglected or marginalised in anglophone cultural studies. The series defines and explores that which distinguishes Wales's anglophone literature, challenges critics to develop methods and approaches adequate to the task of interpreting Welsh culture, and invites its readers to locate the process of writing Wales in English within comparative and transnational contexts.

Professor Kirsti Bohata and Professor Daniel G. Williams

Founding Editor: Professor M. Wynn Thomas (2004–15)

CREW (*Centre for Research into the English Literature and Language of Wales*)
Swansea University

Acknowledgements

This book is the result of our mutual discovery of Ron Berry during the course of our doctoral research at CREW (the Centre for Research into the English Literature and Language of Wales), Swansea University (2006–15). We are indebted to Professor M. Wynn Thomas for initially introducing us to this much critically-neglected writer, who, it must be said, had much to say in regards to the themes of our respective research fields (disability and landscape), piquing our interest from the outset.

During our time working as executive officers at the Learned Society of Wales (2014–16), the topic of many of our conversations in our broom-cupboard office was 'Ron' – as we (and many others in our field) always, with a curious level of intimacy, refer to him. His name was dropped time and time again at AWWE (the Association for Welsh Writing in English) annual conferences as a figure ahead of his time, a painfully-astute cultural observer. But where was the criticism on Berry? It certainly did not exist collectively, in any way that would pay due credence to the myriad perspectives that people had on the man, his writing, and indeed his legacy. Something needed to be done, and in the summer of 2018 we took it upon ourselves (somewhat hurriedly) to 'rally the troops' and remedy the situation just in time for his centenary in 2020. We take full responsibility for any errors made in haste, but it really was a case of now or never.

We are beyond grateful to all of our contributors, some of whom have been ungraciously disturbed in their retirement and asked (begged) to revise material from the 1970s onwards, in our quest to give the fullest account of Berry possible by those who knew him personally.

Professor Dai Smith responded with great enthusiasm in support of the volume, and in the process of writing his brilliant introduction unearthed some undiscovered letters to him from Berry, so that, true to form, Berry defies any easy containment. Dr John Pikoulis very kindly offered us incredible personal photographs of Berry, one of which has made it into the final volume. We are also delighted to be able to present unseen material from new and emerging scholars.

Our gratitude also to Professor Kirsti Bohata and Professor Daniel G. Williams for accepting our proposal for this volume, and to the staff at the University of Wales Press for their support and guidance. We very much value CREW's continuing support for our work as independent scholars.

For granting permissions to use quotations in this collection, we are grateful to the Berry family; to Gomer Press for the use of quotations from *The Collected Short Stories*, *History is What You Live*, *Peregrine Watching*, and *This Bygone;* and to the Library of Wales and Parthian Books for the use of quotations from *So Long Hector Bebb*. We would also like to thank Gwen Davies at *New Welsh Review* for allowing us to reprint in full 'Word-of-Mouth Cultures Cease in Cemeteries'.

We greatly appreciate the full support of Ron's family, Lesley, Simone, Rod, Maggie and Conrad, through all stages of the compilation and editorial process, and are delighted to be able to offer an 'afterword' composed by them as a tribute to Ron, his insight and influence.

Thank you to our families and friends who have had to endure us while we put this volume together. Special thanks to our colleagues in the real and virtual CREW community: Kieron Smith, Clare Davies, Anthony Howell, Gareth Evans, Cath Beard and Daryl Leeworthy, for the heated debates and the beers.

Finally, this volume is dedicated to Ron. We like to imagine that you would be very vocally dismissive, but secretly pleased about it. We hope that this is just the start of Berry scholarship.

Georgia Burdett and Sarah Morse
January 2020

Abbreviations

CS	Simon Baker (ed.), *Ron Berry: Collected Stories* (Llandysul: Gomer, 2000)
FS	Ron Berry, *Flame and Slag* (London: W. H. Allen, 1968)
HH	Ron Berry, *Hunters and Hunted* (London: Hutchinson, 1960)
HWYL	Ron Berry, *History Is What You Live* (Llandysul: Gomer, 1998)
PW	Ron Berry, *Peregrine Watching* (Llandysul: Gomer, 1987)
SLHB	Ron Berry, *So Long, Hector Bebb* (Cardigan: Parthian, Library of Wales Series, 2006)
TB	Ron Berry, *This Bygone* (Llandysul: Gomer, 1996)
FTA	Ron Berry, *The Full-Time Amateur* (London: W. H. Allen, 1966)

Notes on Contributors

Tony Brown is Emeritus Professor of English at Bangor University, where he is also co-director of the R. S. Thomas Research Centre at Bangor. The founding editor of *Welsh Writing in English: A Yearbook of Critical Essays* (1995–2007), he has lectured and published widely on Welsh writing in English, especially on the work of R. S. Thomas and Glyn Jones. He is currently completing a book on the English-language short story in Wales.

Georgia Burdett completed her doctorate on representations of disability in contemporary Welsh writing in English at Swansea University. She is a self-employed tutor and therapist for children with autism in Powys, and her reviews and articles have appeared in *Planet: The Welsh Internationalist*.

Daryl Leeworthy is a writer and historian. His most recent book, *A Little Gay History of Wales*, was published by UWP in 2019, and his biography of the screenwriter and feminist icon Elaine Morgan is published by Seren in 2020.

Sarah Morse was introduced to Ron Berry's work by the Library of Wales series. She completed a PhD on the representations of landscape and the environment in the work of Gwyn Thomas and Ron Berry in 2010. A Senior Executive Officer at the Learned Society of Wales since 2011, she is also currently Chair of Seren Books / Poetry Wales Press.

Tomos Owen is a lecturer in English Literature in the School of English, Communication and Philosophy at Cardiff University. His research focuses principally on the literatures of Wales and on modern and contemporary writing. He has published on topics including London-Welsh literary culture and industrial fiction, and on authors including Amy Dillwyn, Caradoc Evans, Arthur Machen and Dylan Thomas.

John Perrott Jenkins followed a career in teaching and publishing on English and American Literature with a PhD on the Welsh industrial novel. His interest in how cultural assumptions contribute to shaping gender identity in the anglophone Welsh novel have informed his forthcoming article on Menna Gallie's novel *Strike for a Kingdom*, and he is currently preparing a study of representations of masculinity in Valleys fiction.

John Pikoulis was Senior Lecturer in English Literature in Cardiff University until 2006. He is the author of *Alun Lewis: A Life*, and the critical study of Lewis's life and work, *Alun, Gweno and Freda*. He was long-term chair of the Universities of Wales Association for the study of Welsh Writing in English until 2002, and co-chair of Academi (later Literature Wales), as well as chair of the Board of the *New Welsh Review*.

Barbara Prys-Williams grew up in the Amman Valley when it was a thriving coal-mining community. An early student at CREW, she gained a PhD in 2002; her thesis on twentieth-century Welsh autobiography written in English was subsequently published in UWP's Writing Wales in English series.

Dai Smith first met Ron Berry in 1979. He has written and broadcast extensively since the 1960s about the history, the culture and the society of south Wales. He was Chair of Arts Council Wales from 2006 to 2016. His novel *The Crossing* will be published in 2020.

1

Ways Out: Ways In: Ways Back:
An Introduction

Dai Smith

He dealt the pay clerk a wristy backhander across the mouth. Inside the office, the portly cashier strutted about-turn like a bantam cock.
'Lloyd! What on earth . . . Clear off! Go away from there!'
Pushing his head through the pay hatch, 'Gabe,' he said, 'the name's Gabe Lloyd. This isn't the first time I've been robbed by you clever bastards. My water allowance, fifty pence a shift [. . .] My money, I want it today, *now*.'
The cashier plucked out a fountain-pen. He sloped his jowly head over the ledger. 'Petty cash,' he ordered the clerk, who sorted £2.50 in coins and slid them across the hatch counter. Pen wagging, the cashier vowed a priestly edict, 'Lloyd, you will be sorry.'
'Very nice of you,' said Gabe. 'He isn't the first mammy's boy I've slapped across the chops. You sods fiddling in this office, you'd rise the bile in any man. You know sweet fuck all about what it's like down under [. . .] The pair of you couldn't fill enough coal to cook a dinner.' Gabe turned to the pay queue [. . .] Gabe rattled the stack of coins from hand to hand, 'These office blokes, they've never filled a dram, never cleared a top hole, they couldn't pack a waste or a cog, they've never cut up a rib face, they'd be smothered in diarrhoea working a low seam [. . .] How they going to *think* like us, ah?'[1]

To read Ron Berry (1920–97) for the first time is to invite a 'wristy backhander' across the chops of anyone daft or 'twp' enough to be complacent about the conscious intent of the writer or indifferent to the accusatory nature of his subject matter. The latter was, almost exclusively, and in diminishing circles of place, the south Wales coalfield, the Rhondda valleys, the topmost settlements of Rhondda Fawr and an enfolding, unfolded landscape, then and now. Berry dealt with all the travails of that place's fabulous twentieth-century history by means of individual witnessing:

> Gabe walked home, thinking, I'm different from my father. Different from my grandfather. They believed in the rank and file. I say, never mind about the rank and file. It's all mouth, always was, always will be. This life is for me, mine to do as I want with it.[2]

In his writing, Berry recounted everything that he saw and knew at first hand but did so, almost uniquely, without resorting to the literary clichés or sociological solecisms trotted out by any insider sentimentalism or outsider observation. Yet his fearless witnesses, his Gabes – 'It's me, first, second and last' – are never the free agents they yearn or claim to be.

Berry knew this, too, even as he breathed the life of defiance into his characters. They may be, often literally, crushed materially and discarded culturally, or redeemed, fleetingly, by mutual love, but they are, always, given an identity bigger than their sole existence by the framing of their distinctive society, landscape and mindscape both. As in so many ways increasingly apparent to us from his work, and as this revelatory book of essays underlines, Ron Berry went to the heart of universal matter from the beat of his specific place and time. He found *ways out*, some answers, by delving so deeply into questions, *ways in*, and now speaks to the concerns of our time and place more clearly and insistently, *ways back*, than he was ever heard, for the most part anyway, in his lifetime.

Not that relative disregard seemed, when he first came to public notice with the appearance of his debut novel, *Hunters and Hunted*, in 1960, to be his likely fate. After all, he was another welcome working-class writer, a really authentic one this time, and with his own very contemporary working-class truculence. There was, from the late 1950s on, a conveyor belt of British post-war novelists setting out to reveal the disillusioned history of a welfare world. And a number of them went on, via the stage and films and television, to a modicum of worldly success and the kudos of fame. Ron Berry, along with Sillitoe and Braine and Delaney and Wesker and Storey and Barstow, had all that, but so briefly that it scarcely registered, and after 1970 there was not another novel until his final one, *This Bygone*, in 1996.

An Introduction

So why the gap? It was certainly not because he was not writing. He wrote incessantly, on and on, as the bundles and bundles of unpublished novels and memoirs and non-fiction testify in the archive of his work, which is now deposited at Swansea University. So, to put it another way, why the neglect? Some of the speculations in this current volume point to the wilful ignorance of 'metropolitan' critics and London publishing houses. If so, it was not a lack of interest or even respect from which he alone suffered. With very few exceptions, then or now, writers with specifically Welsh material attract limited attention beyond Wales, whilst within Wales in his lifetime publishing opportunities were few and those that were available were largely for his stories, with the novels entirely spurned. Why? The answer is that neither his content nor his style matched, for the outside world, either time-worn expectations or changing contemporary fashion, whilst, on his own patch, and never one to compromise, he was decidedly, and vocally, a literary enemy of the 'Anglo-Welsh' and a quizzical scorner of national parochialism in all its myriad forms.

In the mid-1990s, his last decade, Berry sent a number of publishers, in and out of Wales, the typescript of *This Bygone*, to no avail. Then Mairwen Prys Jones, a perceptive editor at Gomer Press, accepted it at the end of 1995 and pressed for a production grant from Arts Council Wales. Two anonymous readers, puzzled or half-hearted, could not wholly recommend it. There was to be one last throw of the dice. I was asked to be the Third Reader (anon.) and, in early 1996, having read my two predecessors' squirmingly uneasy views I sent in my two pages' worth. This, slightly redacted here, is what I wrote:

This Bygone

> I have no doubt this novel deserves a production grant and subsequent publication. It is a major, late work by a novelist who has always made demands on his readers – in part because his themes sit so uneasily within the 'Anglo-Welsh' literary canon. Clearly, and not merely because it is the name at the end of the typescript, this is Ron Berry through and through – and, therefore, it does indeed have some of the 'faults' of authorial intrusion, and an elided, testing prose narration to place alongside the direct colloquial speech of his characters. In another way, this is to say that it is a novel of reflection in thought as well as in representation. The story of Dewi Joshua, his mother Zena and his two loves, Elsie and Greta, is a counterpoint to an assumed History. The

details of that history, from mid-1930s to later 1940s in south Wales, flit by like a newsreel.

It is not that they are unimportant for many in the novel; Elsie dies in a freak German air raid, she and others are directly affected by that accurately observed, clichéd, March of Time. It is more that the cliché is exposed as a distant, unwanted rumble and that the texture of actual life (food, sex, clothes, local corruption in business and in politics, landscape and weather) is depicted as the real stuff of existence. This may, in some ultimate scheme of things, be questioned but the passion of Berry's viewpoint reeks with authenticity. For this reason alone the work (almost as autobiography – in fiction) is without peer in contemporary Welsh writing. Nothing is false. Nothing rings phoney. Nothing is book-derived.

In my view this is Ron Berry telling us, as he did in *Hunters and Hunted* for the early 1960s, that most of the life of miners, and their societies and their lovers and their wives, is about being cursed or blessed with elemental drives within the specific historical context of industrial Wales. Here, he insists it was like that even in the now mythical 1930s. The story he tells has power, drive and interest in and for itself, but what makes it special is the brilliant account of work underground as Dewi progresses from collier's boy (he marries Llew's widow, Elsie) to collier to small mine-owner as nationalisation and the winter's snow arrive together in 1947. I know of no writing about work as experienced underground that touches this. This is written as if Orwell was more than an observer or if Lawrence had actually wielded a pick instead of pen. In the context of the novel it offers the illumination of the integrated nature of that work and these lives in that Bygone. And the end is the bitter-sweet pregnancy of Greta as south Wales senses a new (false) start.

If an Arts Council stands for anything it should stand for supporting an achieved writer who can link us all up to threads of literature that have been frayed as surely as their material platforms have been set adrift. I understand, to an extent, the commercial reservations of the other two readers, but to turn one on his or her head it would be a foolish publisher who did not take on such a bravura mining novel at this stage of the lives of both that south Wales and that writer. No novel like this one will be written in the future and I strongly urge you to support its publication.

Now, at the very end of his life Ron Berry did receive the fuller critical recognition he deserved. John Pikoulis's magnificent feature article on the novel for *New Welsh Review*, herein revised and reprinted, was an advance standard-bearer for a new generation who would begin

AN INTRODUCTION

to discern how his originality of style matched the depth of his purpose. It was not as if he had not been telling us already. At BBC Wales I had commissioned a thirty-minute documentary about Ron in the *Read All About Us* series in October 1996, and way before that, in June of 1990, I had done a half-hour interview with him on Radio Wales's *First Hand* arts programme. I could also look back down the years, via my essay 'A Novel History' in 1986, to the profile I had written, as its Arts Editor, of Ron for the fortnightly *Arcade* in 1980, and in which magazine his superb piece on 'Peregrine Watching' shortly appeared. I can say then, without any doubt, that he knew how much he was appreciated by those whose views he trusted, and none more so than his great boon friend, Alun Richards, who worked so hard over a number of years to see the autobiography, *History Is What You Live*, posthumously published in 1998. Ron was, too, deeply appreciative of the sensitive, pioneering work Simon Baker was doing in his lifetime to compile and introduce the *Collected Stories*, which came out in 2000. This was a tide turning at the ebb, and more was to set it to a rise when *So Long, Hector Bebb* became the very first novel, with a three-cheers 'Foreword' from the admiring Niall Griffiths, to spearhead the *Library of Wales* series in 2006.

If Ron was truly set before us to read again we needed to hear, too, what he had, often reluctantly, reflected himself as to his prolific output and its meagre antecedents. For the latter he acknowledged no native tradition, since he had read nothing, and never did, of such as Jack Jones or Lewis Jones or Gwyn Jones, and had no stomach, as he sourly opined, for Emyr Humphreys's 'tidy sticking plaster' prose or 'the straightforwardness of Raymond Williams', which prevented any extended reading. Instead, there was this confession-cum-boast from the radio interview I had with him in 1990:

> I was an omnivore [from the age of 16, after the end of his education]. I read everything [. . .] from the Ystrad [Workingmen's] Library and the public libraries. I remember picking up Walt Whitman from the shelves when I was seventeen. That was a revelation, never seen anything like that before [and he quoted Whitman all his life thereafter] [. . .] My influences were American authors, English authors [Miller, Faulkner, Algren, Hemingway, Caldwell, Fitzgerald, Patchen, but also D. H. Lawrence, Waugh and Giono, all these and others later, especially Cormac McCarthy, often referenced by him] [. . .] they certainly weren't Anglo-Welsh in the traditional manner. I had no touch with them, no contact.[3]

Except, of course, with Gwyn Thomas. And therein, I believe, lies the biggest clue to the enigma of Ron Berry. He insisted, of course, that the older Rhondda writer (b.1913) had no direct knowledge of the 'muck' and toil which had been his own, more common lot in life, and that Gwyn Thomas had created a different 'reality' from the one lived by most twentieth-century Rhonddaites. Yet, that was exactly it, the very thing he recognised in himself, one also 'foul-hooked by language', the fact that Gwyn 'had made gold out of dross'. He was, said his knowing admirer, 'one of the greatest . . . we all owe something to Gwyn'. The 'something' was language itself: as a way of transmuting the commonplace of handed-down existence so that it served as a frame for the more significant reality of dreams. Such dreams were about the consciousness to be angry, the desire to be expressive, the aspiration to be free, the understanding of bonds, those that tethered us fast and the liberating ones of freely given loyalty and love.

This tension was all held within the entrammelled personality of the man himself, as Barbara Prys-Williams forensically analyses it in her essay 'Ron Berry's Rumination on His Conflicted Life and Times': complex and obdurate, rooted and evanescent, and, as I can testify, wary as well as welcoming, feisty and inquisitive. Just look at the superbly evocative head and shoulders watercolour by his friend Jim 'Chunks' Lewis on the cover of the *Collected Stories* – lips tightly pursed, head cocked to the side, one eye hidden, the other fixed and unrelenting in its gaze. What you think you may be getting is not quite what he may be seeing.

That is to say, any more than his lived-in Rhondda is the same as the Rhondda he entered and left through the mind. This inner Rhondda is one conjured up to yield its meaning, rather more than its mores, by the razzle-dazzle of language he had alchemised to employ for shamanistic effect. The prose he thereby invented has been, like Thomas Hardy's flirtation between the demotic and the dictionary, off-putting, unsettling to readers unaccustomed to literary neologisms being scattered amongst vernacular dialect studded with rococo adjectives, or by baroque nouns, themselves missing the definite or even indefinite article, turned into participles shouldering aside the clarity of verbs. When I talked to him in 1990 of the social and political and economic paraphernalia of the Rhondda of his growing up, of the interwar years, its history of fact and legend, he shrugged with indifference at a historian's hungry interest. It was not, though lived through, what held him in any kind of thrall. He moved the conversation on, and simply said: 'I've been obsessed with language, and it's been crucifying sometimes, and sometimes it's a kind of ecstasy. That's what I look for still in writing – the use of language.'

His subsequent usage was, through fractured syntax and staccato dialogue, incantatory and hypnotic. What he was doing with language, however, was finding a means – one not marred by the rhetorical inflation of the melodramatic, the romantic or the epic, or diminished by the coy sentimentality of kitchen-sink historical fiction – of capturing the intimate feel and the passing uniqueness of one of the world's most significant industrial communities. Now gone entirely, as he knew it and saw it, and of which he was the most profound remembrancer: in John Pikoulis's apt phrase, 'the poet-laureate of the south Wales that was'. Ron Berry himself was acutely aware of how much of the 'evidence', his term for that individual ingestion of the history which lived you, was deep inside him, and that to make it outwardly known he had to 'crystallise' it, his descriptor, into books. That did not mean any kind of documenting of the public and linear narrative of strikes and hunger marches, of pit disasters and wage settlements, of Labour governments and Aberfan, of pit closures and consumerism, of sacrifice and hedonism, of the decline of religion and the seep of economic decline. Instead, all of that received history is folded, often to brilliant structural effect, into the lives of the heroic and the bullies, and the victims and the survivors, whose singular raw material as individual receptacles for the visitations of wider events and social change we are made to perceive as both holistic and fractured. Thus, in Daryl Leeworthy's concentration on the individual release offered by sport in this working-class world – cycling and soccer in this case, not the rugby of grammar schoolboys – it is, also, to the way in which Ron Berry's capitalised 'South Walian imagination' dealt with 'economic and social change', his central themes, insists Leeworthy, that we are directed. The essay's historically attuned emphasis, to the fiction as well as the life experience, astutely restores human agency to both individuals and society – hunters and hunted.

It transpires, the more we look past the bloody-minded, self-directed, fuck-you attitudes of his (largely) masculine characters, that everywhere, in the novels and especially in the stories, we are set to be disorientated by the dynamics of relationships which are more dialectical than contradictory. Tony Brown looks at the short fiction in his masterly 'A Man's World', which rightly stresses that the overwhelming human focus of the stories is on the life of working men, in the pit, down the pub, at war or at play, but, too, that the stoicism of these lives is compounded by a fierce, self-defeating rebuttal of all that the 'poxy' world can throw at them. As time passes it brings on a narrowness of outlook as to believable possibilities, whether social or political, that leads to unease, almost anguish, yet somehow cannot be avoided. It is the 'evidence', Ron Berry would say, which must be assayed against any fool's gold that might still be panned. Again, language is his testing instrument: one moment Berry is vigorously colloquial, the next he adopts a much more formal register.

Georgia Burdett's essay, on Ron Berry's self-isolation as the ultimate insider/outsider, daringly uses, as a provocative counterpoint to his authority as a full participant, his own physical disability in order to align him with others whose bodies, wounded or 'crippled' or disabled, prevented their holding any of the Rhondda's assigned archetypal roles. Instead, like him, they discover disability to be another form of witness. Such a switch, from destiny to action and back to fate, is at the core of his so-called boxing novel, *So Long, Hector Bebb*. A detailed account of the 'fight game' and its actors, a sort of Rhondda meets the Bronx, a whirling fury of narrative pace and broken hearts and bones, is paralleled by Hector Bebb's removal from the valley (civilisation) and immersion in a timeless landscape (death). John Perrott Jenkins has examined the drafts and re-drafts of this seminal novel to establish the writer's craft in finding an 'architectural design' to build and then undermine his teetering literary monument to the induced flaws of 'hypermasculinity'. This is an essay, quite unimaginable in the language of its own critical discourse when the novel itself was published in 1970, which shadow-boxes its prey with nominal feints and textual allusions to produce a bout of intriguing, anthropological and cultural resonance. Once again, this time with bells and whistles attached, we also see how Ron Berry enriches the 'parameters of realism' within which he first finds his way, and then moves out and on towards 'mythic patterns and trajectories'.

It would be too glib to conclude by asserting that these stunning essays, as a whole, give us a Ron Berry who, as a writer, was clearly ahead of the expectations of his own time. Nonetheless, what his mind saw and his heart felt, as an industrial world was battered out of its known shape, can only be described as visionary. Everywhere in his work are new viewpoints, new questions and fresh perspectives. It is the bird's eye view which Tomos Owen attributes to him in an essay that overturns the anthropocentric assumptions he had come to mistrust. 'Land of My Feathers' really does give wing to Ron Berry's alert and swooping intellect, soaring above the valley settlements, literally and metaphorically, to comprehend a natural world before humans made another to inhabit, and then set out to destroy that one, too.

I have long felt that the sharpest viewpoint to account for Ron Berry, the man and the writer, would be the one which focused on the huddle of Blaencwm (or the more orthographically correct Blaen-y-cwm, a typical shift) set, with its own birthing pit, beneath the mountainous overlordship of Pen Pych at the cul-de-sac end of a valley whose populous, urban sprawl to the south had already brought the Rhondda, through its economic power and its riotous statements of social intent, to worldwide attention by the time of his birth. The Rhondda was, other than Cardiff, the most populated urban area in Wales then, with around 170,000 people at its 1924 peak. However, to a discerning eye and with a native eye for localised distinctiveness, it was never all of one piece. Where Berry grew up, in Blaencwm, it was of the valley, and yet was not the valley: 'In 1920 the village had one pit, a drift mine, one hundred and seventy-two homes, a grocery/post office, sweetshop, two chapels, and a pub.' Here, in Blaencwm, was, readily to hand and all around, a more primeval past, its geological evidence and antediluvian shapes dovetailed into the bare semblance of a modern world. In this spatial and temporal sense, the Blaenddu (Blaencwm) of his fiction was indeed not as time-bound or socially structured as nearby Tosteg (Treorchy), and Ron instinctively preferred the one to the other, though he imaginatively reached out both ways. And he stayed close, inside the valley's dualistic, cheek-by-jowl historical formations, even as the primary reason for the original settlements was disappearing, until to his never-ending horror, as if giving ironic echo to man's underground depredations, the closure of a world of work was capped by the above-ground destruction of the natural habitat. From early to late on in this unthinking process of despoliation, again as the invaluable archive reveals, Ron Berry was an environmental activist, nigh on an eco-warrior, who railed and raged against the 'contoured and conifered' landscape which the peddlers of profit and philistinism brought to the valley, *his* particular part of the valley, worst of all, from the 1960s to the present day. A blanketing death-pall of pine afforestation, 'the largest urban forest' in western Europe, blocked out the light, blighted the habitat of animals, denied open access, destroyed pathways to beauty and contemplation, and altered the 'dialectic of man and his environment' once again, as Sarah Morse fully demonstrates and details with her scholarship and a moral passion to match that of his own ecocentric writing in her essay, '"Green always comes back": Ron Berry's Ecocentric Writing'.

A century on from his birth the significance of Ron Berry's full achievement has, at last, and for sure with this volume of essays, been acknowledged, dissected and valued. Hats were tipped to him in his lifetime, for his resolute courage as a man and as a writer, but nothing like this present acclaim from essayists adept in psycho-biography, in historiographical context, in the probing of literary criticism and the cultural scope of anthropology. Ron Berry would have raised a rather daunting eyebrow at a great deal of the above, but he would have followed it up with his grimace of a grin. 'About time, too', he might have thought, if not said.

And yet, in case any of us care to think that we have had anything remotely like the final word on this remarkable writer, Berry has asked me to give him the last word. I mean, literally so, for as I came to the end of writing this introduction and replacing on my shelves the books I had been consulting, from the pages of his masterpiece *Flame and Slag* (1968), an envelope containing a handwritten letter, from Ron to me, fluttered on to my desk. It had somehow escaped my attention, probably because of its hiding place in the book, when I had assembled selected letters between Ron, Alun Richards and myself, for my *In The Frame* in 2010. The essay of mine to which he refers, and in which he and Gwyn Thomas featured prominently, was 'A Novel History'. Here (more or less) is that letter:

15th Jan '86

Dear Dai,

First, thanks for the Xmas card, and then the essay. Being the product of genes [. . .] no other cross available, we're all jigged by coincidence. According to a programme about cells on telly last night, it's called gastrolation i.e. 'in the beginning'. More important, for everybody, than falling in love, the imprimatur before birth, becoming history via death, even death itself integrated, warranted prefix. And bank on science to pacify the mind. Maybe mine (mind) is the wrong shape. I balked a bit [as] to your theory about how Gwyn Thomas came to write the way he did. It's too dangerous to hunt causes and effects. Gwyn clicked on magic. Cultivating magic (his aesthetic), he was stuck with it. He might have, to our loss, remained stuck on the novel he failed to publish, had Gollancz *published it (<u>Sorrow For Thy Sons</u>, 1936), or anyhow stuck with the form, the style, that way of expressing Gwyn Thomas, there being no other.*

Likewise, impossible, isn't it, for me to believe <u>Flame and Slag</u> would contribute towards the making of a case. Old Glyn Jones, long-head on the Anglo-Welsh pasture, built his pros and cons for <u>The Dragon</u> book, leaving a seethe of would-be-disciples peddling cribbed arcana in <u>The Anglo-Welsh Review</u>, the detritus back-boning just about every damn thing written by Welsh men/ women who see themselves as 'creative'. The AIDS of nationhood.

Best Wishes
Yours,
Ron

Notes

[1] 'The Old Black Pasture' (1996), in Simon Baker (ed.), Ron Berry: Collected Stories (Llandysul: Gomer, 2000).
[2] 'The Old Black Pasture' (1996), in Baker (ed.), Ron Berry: Collected Stories.
[3] The interview with Berry was conducted for the Radio Wales arts programme Firsthand, in 1990; there is no hard copy.

2

HISTORY IS WHAT YOU LIVE: RON BERRY'S RUMINATION ON HIS CONFLICTED LIFE AND TIMES

Barbara Prys-Williams

Most satisfying autobiographies deliver in two important ways: being both explicit records of a process of illumination whereby a writer has come to self-knowledge, and a vivid revelation of the particularity of the writer's identity that can be grasped and understood by the reader. In *History Is What You Live*,[1] Ron Berry's quirky idiosyncrasy sparks out from the first page with energy that threatens to short-circuit. Overall he communicates distress, puzzlement, some fiercely partisan judgements and much celebration. Certainly, too, Berry seeks to understand his baffling self, writing with candour of much that is painful to record and tracing what he sees as discernible trends and pivotal events in his formation. Yet some important detecting and interpreting of pattern is left to the reader. One feels, simultaneously, a considerable resistance in Berry to psychological explanations of his areas of dysfunction, combined with a yearning both to understand and to be understood. Uneven though it is, the self-scrutiny of this touching, obdurate, complex man makes rewarding reading.

Rarely has there been an autobiographer more deeply fascinated by the differences between human beings or more prone to tease out the nature of his own identity through evaluation and implicit measuring against others. However, there is an important area of non-disclosure; Berry takes an impish delight in signalling (and emphasising through italics) some ten pages before the end of *History Is What You Live*, that he is 'married with . . . children' (*HWYL*, 136), not earlier or further mentioned in any way, apart from in his dedication of the work. From his own assessment, Berry was a man of proven prickly temperament. He may have feared that a more intimate account of family life might have involved the exposure of living people to possibly unflattering public scrutiny.

History Is What You Live was published in 1998, the year after Berry's death. Probably, from various dating in the text (most usefully and explicitly on p. 97), the writing and redrafting was spread over nearly a decade, the final one of his life, that saw the virtual demise of the coal industry in south Wales. Part of his intention is to act as elegist to a vanished people and way of life. The historical background contributes vitally to Berry's implicitly explored and hard-won values system. 'Everything passes', Berry seems to be saying, 'but let's celebrate what we have known'. The themes stated, modulated, recapitulated and built to a climax in the final pages are evanescence and loss. Conceptually, the landscape around the village of Blaencwm in the Rhondda, particularly its mountains, is the organising framework of the book. Berry's exact and vividly visual memory imbues that landscape with often poignant meaning: one feels his urgency to record what only he in his uniqueness can know, before the recalling, perceiving and connecting mind and feeling response that is Ron Berry is snuffed out. There is, too, a fervid eagerness and a baffled need to record, as tellingly as he knows how, what it feels like to be him. Olney posits, in his fascinating *Metaphors of Self* , that in the autobiographical process: 'One cannot hope [. . .] to capture with a straight-on look, or expect to transmit directly to another one's own sense of the self; at most one may be able to discover a similitude, a metaphor for the feeling of selfhood.'[2] Berry's metaphors of self are often telling, sometimes revealing a sense of spiritual and emotional hunger amounting to starvation. There is a feeling that, whatever he knows himself to be – cranky, wilful, obdurate – it is because, with his genetic endowment, in his particular historic time and environment, he can be no other, if he is to assuage his voracious longing for genuine experience that may, in the end, feed him.

Berry wants the reader to understand and become part of the process of change and loss that he mourns. We accompany him to different spots in and around Blaencwm and its surrounding mountains at different times in his growing up and adult life. We feel something of the inevitability of change as he describes the petrified mussels, dating, he declares, from 250,000,000 BC, which were found on the slag heap of Tŷ Draw colliery, now a grassed-over part of Graig y Ddelw (*HWYL*, 30). He interprets his habitat in an imaginative and loving way, so that we can see its value through his eyes. We come to understand the richness (and the violence) of the mining culture. As Berry lists the range of skills painstakingly imparted to children, the sense of the diversity of talents in the community is conveyed, as well as the affectionate involvement that the transmission of know-how represents: 'Learning takes time and time again' (*HWYL*, 46).

We experience the feelings and memories called forth in Berry by so much that is, at first sight, mundane in his environment, and feel that he possesses the landscape through those memories. Follow any linear course and it will yield significance. There is the tunnel where Grandmother Berry's first husband was killed; the cutting beyond where violets and early catkins could be found; the spot where the best willow twigs, for making whistles, grew; the hollow oak where early sexual adventures are remembered; the railway footbridge from which gentle and generous Percy Prior, one of Berry's early mining 'butties', committed suicide when suffering from 100 per cent dust (*HWYL*, 40–1). Time and again Berry wanders in memory the mountain tops that hem in Blaencwm – Graig y Ddelw, Mynydd Tŷ Isaf, Cefn Nant y Gwair and Pen Pych – musing on their different delights. He trains us to see the meaning of different landmarks: what seems mountain is often grassed-over slag heap, 'herring-boned with huge drainage ditches since Aberfan's tragedy shook the bowels of absent experts' (*HWYL*, 30). He evokes the delight he felt as a boy on Pen Pych: 'Wheatear territory this, since time stood still' where one might also see 'planing skylarks' and 'mock-crippled pipits flopping between tussocks' (*HWYL*, 31). He mourns that his grandchildren will never experience these joys because of the environmental vandalism of the Forestry Commission, which has planted dark sitkas along all the tops – ousting such enduring life as 'hardwoods older than Cardiff city [. . .] whinberry ledges, ivied buttresses [. . .] The leavings of prehistory sacrificed to Mammon masked as a quango' (*HWYL*, 29, 31). His habitat is altered beyond recognition.

He recreates the feel of Blaencwm when the Rhondda was a single-industry, thriving valley, commemorating all that he knew of the suffering and endurance of the small but typical cross-section of the mining fraternity he worked with at the Graig level. As a secular requiem, he intones the names of many of the dead friends who worked with him there, and the nature of their dying: rheumatic fever, dust, accident, TB (*HWYL*, 41–3). He muses on what he learnt of the variousness of human nature as the junior in the close butty relationship: Sid, a stingy payer, who 'had the one-way mind of a ratting terrier and the twpness' (*HWYL*, 55); 'the most insular year of my life' with open-handed Percy Prior, 'whose entire self was given to coal. Foolishness everything else . . . What I learned from him was *doing*' (*HWYL*, 62–3); sociable Jimmy Shanklin, fun to be with, yet whose careless shoring caused Berry's first accident (*HWYL*, 56–7); on machine cutting with club-footed Eddie Jones Cochyn, with whom he came 'near to feeling inseparable from mining for the rest of my bread-winning days [. . .] Native born slot fit . . . *Humanitas Jerboa*' (*HWYL*, 67–70). The macho code of the Rhondda inflicted extra hardships: 'For two years I carried a burning sore on the small of my back. Healing scabs were knocked off . . . Boys were not allowed to kneel in the Five Deep. Kneeling signified moral weakness' (*HWYL*, 55). He communicates vividly a sense of typical, everyday dangers, such as their headlong dash when the subterranean lake comes flooding into Five Deep 'and the black lake filled the district, dozens of stalls [. . .] supply roads, airways, water rising steadily up the Five Deep, drowning the toil of half a century' (*HWYL*, 65–6). By 1990, the whole colliery is gone: 'And now, since then, time has obliterated Graig level, the arched stonework blown in, the whole mountain's flank thick with conifers' (*HWYL*, 66). Indeed, by the time the autobiography is completed, 'King Coal is dead, sole reason for both Rhonddas, leaving twin valleys of commuters (20 per cent unemployment of course)' (*HWYL*, 30). The Methodist chapel has become a bus garage. Berry weaves in regular elegiac refrains: 'All gone now though, gone, Treorchy, Trealaw and chapel cemeteries' sempiternal harvest' (*HWYL*, 34); and, even there, winds and weather remove the names from the gravestones, as they have effaced all record of Grandfather Noah's last resting place (*HWYL*, 37).

As Berry worries away at what he is and why he is it, the reader becomes quickly aware of his certainty that one of his key endowments is the acute recording of sense impressions, particularly visual ones. By the end of *History Is What You Live* one has a sense of a memory bank overflowing with intense recall, a human personality unusually endowed in recording, being nurtured by, and finding meaning in, what he sees. Berry, like Larkin is poignantly aware of the 'sure extinction that we travel to';[3] his recording on paper of the sights, in particular, and sense impressions in general that have touched and changed him (many now passed away from the face of the earth), is his own personal stay against evanescence. He writes vividly of his earliest awareness of himself as a bundle of sensations: 'Smells, tastes, sounds, sights, sensations crowding my infant ganglia, confirming oneself as singular. A soul bud. Chopped mint, drops of blood, sand on the flagstone floor, the pure tugging of candle flame, bladders of air behind gulps of stingy-nettle pop, soapsuds burning eyes' (*HWYL*, 14). The reader witnesses Berry's recall of a time when the external world seemed a secure, tender and nurturing place, that reflected a promise of sure sustenance: 'Loving-kindness shone from externals, from buttercup chains, Selsig minnows and loaches, jack-frosted windowpanes, woollen vests, hawthorn berries' (*HWYL*, 16). Sight imbues the autobiographer Berry with a sense of continuing wonder at the potential glory of the world. A poignant tracing in *History Is What You Live* is that, while the receptivity remains, a sense of having a secure place in that world vanishes forever and vanishes early.

The aggression and dis-ease which Berry finds so fundamental in his understanding of himself is frequently recorded in *History Is What You Live*. Certainly, the deepest security that Berry records in relation to his adult life is in his male friendships. His macho Rhondda background has given him very particular models of male identity. We have already explored the range of 'butty' relationships Berry experienced before he was twenty, a very formative period in anyone's life, and the culminating one with Eddie Jones Cochyn, which was a close and trusting one. He recalls in impressive and minutely discerning detail all that he remembers of the individuating elements of a wide range of early peers, almost all male, and, in many cases, what later flowered or withered in them. He remembers with warmth how he was saved by his comrades, being given the means to pay the fine incurred after assaulting the colliery manager, when inwardly he believed 'Prison seemed fitting . . . Cardiff or Swansea': 'Very many of the colliers who chipped in have passed away. I knew them all by name' (*HWYL*, 88). His early relationship with cycling mate Vernon Rees, a fellow miner, taught him a great deal about himself: 'Cycle racing exposes limitations, reveals what's in the blood' (*HWYL*, 73). The discovering of what those limits were is written about with great insight. The most detailed analysis of any in the book is of his relationship with Cliff Williams, tubercular from his teens from work underground, with whom he drifted and learnt harshly realistic life values.

Aggression in the tough mining environment could almost be regarded as a necessary evolutionary adaptation for survival, yet Berry recognises something pathological in his own inordinate aggression. From adolescence he is aware of a need to defuse himself: 'Innately vexed, equally liable to bouts of savagery and brightly meaningless standstill, sweaty bike rides depolarised some of my adolescent aggro' (*HWYL*, 68). In the workplace, he is aware that he 'hankered for conflict', leading him to challenge the 'heftiest bullying haulier in the Graig [to a] stand up fist fight' (*HWYL*, 70). His image of feeling like 'a solitary piranha among inedible weavers' (*HWYL*, 70) suggests how innately aggressive he feels, and yet how impossible it seems to find ways of channelling that aggression. Seeing his ego as 'intact like a blocked biro' (*HWYL*, 85) implies recognition of his dysfunctionality – 'a chrysalis waiting for Cain heat' (*HWYL*, 72). The charting and detecting of pattern involved in writing this autobiography helped the man-who-held-the-pen to see how compulsively he resisted all authority, from the regular 'mitching' from Upper Rhondda Junior Technical school (*HWYL*, 20), to his hitting the colliery manager when refused any job but one in the silicosis-inducing hard heading (*HWYL*, 88), through to threat of military detention for 'flout[ing] discipline' (*HWYL*, 114) for refusal to salute officers, which results in his walking out on it all (*HWYL*, 114–16). At different times he is twice sent to psychiatrists and, though longing for help – there is positive envy of Chunks Lewis, at a later time, whose breakdown is 'classified, treated' (*HWYL*, 129) – he is unable to accept the proffered help. Typical exchanges with the psychiatrist run like this:

> 'Name, rank and number?'
> 'Yours in exchange for mine.'
> [. . .]
> 'Why do you resent authority?'
> 'Why do you have authority?'
> [. . .]
> Are your parents alive?'
> 'Are yours?'
>
> (*HWYL*, 117–18)

Such intense resistance to authority often has its roots in early relationships with parents – as he seems to be well (and resentfully) aware. There is much to deduce from what we are told of these filial relationships.

Through the lens of hindsight, Berry is almost in awe of the agonising mental states he endured in his young adult life. He describes winter in a distant place doing a mindless menial job:

> Against seepage of despair, I plugged bitty Cloud 9 aspirations. My worst flood of depression arrived in Huntingdon. The universe turned grey. Total greyness one Saturday night in a cinema, robots mouthing on the screen and hoar spreading from within [. . .] Too sane for suicide, I got drunk. (*HWYL*, 127)

It therefore seems possible that Berry perceives depression as stemming from anger, and particularly, from that aggression being turned self-destructively inwards. Throughout his autobiography, there is an appalled fascination with madness. Having described a mortuary attendant at his place of work being carried off in a straitjacket, there seems to be satisfaction, even triumph, in his observation: 'Most of us are blocked off from insanity. We abide, we hold our ground' (*HWYL*, 132). Yet, there is also recognition from his end-of-life perspective that at times it has been a near thing. On a long ramble on the mountain with Cliff Williams:

> Like pilgrims we visited a dugout built towards the end of my squeezed escape from the Merchant Navy. The turfed roof had collapsed [. . .] Had I tried to live in this dugout, God knows what brute stuff would have surfaced. That secret, desperate hideaway in the hills, bizarre to the point of exit. (*HWYL*, 124)

As he catalogues what the world would judge as bungle after deliberate disaster, Berry would also seem to have been aware, on the fringes of his vision, that there had been in him a determined failure to thrive. Although at or near the top of his class at primary school (*HWYL*, 17), he fails the eleven-plus and regularly truants in his final years at his technical school (*HWYL*, 20). He strikes the colliery manager and is thenceforth *persona non grata* in local pits (*HWYL*, 88). It has to be said that his resolute evasion of a second voyage in the Merchant Navy seems a clear indication of perspective and sanity (*HWYL*, 101). He deserts from the army (*HWYL*, 114). When offered government training, against all advice, because of his damaged knee, he chooses carpentry but does not complete the course (*HWYL*, 119–21). He later completes another government carpentry course but exercises the skill only briefly before selling his tools. When accepted for a one-year course at Coleg Harlech, he gives up his study of history after two terms (*HWYL*, 134–7). He is accepted as a mature student at teacher training college and gives up on that (*HWYL*, 143). A regular image of him perceived by others is 'waster' (*HWYL*, 102), and, by himself, a drifter:

> Since birth I think I've been possessed, measured for twilight drift instead of making a wage, the worst crime of all in chapel-hagged Wales. 'Him, that one, he's like Uncle Dan', they used to say, my own kin passing judgement. Solitary old Uncle Dan, tramp from youth to pension age, unkempt, [. . .] despised. (*HWYL*, 36)

There is a psychologically acceptable explanation of his self-thwarting behaviour that would be in keeping with the levels of emotional distress Berry sometimes describes; it is both more publicly and privately tolerable to find good reason for emotional pain in one's everyday situation, rather than be driven to accept that it is fuelled from inner psychological sources over which one has no control.

Berry's end-of-life, hard-won ability to value himself exists alongside a desire to look unflinchingly at his troubled younger self. In his adolescence, he admits to a kind of neediness in terms of emotional hunger, and sometimes that hunger is orally linked. He describes 'gorging [himself] on flora and fauna' (*HWYL*, 58). He identifies the obsessive thirty-mile cycle rides he and Vernon Rees undertake every evening for a period after a day in the pits, as a result of 'tap roots starving' (*HWYL*, 76). He declares that, 'We find out what we are from hungering enough' (*HWYL*, 32), and that 'I've starved for other things than bread' (*HWYL*, 111). A very powerful image of frustrated oral aggression is the already noted one where he sees himself as a solitary piranha amongst inedible weaver fish (*HWYL*, 70). One of the most vibrant images of the whole work is to do with feeding. He describes succour after fear when, as a toddler, he accidentally starts a fire and is comforted, presumably by his mother, Mary Anne: 'Afterwards, snug as buddhas by firelight, we [he and his cousin] ate toast and jam' (*HWYL*, 15). He describes with pure love his perception of Mary Anne's brief period of untrammelled happiness in the early years of her marriage as she sang songs such as 'Myfi sydd fachgen ieuanc ffôl': 'That pulsing old love song, her young-wife contentment, fulfilment of her days. Mary Anne's headaches came later when there were seven mouths to feed' (*HWYL*, 14). There is one lyrically expressed occasion of personal pride for Berry, accompanied by a photograph in the text, when he clearly felt special to Mary Anne:

> On July 2nd 1927, Treherbert Hospital carnival. The Junior First Prize silverplated cup was bigger than my head. I heard women on the pavement 'Well, yes, George's boy, him dressed up as a little costermonger, them pearl buttons, silk scarf and blancoed daps . . . Great idea mind. Trust Mary Anne, wonderful dressmaker she is.' (*HWYL*, 16)

The early ousting from the paradise of mother's special love has been tellingly described by Laurie Lee in *Cider with Rosie*. We can hypothesise a similar sort of deprivation for Berry – but coming about earlier than Lee's – from what we can read between the lines in Berry's narrative.

Berry's earliest memory is of a time when, a one-year-old 'still frocked and napkined, on Mary Anne's lap', he is 'lost and found next to my unborn sister Marian' (*HWYL*, 13). He is ousted at the breast by this child, who is further special in being given a merged version of her mother's name, and quickly becomes special in other ways – 'From childhood, Marian blazed quick delight, energy' – but dies before her twenty-first birthday (*HWYL*, 36). Through collating various pieces of factual information, we discover that this beloved child died at just the time the difficulties in communication with his father, which Berry described as being 'hopelessly alienated' (*HWYL*, 68), moved into a period of stronger rejection by both parents:

> Familial values sundered between '41 and '43. In my case, eldest son found wanting, fallen far short of expectation [. . .] Villagers saw me as unsound, a young man of little account [. . .]
> It was a time I had to live through. (*HWYL*, 101–2)

In a section where Berry has been pondering in a mystified way about grief, he observes: 'When Marian died the old man wept and wept. She was his favourite' (*HWYL*, 36). One can imagine the misery of being the eldest child 'found wanting', out of work and drifting, when parents were grieving intensely for the seemingly preferred child. In such circumstances, the earlier displacement at a time of acute vulnerability would be bound to resonate.

Although there is always love and understanding in the way he writes of his parents, there is, too, a striking distancing in his use of his parents' first names, George and Mary Anne, throughout. Surely this is a most striking 'failing [. . .] to salute [. . .] officers' (*HWYL*, 114). Certainly some of the most traumatic events in the book are to do with his parents' rejection of their oldest child, sometimes recorded in a way that reveals the pain, sometimes set down noncommittally. When he abandons the army, he takes fifteen days to plod painfully home, his long-injured knee causing near agony. When, at last, he makes it to Blaencwm:

> Local coppers had already made enquiries. Greater than my father's, Mary Anne's rejection was absolute. I slept in a railway signal box [. . .] Ten days in military detention awaiting trial, ten days and nights of yet more delving inwards [. . .] Stress times, insomniac's end, a time of repair even as flags of faith disintegrated, as ramparts cultivated since infancy toppled. (*HWYL*, 116)

Those 'ramparts cultivated since infancy' seem to be to do with defences set up against awareness of a lack of love. He later records in turn his parents' lack of interest in or any sense of celebration of his success, at last, as a writer (*HWYL*, 33, 145).

From what he takes trouble to record, albeit in an unshaped and unfocused way, it seems probable that Berry was aware at some level that problems of mental distress often have their sources in early childhood, born crucially of early relationships with parents. What I have outlined of recalled rejection or coldness in later years would have particular resonance for someone who had been unsure of the strength of parental attachment in his early childhood. He interprets most sympathetically the burdens of life for people like his parents: 'Working class parents had to be colossi of dedication and survival' (*HWYL*, 14).

In most respects, Berry seems a 'native born slot fit' (*HWYL*, 67) in his Blaencwm environment, yet he clearly had ambivalent attitudes to his Welshness, in part related to his incompletely acknowledged anger with his parents, particularly his mother. He comments appreciatively of his sculptor friend, Bob Thomas, that he 'creates realities more everlasting than any Welshman since matriarchy ruled. Funny inheritance, Welshness' (HWYL, 125). The fact that the Welsh language was used as a means of control by his Welsh-speaking mother has left feelings of resentment: 'Mary Anne spoke secrets in Welsh to George . . . Language used subversively leaves a legacy of mistrust' (*HWYL*, 26).

But he seems totally accepting of his great aunt's (Granny the Farm) 'pidgin English' and of her grandchildren who 'were our playmates every August when we stayed at Ynystawe, Wynford and Nellie, giggling Welsh monoglots. No hassle at all about communication' (*HWYL*, 37). Measured against this model, the Rhondda seems a different country: 'This Wales wasn't Welsh. Some Blaenycwm families clung to Cymraeg with private hints, Janus-murmurs, hopelessly fragile against the ups and downs of Rhondda's coal klondike' (*HWYL*, 26).

His evocation of his Valleys idiolect rings true as a bell: 'Yes, aye, illustrious vocation' (*HWYL*, 70); his interspersing of characteristic 'Ach y fi' to indicate particular repugnance expressed by relations (*HWYL*, 145); his use of sobriquets, as in Eddie Jones Cochyn (*cochyn* being a common Valleys appellation for a redhead) and Dai Lewis Short-Arm (*HWYL*, 44). He has been stirred by aspects of this culture, as when he records his small-child response to his mother's singing of Welsh love ballads (*HWYL*, 14) and his appreciation of Mari Lwyd nights (*HWYL*, 35). He tellingly evokes domestic habits of a south Wales mining community, when he describes 'gnarled Granny treading *pele*' (*HWYL*, 18) in clogs, creating and shaping combustible 'bricklets' from coal dust. Unmistakably, his native scene exerts a strong pull. His essential moulding is the typical Welsh industrial experience, based on the geological given of coal seams mined in the valley, where industrial waste accumulates, but with the possibility of escape within moments of hard climbing to the beauty of the surrounding mountains. He writes pityingly of a fellow worker who was 'affable in the loud, meaningless way of townies deprived of privacy from childhood' (*HWYL*, 132). While Berry gave short shrift to idealised or stereotyped notions of nationhood or religion, he does show every sign of valuing very highly most aspects of his own particular patch of English-language Welsh native ground, with its particularities and idiosyncrasies.

Some of his resistance to strong Welsh identification is to what he perceives as the 'chapel-hagged' nature of Wales (*HWYL*, 36). By the end of his life, Berry inhabits hard-won positions established from testing human experience. His exposure to religious narrowness and bigotry from early childhood onwards revolts him. He presents searing examples of punitive fanaticism in his own infants' school head, who 'polluted innocence as surely as law and order comforts bigotry' (*HWYL*, 16), and there was 'Mr Minty for hate, Mr Elliott for Blood of the Lamb' (*HWYL*, 27). His Merchant Navy experience of appalling inhumanity and fecklessness, when added to his compassionate sense of the blighted lives of so many miners, does not give him any sense of God alive in his world. Resistant himself to bending the knee to any power or person, he is incredulous, when Stukas dive-bomb ships in Bone harbour, to see 'slum hardened Scousers huddled below begging protection from the Holy Mary' (*HWYL*, 99), and comments, 'Maybe Man's a natural groveller'. He describes how, as a collier boy, he rejected 'everything that smacked of other-worldliness', for 'Life's the clincher, inner and outer yeasting the matrix of YOU and ME. Christian adults preached cramp while trees, plants, fowls of the air and fishes in water, all things alive-O, alive-O gouted sap and spunk' (*HWYL*, 58). As his only models for religious experience seem to be intolerant institutional ones with 'Thou shalt not' writ large, he does not connect his own feelings of overwhelming awe and fusion with a life force with what others might classify as an experience of the numinous:

> Once as a small boy, enraptured by swarming swifts in Wion gully, I felt universal, holier than ages, mightied by wonder. Another ecstasy a sunny morning before school, crawling over a hillock to watch a green woodpecker hammering its crimson-splashed head at the bole of an oak, yaffle and boy sounding alpha, alpha, alpha! (*HWYL*, 31–2)

Berry, from what he signals from the title of his autobiography onwards, would seem to belong firmly to the group Paul John Eakin in *Touching the World* describes as 'featur[ing] the active, conscious construction of the point of intersection between the individual's life and the larger movement of history of which it is a part'.[4] Weintraub recognised Goethe as the first autobiographer to insist 'that his life would have been something entirely different had he been born ten years to either side' of his actual birth date, in his case 1749.[5] Berry's coming to young manhood at the outbreak of war was crucially formative: 'The world I knew was a shambles, rags and tatters of pride, of convenience and shitten principles [. . .] Civilisation, I thought, was becoming extinct. Even my allocation of it, night shift behind the Longwall cutter in Graig level' (*HWYL*, 85). Up until the time he lost his job to a younger, cheaper man, at a time when Bevin's Essential Works Order had given enormous powers to government control of workers, Berry seems to have seen himself as a typical hard-working, hard-playing miner, a good butty and a good mate. His image of his huge capacity to push himself to his limits cycling, experiencing the knock (delirium caused by fatigue and hunger) to such a degree that he briefly loses sight and feeling, establishes him as someone who has it in him to be totally, self-punishingly committed (*HWYL*, 77–8). Yet his more enduring image of himself over a longer span is as a 'meanderer' (*HWYL*, 138), and he hardly quarrels with others' view of him as a 'waster' (*HWYL*, 102). Bevin's Essential Works Order 'dry-rammed up the ring of personal choice and rang ding-dong knell on anyone cherishing him/herself as precious' (*HWYL*, 86). He loses a job that he does well on the cutter, and, at a time when he is made brutally aware of the health risks of any underground work as his friend, Cliff Williams, develops TB with haemorrhaging, is offered only work which everyone knew was a virtual death sentence on the silicosis-inducing hard heading: 'Miners were expendable in 1940. And *all* the men who worked that hard rock heading are in Treorchy cemetery' (*HWYL*, 87).

As a result of striking the manager who will offer him no alternative work to this, he will never be offered another local pit job. In recreating from the present his mood at that time, he powerfully evokes an objective correlative to his remembered misery in the nature of the war events he chooses to list:

> After the court case, nothing much seemed to matter. Intimidation and fear, sanctimony and cant were everywhere. Fifth columns, pimps in office, Britain's aristocracy shipping their children overseas, ration cheating, MI5 round up of Rhondda Italians, the blitzing of towns, these were the slush of War. (*HWYL*, 88–9)

The searing clincher of what becomes a lifelong obsessive need to be his own person, required to defer to no one, was his experience in the Merchant Navy, for which he volunteered 'to avoid wearing uniform' (*HWYL*, 98). With hindsight, he sees that 'only the naive, bedevilled or frenetic' (*HWYL*, 98) joined the Merchant Navy in the winter of 1941. Berry's one and only trip was cataclysmic in its horror and the way it modified his life attitudes permanently thereafter. He suffered constant, gut-wrenching seasickness. There was constant, at times wild, drunkenness in everyone, from the captain down; predatory, power-based sexual behaviour was indulged in; rations were stolen from the lifeboats; the bonded cargo was broken into, and food, drink and equipment intended for Monty's Desert Rats was sold; Big Mac indulged his taste for north African child prostitutes and looted a motorbike which travelled back to Britain with him (*HWYL*, 98–100). 'We were defending Western civilisation' (*HWYL*, 99), Berry observes drily.

This experience seems to set in amber the utter distrust and total resistance Berry felt towards the following any sort of herd reaction, or knee-jerk responses to notions of honour or patriotism. His retrospective look at the feelings evoked in his child self and in others by Remembrance Day is wondering and ironic:

> And on Remembrance Day, Treherbert Brass Band glittering, bomping up to the Cenotaph like talkie extras [. . .] with a bugler fluting the Last Post up at Pen Pych, bared heads, stillness all over the country, my throat burning to the gristle, nape hairs crimped, prepared for reverence, ascent of the species via hallucination. (*HWYL*, 35)

Thereafter, for Berry, there can be no sense of serving King and country; honour is nonsense. As we have seen, in his attempt to give meaning to his whole life mythic tale Berry has identified himself as 'Since birth [. . .] measured for twilight drift' (*HWYL*, 36). Yet, until his service with the Merchant Navy, he was absorbable within the bounds of what society at the time would regard as normalcy. A brief summary of Berry's subsequent wartime experience establishes how it 'broke' him in conventional terms, while also consolidating within him an inalienable sense of his own fundamental selfhood.

Through theft of the local library date-stamper, he is able to fend off, for a period, any further Merchant Navy postings, while still receiving food ration coupons (*HWYL*, 101). After further drift, he ends up in the army, where he quickly reports that 'the shuffleboard of army life was breaking me', pushing him to 'unleash fatuity' (*HWYL*, 110) in an essay, causing an increasingly harsh army crackdown. Buckling under the pressure, he goes absent without leave, and is rejected by his parents; yet, in this record, he portrays this period as 'a time of repair even as flags of faith disintegrated, as ramparts cultivated since infancy toppled [. . .] Clinically I was *out* of the mind one normally shares with other folks at all sorts of levels' (*HWYL*, 116–17). Even during the process of disintegration, the nadir of his life experience to that point, with hindsight he acknowledges that at times he had felt 'profoundly warranted' (*HWYL*, 115), able to return to a censorious officer 'the only answer of my life: "I've starved for other things than bread'" (*HWYL*, 111). The process of becoming a reject of society as represented by the armed services in wartime has given Berry some sense of the hard core of self, what he must be true to if he is to survive: 'At the centre, there's a core greening like bronze, a private memorial decked with shrivelled blossoms. They glowed once, in the lost country of childhood' (*HWYL*, 113). One of Berry's final images of self is as an almost lifelong nonconformist, 'shaping the square peg of myself, escapee from round holes since before leaving school in 1935' (*HWYL*, 147).

Berry would seem to perceive the historic times in which he lived as crucially moulding the potential embodied in his natural endowment and early nurture. As we have already posited, the anger with his parents, which was transformed into anger at, and resistance to, any authority figure, reached such levels of intensity when he was caught up in the power structures of wartime that the system's resultant crackdown almost broke him. He would seem to see two wartime happenings as crucially formative. Fifty years after the event, he refers with venom to the harshness of Bevin's wartime Essential Works Order. During his brief service in the Merchant Navy, physical seasickness combined with a spiritual horror to bring about a subsequent tacit refusal to accept the state's decisions for his life. War gave him harsh perceptions on the nature of humankind which he did not modify subsequently. Further, the time in which he lived, in which south Wales coal lost its traditional markets and the Rhondda valleys became largely a commuter dormitory, shaped and transformed his environment. Exceptional times created exceptional pressures. As Dai Smith has so astutely pointed out, one of Berry's purposes is to 'witness and refuse the suffocating custody of the comforting, herded tribe' (*HWYL*, 11).

History Is What You Live is imbued with a sense of mortality, with memories of those now 'gone to clay' (*HWYL*, 100) and an awareness of how little that has been thought worth human struggle endures. As Berry approaches the end of his own life, his final implicit perception is that a self that has written of itself has built a frail defence against the encroaching sea of annihilation. 'Foul hooked on language' (*HWYL*, 130) at one time in his life, he has won through to bear witness to what he and his community have lived through. Although in *History Is What You Live* he has often identified himself with 'wasters', the sediment of society, his final image is a triumphant one: of himself as a young man scoring the penalty goal that won Fernhill soccer team the Cup in 1937, and as an old man, the last survivor of that team, he wins again in another way by making an enduring testimony of what he and his community have known. For all its shortcomings, the fact of *History Is What You Live* – its complex structure, its glowing and loving evocation of a world now past, its linguistic bravura and Berry's final insight into his own complexities – stands in counterpoint to its record of failure. Berry wrote *History Is What You Live* after he had won success as a writer. The self he there explores is the self who has part found, part created, a meaningful pattern, in and from the fragments of his lived life. The accomplishment in that patterning is a triumphant part of his perception of self.

Notes

[1] Ron Berry, *History Is What You Live* (Llandysul: Gomer, 1998). All further references will be made within the body of the text (*HWYL*).
[2] James Olney, *Metaphors of Self: The Meaning of Autobiography* (Princeton, NJ: Princeton University Press, 1972), pp. 226–7.
[3] Philip Larkin, 'Aubade', in Philip Larkin, *Collected Poems* (London: Faber and Faber, 2003), pp. 171–2.
[4] Paul John Eakin, *Touching the World: Reference in Autobiography* (Princeton, NJ: Princeton University Press, 1992), p. 144.
[5] Eakin, *Touching the World*, p. 148.

3

A Man's World:
The Short Fiction of Ron Berry

Tony Brown

The pattern of Ron Berry's publishing career itself tells a story: a series of five novels between 1960 and 1970, all from London publishers, culminating in arguably his most powerful novel *So Long, Hector Bebb*, then a gap of over twenty-five years until Gomer, a Welsh publisher, finally accepted *This Bygone*, published the year before Berry's death. While Berry did produce two television plays in the 1970s, thereafter his television career came to a halt and, anyway, his story 'Ben, the T.V. Playwright and his wife, Lottie' (1993) suggests that, perhaps predictably, Berry had little enthusiasm for the world of television production: a somewhat effete world of 'willowy Cavalier haired' directors who sipped sherry rather than beer and had a tendency to 'wriggle-giggle'.[1] The distinguished film director Bryan Forbes optioned *The Full-Time Amateur*[2] but, though the cash was no doubt useful, the project came to nothing.[3] Through this quarter century of being ignored by publishers and critics, the only form in which Berry was able to express himself in published form was the short story.

Berry had been writing short stories in the 1940s and 1950s, alongside poetry, but nothing of this was published.[4] It was Alun Richards, aware of his friend's situation and presumably his shortage of income, who seems to have encouraged him to fresh work in this form. He had written to Berry in about 1970, as *So Long, Hector Bebb* was being prepared for the press, about a potential new outlet for short fiction: 'Have you heard about *Planet*, this Welsh magazine? They're paying good money for stories', and a few years later Richards included 'Before Forever After' in his *Penguin Book of Welsh Short Stories*, in

1976.⁵ Pushed by circumstances into this new creative channel, between 1976 and his death Berry published some twenty-seven short stories, almost all of them in Wales, in journals (mainly *Planet* and *New Welsh Review*) and anthologies.⁶

Berry had a sharp sense, an acute ear, for the idiosyncratic event or character in the community in which he lived; page after page of his autobiography contains vividly realised recollections which read like embryos of potential short stories:

> She reared eleven children on a hill farm, among them an imbecile daughter fastened to her apron strings till she passed away in her thirties. Granny the Farm (so-called) spoke pidgin English, the prow of her nose hooking towards the jut of her chin, her toothless welcoming smile accompanied by gleeful flaps of her forearms on her black-skirted thighs. During her menopause Granny the Farm cooled flushes with cabbage leaves tied around her head, the yammering daughter trailing her from kitchen to fields.⁷
>
> When Jim Taylor (known as Jim Greek) opened his shop in Hendrewen Road, he landed in clover. Bang on the square, it was a meeting place for youngsters. Jim sold thousands of Woodbines for five a penny. He was middle-aged, living tally⁸ with Mrs. Holly a widow. Her daughter died of TB. Jim Greek's daughters by Mrs Holly also died of TB. [. . .] A few years after establishing the shop, Jim fenced an acre of ground at the base of Mynydd Tŷ Isaf. It was steep and boggy, just below the long sprawl of Hendrewen tip, almost directly above the Co-op stores. [. . .] He built himself a black tarred corrugated shed with a stove, he drained the yellow clay, and he dug up his acre. Jim returned to the land, seeking get-out from the infected house. (*HWYL*, 47)

Other characters or events provide a seed which Berry did shape into fiction. The grim death of Percy Prior, Berry's one-time 'butty' at the coalface, who, diagnosed with '100 per cent dust' (*HWYL*, 41), walked off a railway footbridge and under a train, contributes to the bleak suicide of Lewis Rimmer, who has received the same deadly diagnosis, in 'Time Spent', one of Berry's finest stories (*CS*, 103). Inevitably, some stories draw even more directly on Berry's rich and varied life experiences. Berry's being falsely accused of stealing cigarettes while working as a young man at a hotel near Chepstow, for instance (*HWYL*, 67), is skilfully shaped into fiction as 'Nice Clean Place' (*CS*, 140–4); the remembered episode, however, becomes a study of the contrast between the comfortable life of the English hotel, with its cigar smoke and iced cakes and salmon, and the poverty of Clay Cullen's Valleys' home and of the alienation of the young Clay. For Clay the episode becomes a turning point as he decides, at the end of the story, to join the army. It is a decision coloured by the fact that the setting is the late 1930s and the reader realises that Clay will soon be sucked into conflict, an awareness underscored by the presence in the town of 'derelicts' who served in the First World War. The personal memory is shaped by Berry into resonant fiction.

Berry was, of course, writing in an anglophone Welsh literary culture in which, after poetry, the short story is the major form of literary expression, with most of our leading writers – Dylan Thomas, Alun Lewis, Rhys Davies, Dorothy Edwards, Margiad Evans, Glyn Jones – producing first-rate work in the form. Quite why the short story is such a central form in Wales, especially when compared to the somewhat peripheral position which it has in England, is an interesting matter for debate. While in its linguistic concentration and potential for lyric intensity it is the closest prose form to the poetry which many of these writers were also producing, we should not lose sight of more practical and economic reasons for the development of the form in the first half of the twentieth century: apart from Rhys Davies, for instance, most writers in the period had day jobs, usually as teachers or academics, and – as Raymond Carver once commented – in such circumstances the time and energy for novel writing is in short supply. Moreover, in the 1930s and 1940s, and especially in the war years, there were numerous magazines in which to publish short stories, even though, before the founding of *Wales* (1937) and *The Welsh Review* (1939), these were in London: stories by many of the writers mentioned above appeared in journals such as, for instance, the *Adelphi, New English Review, Life and Letters To-Day* and *Penguin New Writing*.

However, as I have argued elsewhere, there is possibly something innate to the form itself that lends itself to the experience of the Welsh writer in English. (Moreover, once the tradition had been established, the very existence of this body of work serves to provide models for later generations of storytellers.) Almost inevitably, in considering the nature of the short story as a literary form, one finds oneself referring to that early, path-finding study, Frank O'Connor's *The Lonely Voice*, published in 1963.[9] O'Connor argues that in its fragmentariness, its concern with small detached groups of characters or the solitary individual within the community, the short story articulates the experience of what O'Connor terms 'submerged population groups'.[10] For O'Connor, the short story tends to articulate the experience of the marginalised, the isolated, the lonely: 'in the short story there is this sense of outlawed figures wandering about the fringes of society'.[11] A number of critics have built on O'Connor's study, in particular Clare Hanson, who sees the form as one which has frequently expressed the experience of those who are 'not part of official or "high" cultural hegemony', individuals and groups outside the centres of cultural and political power.[12] This is manifestly a resonant set of ideas when applied to Wales's English-speaking writers, authors writing with an awareness that they are not English (and for the most part living and working away from the centres of cultural and political power, in England), but also often acutely aware that they are shut out from the rich cultural heritage of Welsh-speaking Wales. The short story is, in other words, a form which has been seen as expressing the experience of marginality, displacement and loneliness.

However, one's initial awareness in approaching Ron Berry's short stories is of their firm location in a community, albeit those communities, especially in the stories set in the years of industrial decline, are certainly marginalised and powerless. These are places where people know the details of each other's backgrounds and where individuals are known to each other by communally-ascribed nicknames. These are also stories set in the shared world of men working together: on building sites ('Rosebud Prosser', 'Max Thomas', 'Before Forever After'), as part of a hospital maintenance crew ('Protocol Spin-off'), on board ship ('King of the Foc'sle') and, above all, of course, in the colliery, where survival can depend on men's ability to rely on one another's skill, resilience and brute strength. Berry draws on his own experience in portraying the bond between collier and 'butty', the one cutting into the coalface with pick or mechanical coal cutter, the other loading the coal into the tram, on the efficiency of which the men's income depended. The young Bryn establishes a firm bond as butty to his collier Percy Naylor in 'A Hero of 1938'; the two work steadily, and rewardingly, together: 'Bryn filled the trams – three by eleven o'clock. "Grub up. Dab my number on the bugger," Percy said. [. . .] Every Friday outside the colliery office, Percy handed him ten bob trumps on top of his wages. Good collier, good trumper' (*CS*, 50, 52). When the pit floods and Bryn risks his life to save a pit pony, it is Percy who looks after the soaking wet, exhausted Bryn, appreciating what he has done: 'You'm a good un, butty' (*CS*, 56).

Even the violently independent Gabe in 'The Old Black Pasture' ultimately establishes a working bond as butty to Billy Cochyn:

> Gabe repaid his butty by taking on strongman graft. He dragged out the cable before they started cutting each face, he heaved on a crowbar after they flitted out from the coal. [. . .] He relied on Billy. [. . .] For Gabe Lloyd and his butty, safety hinged on experience foretelling chance. (*CS*, 233-4)

When disaster strikes and Gabe is trapped alone by the roof-fall with the dead Cochyn, he sits 'with Billy across his lap [. . .] "Ah, Christ, Billy," he grieved [. . .] letting the slack head loll down' (*CS*, 243). The echo of a pietà is unexpected, but suffuses the scene not only with grief but with tenderness: '"Cochyn, I'll stay company with you. [. . .] Ah, poor old Cochyn"' (*CS*, 250).

The sense of community in these workplaces is enhanced by the fact that there is a jargon and terminology which the men share, and from which of course most readers are excluded. On the building site, for instance, 'Strapper leapt off the RSJ, clean over my head as I prised the shutter away from the soffit with a nailbar' (*CS*, 37). The pit similarly has its jargon: 'Lissen, strip the clod off up'n the left side. Mind to pack the gob wall tight' ('A Hero of 1938', *CS*, 51), 'Butty, you bolt up the fishplates. Got your skyhooks handy?' ('The Old Black Pasture', *CS*, 239).[13] The world of leisure also has its own routines and technical jargon, exclusive to its male participants; Lew's pigeon loft in 'Time Spent' is another place of specialist expertise ('There were slatted flight runs each side of the aisle, the aisle itself littered with scrapers, a hammer, skewed handsaw, tins of nails, stunted cane brush without a handle, and a small tin of maple peas', *CS*, 99), while, when Hopkin goes fishing in 'End of Season', we enter another world of male knowledge: 'Hopkin tied a size 14 Iron Blue nymph on the dropper, size 12 Teal and Green on the point. He smeared his twelve foot tapered leader with a paste of Fuller's Earth and liquid soap' (*CS*, 2).

This outdoor world of leisure is a further site of male comradeship. In 'Clarion Boys', the teenaged Lew Cullen and Rick Taylor, on their days off from the brewery where they are 'fetch-and-carry workers' (*CS*, 145), cycle together the hills and valleys of Glamorgan and take part in road races on behalf of their club, the Moel Exchange Clarion.[14] The two young men camp together on the tranquil banks of the Wye on the night before the race, carefully sharing the cost of the meal which they cook together. The calm is broken, however, when the race is abruptly cancelled because two other competitors, young men like themselves, have been killed in a car crash. Then, after a night of dreamless sleep, as they arise to a 'lovely morning', chance abruptly breaks in again when Rick suddenly has to dive into the river to rescue a fisherman from drowning. Rick had jokingly cried, 'Wake up! Wake, you bastards', as they had walked through the quiet of a graveyard on their way back from the pub the night before (*CS*, 147), but as they cycle home in the sunshine, we, and they, are aware of the vulnerability of the lives of these two young friends in a world of randomness and chance.

In 'November Kill', the two miners Miskin and Beynon amble in the quiet of a Sunday morning, teasing each other about events in the Club the night before: 'They grinned, gently grinding shoulders, appreciating a bond without malice' (CS, 113). The Sunday world, away from the pit, into which Miskin and Beynon walk with their dogs to hunt foxes is a place of freedom and vitality, emphasised by Berry's active verbs and participles:

> Pen Arglwydd mountain jutted up at the November sky, a stillness of dark, bare cliffs intergullied with heathered ledges. Scree slopes gave way to invading bracken. Below the rusting bracken, patches of marshland, mole-tumped pasture, scatters of gnarled oaks [. . .] Alders lined feeder streams running into Nant Myrddin. Silver birches were spreading eastward, seedspill from a large stand of blackening, dying trees. (*CS*, 114)

When they eventually sight a fox, delicately and precisely described by Berry, it seems to epitomise the freedom of the dynamic natural world around the two friends: 'the fox trotting its side-long gait, front and rear legs inswinging, four pads straight-tracking in the peat-stained silt [. . .] Light-footed over cropped turf and up to scree spillage below a gully, the fox climbed swiftly, skittering over stones like a squirrel' (*CS*, 116). When, in pursuit of the fox, Miskin's terrier, Lady, becomes trapped underground, the two men dedicate the next four days to digging down to rescue her, timbering their vertical shaft as they would timber in the pit. While concerned for Miskin's dog, Beynon's ultimate motivation is to preserve the men's times together and their friendship: 'Beynon thought, she's been four days without food and water. It'll break Miskin's heart if Lady dies underground in Dunraven Basin. He'll quit. Sell the dogs. No more weekend fox-hunting' (*CS,* 120). When they finally unearth Lady and the two men sink exhausted in the bottom of their pit, the dog in Miskin's lap, Miskin's simple 'Thanks, butty' (CS, 122) is a simple but profound acknowledgement of what his friend's efforts actually mean. 'The Foxhunters' is set in the same free, dynamic landscape below Pen Arglwydd, as the two friends, Joe and Shad go out into the August heat with their dogs: 'Rolling mountain top under naked sky, invisible grasshoppers churring [. . .] Odd, grasping hawthorns tufted green in the black welter' (*CS,* 194–5), though that dynamism is also a place of brute survival: 'A late brood of crows of crows rose from a dead sheep, the eyes, tongue and intestine ripped out. Small maggots speckled the soiled wool' (*CS,* 194). It is a violence which climaxes in the story when Joe and Shad's dogs put up a fox and, in a vicious fight which ends in a mountain pool, Joe's terrier is savaged by the fox and drowned. Again, one man mourns for what his friend will feel; Shad realises, 'This'll drive him mad. He'll rave. Ah, Jesus Christ' (*CS,* 199). When Joe arrives, the two friends share their grief for the dog, the usual masculine emotional inhibitions briefly set aside: 'They wept briefly, shamefacedly, kneeling besides the little terrier' (*CS,* 199).

One might assume from the title that 'Comrades in Arms' is a similar tale of male friendship. However, while Lemuel Nelson and Redvers Gillard are indeed inseparable friends, they are essentially, to go back to Clare Hanson's view of the short story, a pair of outsiders, marginalised and finally isolated. In the strike of 1926, penniless, they escape Blaen-du by joining the British army and fighting for the Empire, 'subduing factions, zealots, dervishes, in India and Egypt' (*CS,* 57).[15] By the time the two men come back, twelve years later, still 'shoulder to shoulder' (*CS,* 58), the village has largely forgotten them. They go down the pit but remain outsiders. While their contemporaries have settled down to respectable working lives as family providers, Lemuel and Redvers continue to live by the rough codes of their army years; feeling 'immune to consequences', they fill their leisure time with heavy drinking and 'feckless women, widowed, abandoned outcast by fate' (*CS,* 58). Their tenuous links with the community are severed, finally and abruptly, when, outside in a field and under cover of darkness, they have sex with Jilly Hughes, the fifteen-year-old daughter of the pub landlord, passing her from one to the other. As she scurries home, the two men reflect: '"What d'you think, Lemmy?" "Nice bit of kief, not bad at all considering." "She wanted it"' (*CS*, 60). It is one of the darkest episodes in Berry's short fiction. The measure of the extent to which the two men are outside not only the codes of the community, but of civilised behaviour, is underlined in the pub as the locals, learning of what they have done, turn on them. As the hard young colliers threaten them, in an extraordinary scene, the two men's 'feral' nature bursts out; they howl, 'desolate, rabid, nerve tingling', strip naked and, while Lemuel urinates in the bar, he keens 'a primal dirge' (*CS*, 62). The whole episode is an expression, almost a dark celebration, of ultimate outsiderdom. After a period in jail, they find refuge again in the army; while Redvers dies at Dunkirk, Lemuel, his violence diverted into acceptable channels, wins the Military medal, at Alamein. When he eventually returns to Blaen-du, he brings with him a woman who is a Polish refugee, another outsider.

The setting of 'Summer's End: Snaketown' is a more contemporary, gently melancholic story of outsiderdom. Chris, a young dropout from art school ('Couldn't stomach the poncing', *CS*, 6), has returned to his home town, a seaside place of 'slow dereliction' (*CS*, 12), where he lives alone in a tiny flat, making a living as a window cleaner. His parents have separated; Chris has lost contact with his father, Gomer, and, a recurring motif in these stories, he has a difficult relationship with his mother, now working as a local barmaid, whom he blames for his father's leaving. Chris is a 'marginal bloke [. . .] Lonely sometimes' (*CS*, 11, 14), as he tells Esther, the middle-class girl staying locally, with whom he has a fleeting love affair. When, disapproving of the relationship, the family with whom she is staying ship her off home, the 'cool' façade which Chris has constructed crumbles; he faces his renewed loneliness and mourns his lost, defeated father: 'So I wept, sobbed on Tan-y-mor sands, purging for the only time since Gomer went away' (*CS*, 18).

The protagonist of 'My Uncle Dan' is an archetypal loner, though from an earlier generation than Chris. In fact, Ron Berry's relation to Uncle Dan, and indeed to the first-person narrator who tells the story, is a complex one. As is evident in *History Is What You Live*, he is closely based on Berry's own great uncle, his mother's 'tramp brother' (*HWYL*, 26), the man to whom, revealingly, as he drifted from job to job, the family compared Berry himself: '"Him, that one, he's like Uncle Dan," they used to say, my own kin passing judgement' (*HWYL*, 36). In the context of the present discussion, it is perhaps telling that Berry chose to recreate and develop this familial loner into a more detailed (ostensibly) fictional portrait. In the story, Dan becomes an almost iconic figure of marginality: 'Throughout most of his long life he endured the loneliness of a saint' (*CS*, 26). For years between the wars, Dan tramps the roads of south Wales 'with a hawker's licence and a cardboard suitcase display of England's Glory matches, shoelaces, tintacks, dubbin, needles, safety pins, reels of cotton, hairgrips, ribbons and Old Moore's Almanacs' (*CS*, 26). The reasons for his departure from home are never clear, though it seems likely that it is at least in part a rebellion from the feminine world of domesticity and respectability; when he occasionally visits home for a few days, his sister hustles her brother, dirty and unkempt, indoors out of sight until he and his clothes are washed and presentable. But even on these brief visits home Dan does not socialise with the community; he walks 'the village main street, unseeing, perfectly alone, heedless of people and the pub' (*CS*, 28). Later, isolated even more by years of blindness and by the deaths of his generation of relatives, this family black sheep himself dies 'unmourned by a single relative' (*CS*, 29), but quietly leaves each of the next generation the not inconsiderable sum of £45. It is an enigmatic but resonant story, told by a first-person narrator who offers no access to Dan's inner life.

There are a number of other figures in Berry's gallery of marginal men. 'Reardon Jones, MM' is a fuller, more achieved narrative than the portrait of Uncle Dan, but he is another lifetime loner. Having joined the army in the late 1930s, and embraced its warm camaraderie, its 'exclusive male loyalties removed from hearth and home', Soldier Jones is now in his fifties and living alone with his dog in the family bungalow, squalid and packed with rubbish. Having subsided into alcoholism – 'Life had meaning when he was drinking [. . .] the fact of loneliness forgotten' (*CS*, 201) – Soldier loudly and drunkenly expresses himself in 'the familiar profanity of men isolated from women' (*CS*, 200) and has as a result been banned from all but one of the town's clubs and pubs. Ostracised by 'respectable folk', he dies alone; in a touch reminiscent of Caradoc Evans, when the young woman from social services breaks into the smelly house, she finds that the dog has been eating him. At the outset of 'Reaping the Sown', Dilwyn Templin is firmly in the village community, working in the furniture factory and married to Myfanwy. However, Dilwyn, who as a child has for years has been moved from one foster mother to another and lived in hostels with 'strict rules, locked doors', has always 'dreaded loneliness' (*CS*, 74). When the sexually flirtatious Myfanwy goes off with her employer, the local butcher, Dilwyn is left alone in a caravan; there 'A sense of vacancy comforted Dilwyn, emptiness within himself lulled his fears of loneliness' (*CS*, 75). Made redundant by the factory, Dilwyn cocoons himself in the isolated caravan before illness carries him off. Myfanwy comes and chatters at his hospital beside, but ultimately Dilwyn dies alone.

One doesn't, though, have to be alone to be lonely. The irascible Lewis Rimmer's marriage to Bessie in 'Time Spent' seems by now to be merely a matter of habit, of crass insensitivity and the giving of orders ('Use some bloody elbow grease on the bowl of the lav', *CS*, 96). His son left home years before – it seems likely that Bessie is right when she tells her husband, 'You drove our William away' (*CS*, 96) – and the son now has a successful life with his family, miles away. In fact, years before, Lewis has had another son with a local woman, Esther, a betrayal of which Bessie is well aware. Diagnosed, in his fifties, with 100 per cent dust and faced with immediate redundancy, Lewis now confronts the dreadful, meaningless emptiness of his life:

> She meant nothing. Bessie, nothing. William, nothing. Bernard, nothing. It's me, Lewis Rimmer, fifty-seven, that's all, fifty-bloody-seven. Man for man I've filled more coal than any collier in Fawr pit. Now this. Here I am. [. . .] How carry on? What's next? Jesus Christ. (*CS*, 99)

The final expletive is ironic. Lewis has neither spiritual beliefs nor emotional resources to give his life meaning; his only sense of meaningful identity comes from his masculine self-esteem as a collier, and now that is to be stripped from him. In this ultimate existential loneliness he sits silently in his pigeon loft and, while the birds fly free over the valley, Lewis puts the muzzle of his shotgun in his mouth and pulls the trigger.

Thus, alongside the occasional examples of male comradeship, we do indeed find the marginality and loneliness which critics of the short story like O'Connor and Hanson have associated with the form. Ultimately, isolation is of the essence of Berry's short fiction. While Gabe Lloyd and Billy Cochyn, as we have seen, form a firm working bond underground in 'The Old Black Pasture' – Billy's '*real*', reflects Gabe (*CS*, 238), a man of no pretension or emotional falsity – we realise from the outset that Gabe is not a man who establishes friendships; he is in fact another of Ron Berry's loners. Indeed, one might argue that Gabe Lloyd, in this longest of the stories, is closest to being the archetypal Ron Berry protagonist. In the opening lines of the story, the violently independent and unfettered Gabe, a former local amateur boxing champion, punches a wages clerk who has not given him his full allowances on payday, an episode which, paralleling Berry's own punching of a pit manager when a young miner (*HWYL*, 66), not only lands Gabe in court but, when he is placed on probation, renders him vulnerable to management pressure. Like other Berry heroes (one uses the word intentionally), Gabe measures his masculine identity by his physical capacity as a collier. Those who, like the clerks, the cashiers and the managers, do not work underground he sees as less than fully masculine: '[. . .] they've never filled a dram, never cleared a top hole, [. . .] they've never cut up a rib face, they'd be smothered in diarrhoea working a low seam with the top pouncing like fucken Guy Fawkes' Night'; it is a '*Man*'s job' (*CS*, 217, 218). One notes Berry's narratorial endorsement of Gabe's gendered perspective; after being punched by Gabe, the clerk is 'Anguished as a schoolgirl' (*CS*, 216).

Faced by the regime of such men, and behind them the courts, the police and ultimately the state, and seething after his court appearance, Gabe voices to himself words that might stand as epigraph to Ron Berry's short fiction: 'Discipline's for puppydogs and born losers who can't think for themselves. [. . .] Therefore no reason why a man should respect any system at all. Bugger respect' (*CS*, 222, 232). He has no respect for the political system, or even for the rich political traditions of the valleys in which he has grown up: 'Great people, the rank and file, cream of Socialism. Brainwash the dumbos, then just give them orders and they'll make a short-time Christ out of some chesty government leader' (*CS*, 218). The NUM is a 'right shower' (*CS*, 219), and collective bargaining merely a collaboration with management. The only thing in which Gabe places value is himself, his own masculine selfhood ('This life is for me, mine to do as I want with it. [. . .] It's me, first, second and last', *CS*, 217, 218); his only concern for his fellow workers is the satisfaction he takes in their cautious admiration *for* his independence.

That selfhood is put to its ultimate test in the roof collapse at the coalface, which kills Billy Cochyn and traps Gabe. The collapse is carefully foreshowed in Berry's narrative. As Gabe and Billy meet up for their Friday night shift, we are told, casually and quietly, that it is 'their last shift together' and then, a page later, they ride down in the cage: 'Billy Holly for the last time. And Gabe, he missed his Saturday night date with Lucy Passmore' (*CS*, 236, 237).The perspective is almost Hardyan: the two human individuals placed in a dark, timeless, indifferent world.

Stranded alone with Cochyn's body in the darkness of the pit, Gabe's initial struggle is a physical one: he hacks and burrows for hours to access the compressed-air pipe which will save him from suffocation. But beyond this there is the psychological and existential struggle, his habitual, assertive sense of self reduced now to a point of consciousness in the darkness; 'Hang on, gotto hang on to my nerve. Once my nerve goes I'll be useless. I won't lose my nerve. I *won't*' (*CS*, 250). But through the eight days it takes the rescue party to reach him, Gabe experiences periods of being comatose, the torpor being revealingly gendered:

> He drowsed, hungering, cuddling his privates for warmth, the only wistful reach of life in his humanity. Subsequently through his drowse, emerged a large amorphous female, soft concubine of dream to give succour, dissolving benevolence throughout his bones and flesh. (*CS*, 251)

The instinctual, wistful impulse towards sexual comfort renders him vulnerable to a sensual surrender of self, manifested in a female form. His desperate response is to cling to his sense of masculinity: 'It's me, Gabe Lloyd . . . N.C.B. champion two years ago' (*CS*, 251). Gabe asserts the bloody-minded sense of male selfhood that is the essence of his character. No more than Lewis Rimmer, alone in his pigeon loft, does he have recourse to any sort of spiritual faith: when Rosser Passmore, the man whom Gabe is cuckolding, asks 'Tell me true, you prayed to the Lord when you were trapped down there', Gabe answers bluntly, 'Can't say I did' (*CS*, 256).

In fact the Valleys communities which we see portrayed by Berry in his short stories are essentially places which no longer have the structures of belief which once cemented those communities and which largely gave them their identity. 'I've had politics up to here' says one of the ex-miners who sit in the pub in 'Natives' (*CS*, 77). One of his drinking mates, once the librarian at the Miners' Institute, recalls the days when a collier 'filled out coal on a diet of Spinoza, Immanuel Kant, Nietzsche, Voltaire and Charles Darwin' (*CS*, 79), and there are men on building sites who recall Robert Tressell's *Ragged Trousered Philanthropists* (*CS*, 35, 133). But the Institute was pulled down years before, and the rich political and philosophical awareness that that such libraries brought into being is long gone. Former heroes of

Labour are seen as lost leaders who have taken their 'handful of silver'. For Rupe Maindy in 'Protocol Spin-Off', Nye Bevan is 'a disgrace to the brotherhood of man' (*CS*, 178). Rupe, while a member of a maintenance crew at Hammersmith Hospital, has seen Bevan, now a cabinet minister, open a new nurse's hostel; the workers are kept well away from the elaborate buffet 'fit for royalty' which is provided for Bevan, who, after a short speech, sweeps away in his Daimler, back to Whitehall. While one should of course be duly careful not to attribute the views of a character to his creator, Rupe's story is closely based on an episode Berry himself experienced when working at Hammersmith Hospital, and his antipathy is strikingly similar when he relates how 'Nye came, shielded by a gaggle of easy smilers [. . .] a bulky man dispensing and receiving platitudes' before he 'purred away in his Daimler [. . .] back to his Ministerial affairs of state' (*HWYL*, 133–4). As market forces bear down on the miners in what proved to be the last chapter of the coal industry in south Wales, those very pressures splinter the solidarity that had unified the workers in previous generations: 'Outright greedies, some of our Welsh colliers. Tories wearing cap-lamps' ('Lew's Old Man', *CS*, 150). For the narrator of 'Before Forever After', on his building site, 'Times change. [. . .] We inherit chaos. It's unconditional' (*CS*, 35). As Gabe Lloyd has realised, in such a world, the old comradely bonds gone, it's every man for himself.

It is ultimately a stance which, epitomised by Gabe's lack of recourse to any notion of transcendent hope in the blackness of the pit, extends beyond politics to the world of the spirit. It is striking, in fact, how few references there are in Berry's stories, even in those set in the 1930s, to the life of the chapel, and those few are invariably lacking in much sympathy. In 'Lew's Old Man', Dai Rees Bowen battles fanatically in the face of an imminent collapse at the coalface, disregarding the fact that he is bleeding profusely from his injured ear, 'hanging like meat scrag': 'Touched by madness, he went beyond reason' (*CS*, 155). Dai is a deacon in Bethesda chapel, and the lack of reason he has exhibited in the pit is seen by his own son as of a piece with his rigidity of belief, 'Bethesda mania perhaps, some kind of dipsy-do' (*CS*, 156). Rupe Maindy in 'Protocol Spin-off' recalls the grandparents of the current generation, walking to worship on a Sunday, their Bibles under their arms: 'The chapels were crammed with believers. *Hwyl* poured from the Chapels of Wales' (*CS*, 179). But this son of a Pentecostal believer is eloquently scathing about the Christ celebrated in those chapels:

> His suffering arrogance down the ages, prescribing guilt and the comfort of redemption for the sentient hominid. His boggling control stroke, that we are beholden to His unknowable Sire, since when countless have perished in his name, or surrendered in artefacts of the infant psyche, in cathedrals, churches, tabernacles, chapels [. . .] in corrugated iron shacks on the outskirts of commerce and privilege, where the already beaten station themselves to the dumb hereafter. (*CS*, 178–9)

The words, again, are those of a character, not of Berry *in propria persona*, but there is an imaginative energy here which, especially when located alongside Berry's vision elsewhere in these stories, bespeaks a deep creative involvement. Berry portrays a post-Christian south Wales, where hymns are not sung in chapel but in the pub or club of a Saturday night, 'Calon Lan' alongside 'Blue Moon', choruses from 'The Desert Song' and 'Rock Around the Clock' ('Natives', *CS*, 80–4). These working men live in an existentialist reality, determining the direction of their lives as best they can by their own determined, individual efforts: 'Nature herself has to be man-handled, forced, controlled, exploited, and coal-getting's the essence of it, less than a short spit away from deep sea trawling' (*CS*, 88). This is a world governed solely by time and chance, where life, like that of Cadwgan Pugh in 'Left Behind', can be snuffed out at any moment by a massive slab of rock in the pit 'slamming down out of millions of lightless years, without warning' (*CS*, 88). After Cadwgan's death and the pious simplicities of the minster at the funeral service, his widow, Nita, 'bankrupt past all telling' (*CS*, 91), walks in the dark of night up to the chapel and burns it down, ending her own life in the process.

Ultimately, the only reality in these stories which transcends the mundane, material world of work and of the domestic is the natural world of the fields and the hillsides. In *History Is What You Live* Berry explicitly compares this world with the visions preached from the pulpits of the chapels. Recalling his own times with his dogs on the hillsides, he comments:

> Father, Son and Holy Ghost meant naught. Multitudes sang the trinity. They sickened me, still do, from archbishops down to the tidiest back street chapel-goer. Life's the clincher, inner and outer yeasting the matrix of YOU and ME. Christian adults preached cramp while trees, plants, fowls of the air and fishes in water, all things alive-O alive-O gouted sap and spunk. (*HWYL*, 58)

It is a remarkable moment, a celebration not of any Wordsworthian notion of nature as a manifestation of a transcendent spiritual reality, but of the processes of life itself, of natural physical life, and of individual selves as part of those processes. It is into the freedom and energy of this realm that, as we have seen, men venture with their friends and their dogs.

And it is explicitly a realm of *masculine* freedom, a place where few women are allowed to venture in these stories. When, in 'Boy and Girl', sixteen-year-old Emyr takes his girlfriend, Gwyneth, out on to the hills, while he strides ahead, revelling in the natural world around him, the streams and the birds, Gwyneth cannot keep up. Her constant cries of 'Wait for me!' irritate him and, we are told, 'shrivelled his rapture' (*CS*, 259). Albeit the narrative is in the third person, the point of view is essentially Emyr's. As he looks down, waiting once more for Gwyneth to climb up and reach him, he sees her beckoning hand as 'demanding, the familiar gesture, token of her imperious dream' (*CS*, 260); 'Humourlessly' reflecting that she will be 'plastered with cuckoo spit' as she ploughs after him, he decides that she can 'follow if she wants to, or otherwise. She can please herself' (*CS*, 261). Quite where the narrative sympathy is here is not easy to determine. When Emyr wonders to himself 'why she resented being a girl', the irony seems obvious, but then she sits on a stone in front of him, she is described as tucking her legs under him 'like a houri'. But Emyr's lack of comprehension of the girl is as evident as his insensitivity; when we see them years later, it is unsurprising that their marriage has collapsed into animosity and resentment. When Emyr decides to leave his wife and 'live tally' with Ruth, the barmaid at the local pub, one of the first things they do is to drive up into the hills, where 'Brave Ruthie' swims naked and is well able to keep up as they walk (albeit he is by now forty-eight, while she is over ten years younger). As they drive home, the car window open and Ruth urging him to sing, Emyr exclaims, 'Thank the Christ' (*CS*, 267). For once, a man and a woman have shared the freedom of the hillside together. But despite the upbeat ending, whether Emyr has any greater understanding of women is not evident; he talks to himself of Ruth's feeling for love and sharing, but he also sees her as being 'my woman. Mine while I live and breathe' (*CS*, 262, 265).

For Berry, female presence in the natural world is usually unwelcome. When Shad and Joe, out with their dogs, see a naked young woman sunbathing by a distant stream, they are initially appreciative: 'She's a what's-a-name, a naiad. Lovely thing' ('The Foxhunters', *CS*, 196). But when the dog is killed by the fox, in the irrationality of his grief, it is the girl whom Shad blames: 'Ah, Jesus Christ . . . jinx, that bloody girl, that bloody stripper out here' (*CS*, 199). The negativity towards women of those other two hunters who come 'out here' together in 'November Kill' is more deeply rooted. Both Miskin and Beynon's mothers left home when they were young boys: one has gone off to Spain and the other is 'Shacked up with some bloke in Swansea' (*CS*, 115). The animosity is never far from the surface: 'She's cranky, worse than my mother' (*CS*, 114), Beynon suddenly says when one of the dogs – named 'Lady' – snarls, and it is an animosity that colours their whole attitude towards women. As the two pals sit in the bar of the social club, conversation again turns to their mothers and Miskin asks, 'D'you think all women are the same, I mean selfish?'; Beynon answers bleakly, 'Christ knows. They go their own way like cats' (*CS*, 120). They are not the only men in these stories to be portrayed as damaged by their relations with their mothers. Rosebud Prosser remembers his mother as 'a saint', but as he himself has come to realise, living with her until she dies has inhibited his chance of marriage or even satisfactory relations with other women ('Rosebud Prosser', *CS*, 173). Other mothers are more overt in their constraint of their sons; both Lemuel Nelson and Redvers Gillard's flight from the village is as much driven by maternal pressures as by economic, from the 'Mouth [. . .] indoors' and the 'haggard fury' ('Comrades in Arms', *CS*, 57). On the degree to which their creator's gender attitudes were themselves coloured by such pressures one can only speculate. As Barbara Prys-Williams has pointed out, it is evident in Berry's autobiography that his relations with both his parents was an emotionally distant one (he refers to them throughout as 'George' and 'Mary Anne'), but it is his mother's rejection of him, after Berry goes AWOL from the army, that is 'absolute', greater than his father's.[16]

Almost inevitably, wives are rarely seen in positive terms, though when Lewis Rimmer sees his wife, compared with the young woman serving in the local chemist's shop, as looking 'like a bag of slurry tied round the middle', his appalling comment is not endorsed by the narrator, and indeed the reader is given a different perspective on Lewis and his eyeing of the young shop assistant when she winces as she looks at 'the rawness of his ugly old face, his huge, black-nailed, gripping fingers' ('Time Spent', *CS*, 93). While Lewis treats his wife as oppressively as Emyr treats Gwyneth, other wives are seen by men as putting 'the snaffle' on their husbands ('Natives', *CS*, 80). Marriage is almost never portrayed as emotionally or sexually satisfying in these stories. In 'Reaping the Sown', Dilwyn and his wife Myfanwy make love in the countryside, in the context of these stories itself an ominous location for a man to engage with a woman. When they emerge from swimming naked in a chilly pool, Myfanwy giggles at the fact that Dilwyn's penis has 'shrivelled'. She takes the initiative in the love-making – 'Lay down, I'll be jockey' (CS, 66): 'Myfanwy's fingernails scrabbled welts on his chest. She slid to and fro, her blonde hair shawled over her face' (*CS*, 67). 'Do you think I'm over-sexed?' she asks; when she grabs his testicles and makes love to him again, he climaxes prematurely, leaving her unsatisfied: '"Wait for me, Dil, wait, wait!" "I can't!" She gagged, whimpering, "O Jesus . . ." He felt defeated. "I'm not made of stone." [. . .] Myfanwy argued, "It's always the same"' (*CS*, 67). This sexual incapacity, the ultimate masculine failure, is the beginning of the downward slide of Dilwyn and Myfanwy's marriage which, as we have already seen, ends with Dilwyn in his caravan, alone and indeed defeated. If this is perhaps the bleakest of Berry's stories, the title of 'Before Forever After' suggests that, almost uniquely in these stories, the relationship between Rebecca and Strapper, crippled by an accident on the building site, will indeed be a happy one, despite his workmates' initial misgivings about her ('She's got him for a stud, pure and simple', *CS*, 37). At the same time, one registers that that happy ending has involved 'Big Strapper' becoming physically dependent on his wife; at the end he drives off in the little three-wheeler provided for the disabled; Rebecca follows on her motorcycle.

Berry not only writes in these short stories out of a world he knows, but does so with a consistent force and discipline, imposed by the form itself, not always maintained elsewhere in his fiction. He writes about that world with a shrewd, sometimes mordant and occasionally acerbic perspective, a perspective present in the very texture of the writing. Along with the occasional clipped, staccato syntax character-istic of his work, Berry is also capable of writing, particularly when describing the vitality of the natural world, in a style which is fluid, fresh and lyrical. His is a vigorous and direct voice that is at times unafraid of a descriptive incongruity that can verge on the surreal: a pony's eyes in the soft flare of a lamp in the pit gleam 'like spoons' (*CS*, 50), a woman's 'delicate [. . .] nostrils [are] red-raw as the inflamed poop-holes of sickly babies' (*CS*, 190), a setting sun disappears 'like an apricot slice on the horizon' (*CS*, 225). The colloquialisms of the pit and the pub jostle with idiosyncratic coinages ('swilkered', 'chogged', 'milpuffy', 'dappered') and an altogether more consciously formal register ('couchant', 'trudgeoned', 'ectoplasm', 'prognathous', 'echelon', 'vagaries') which serves to distance the narrator from the working world of the Valleys and makes us as readers aware of a slightly detached, perspective-giving voice. Berry's refusal to be constrained by the niceties of literary decorums, one feels, is of a piece with the obstinate refusal of protagonists like Gabe Lloyd to be subject to the constraints of social codes and conventions, the writing a version of their stubborn, often lonely, struggle to shape, control, *man*-handle a world.

Notes

[1] Simon Baker (ed.), *Ron Berry: Collected Stories* (Llandysul: Gomer, 2000), pp. 105, 107. All further references are to this edition and are incorporated into the text (*CS*).
[2] Ron Berry, *The Full-Time Amateur* (London: W. H. Allen, 1966).
[3] Alun Richards, 'In Good Pasture: A memoir of Ron Berry and friends', *New Welsh Review*, 38 (Autumn 1997), 20. See Dai Smith, *In the Frame* (Cardigan: Parthian, 2010), p. 174.
[4] See Robert Thomas, 'Make it true, make it new', *New Welsh Review*, 38 (Autumn 1997), 14.
[5] Richards's letter is reproduced in Smith, *In the Frame*, pp. 198–9. The first issue of *Planet* was published in 1970. See also Alun Richards (ed.), *The Penguin Book of Welsh Short Stories* (Harmondsworth: Penguin, 1976), pp. 264–79.
[6] *Collected Stories* includes one unpublished story, 'Boy and Girl', which Berry left in manuscript, and one story published posthumously in *New Welsh Review*, 'Who Belonged Just Long Enough Ago'.
[7] Ron Berry, *History Is What You Live* (Llandysul: Gomer, 1998), p. 37. Further references will be included in the text (*HWYL*).
[8] The term 'living tally', refers to the act of cohabiting outside of marriage. This may or may not have involved the paying of rent.
[9] Frank O'Connor, *The Lonely Voice: A Study of the Short Story* (London: Macmillan, 1963).
[10] O'Connor, *The Lonely Voice*, p. 20. An American critic, Thomas Gullason, writing contemporaneously with O'Connor, comes to strikingly similar conclusions: he writes that 'the novelist has been called "the long distance runner", and he is not lonely. The short story writer has been called a "sprinter", and he is lonely'. See Thomas H. Gullason, 'The Short Story: An Underrated Art', in *Studies in Short Fiction*, 2 (1964), 13–31.
[11] O'Connor, *The Lonely Voice*, p. 19.
[12] Clare Hanson (ed.), *Re-Reading the Short Story* (London: Macmillan, 1989), p. 2.

13. Uniquely, footnotes are supplied to the mining terms in 'Lew's Old Man'. This was evidently at the request of the editor of *New Welsh Review* when the story was first published. (These are maintained in *Collected Stories*.) See Ron Berry's scornful letter in Smith, *In the Frame*, p. 249.
14. The friendship of Lew and Rick clearly owes something to that between Berry and Vernon Rees in the late 1930s, when the two young men cycled regularly 'thirty odd miles every evening' and took part in races. The friendship, one of several close male friendships which Berry refers to in his autobiography, was he says 'a starry phase for all my life' (*HWYL*, 71–7, 105).
15. Berry's naming of the pair carefully associates them with British military imperialism: not only is Lemuel's surname 'Nelson', but Redvers presumably was given his unusual name in tribute to Sir Redvers Buller, VC, who had been Commander-in-Chief of British forces in South Africa in the second Boer War.
16. It was presumably his mother who refused him access to the family home at this point. See *HWYL*, 116. On Berry's relation with his mother, see Barbara Prys-Williams's essay in the present collection.

4

READING HECTOR BEBB: MASCULINITY AND MYTHIC PARADIGMS IN *SO LONG, HECTOR BEBB* (1970)

John Perrott Jenkins

In late 1970, a *Times Literary Supplement* reviewer, perplexed by Ron Berry's bravura novel, *So Long, Hector Bebb,* judged it to be a 'confusion of voices'.[1] With its fourteen narrators, unsentimental Valleys setting, and raw, sometimes brutal narrative, it proved a fictional bridge too far for the hapless reviewer, and was soon brushed from the manicured paths of metro-approved culture. Berry continued to have strong advocates in Wales, however, like Dai Smith and John Pikoulis, and since the novel's re-issue by Parthian in 2006, at a time when Welsh anglophone writing was acquiring publishers and admirers, it has enjoyed justified critical plaudits. Daniel G. Williams, for example, judges it to be 'the most experimental and successful of all Welsh boxing novels';[2] Craig Austin wonders if it is 'maybe *the* great Welsh novel';[3] and for Niall Griffiths, it is 'one of the greatest novels to come out of the twentieth century'.[4]

Yet for all this acclaim, little has been written about the composition of its brilliantly conceived central character: the hypertrophic, iconic male, Hector Bebb – the novel's eponymous focus. In her *Narrative Fiction: Contemporary Poetics*, Shlomith Rimmon-Kenan distinguishes between 'story' and 'text'. She suggests that while 'story' is 'a succession of events in chronological order', in the text 'all the items of the narrative content are filtered through some prism or perspective'. In other words, 'the text is what we read'.[5] This chapter proposes that a gender-orientated reading of *So Long, Hector Bebb* offers a prism or perspective into appreciating the rich possibilities that constructing a figure like Hector Bebb offered a former 'Shoni Tarzan' like Ron Berry.[6] It begins from the premise that Hector Bebb is endowed with male-approved hypermasculine signifiers at once of his present and the past, his times and earlier times; that he exemplifies a phenomenon Christopher E. Forth calls a 'violent yet rejuvenating alternative to an inauthentic life devoted to politeness, consumption and appearances'.[7] If this were all it would be achievement enough. But for Berry, Hector Bebb also functions as a means of probing, through those same gendered attributes, the problematic relationship between the male self and the 'other': the male and the female, the animal and the human, the animal in the human, the natural and the civilised, the primitive and the domesticated.

Berry begins his enquiry by constructing Hector Bebb through the medium of boxing, an activity where the sole purpose is to inflict physical damage on an opponent. By association, it functions in the novel as a metonym for unequivocally hypermasculine practices and rituals that in their sheer brutality, through the ages, separate a man from other men and, most certainly in this novel, separate men from women. Identifying the peculiar qualities of such masculinity, Joyce Carol Oates observes that they are intensely self-referential and ritualistically dangerous: 'In the brightly lit ring, man is *in extremis*, performing an atavistic rite or *agon*.'[8] In one respect, the entire text of *So Long, Hector Bebb* itself functions as a brightly lit ring. Under its intense spotlight, the reader is invited to observe in Hector Bebb a hypermasculine presence *in extremis*, performing a sequence of atavistic rites: inflicting severe physical and cerebral damage on opponents, killing a rival – his wife's lover – by main force, and living wild as a fugitive on the hills, which lead inevitably to his isolation and death.

In his short appreciation of the novel, Craig Austin comments that 'there are no heroes here'.[9] This essay proposes that, to the contrary, it is precisely as a hero, in a paradigmatic, mythopoeic, tragic sense, that Hector Bebb is conceived. Ian Watt notes the power of mythic archetypes to embody 'a single-minded pursuit by the protagonist of one of the characteristic desires of Western man'. Such figures, Watt argues, embody 'an *arete* and a *hubris*, an exceptional prowess and a vitiating excess, in spheres of action that are particularly important in our culture'.[10] Hector Bebb is such a figure. When an example of elite manhood appears in 'the here and now', Christopher E. Forth remarks, 'it must bear the residual traces of these other times and places'.[11] And through a form of 'mythic realism',[12] Berry interfuses the verisimilitude of Hector Bebb's construction as consummate boxer with paradigms, both mythic and legendary, of the male as warrior, 'from other times and places'. The result localises but also universalises his 'exceptional prowess and vitiating excess', his *arete* and *hubris* as features of the elite but doomed male.

Within this heroic model, Hector Bebb follows a broad but recognisable mythic trajectory of early neglect, initiation and emergence as an exemplary model of an admired physical manhood, followed by exclusion from a social and legal framework to which he cannot be reconciled. In death, his rare distinction attracts continued devotion. The mythic archetypes underpinning the surface narrative of Hector's construction begin with his parentage. Writing on the 'hero', Fitzroy Raglan (Lord Raglan) points out that heroes are often conceived in atypical circumstances – sometimes adulterously, sometimes by deception, and sometimes of undetermined paternity.[13] Hector Bebb's parentage is unusual. He is possibly conceived out of wedlock, neglected by his mother and abandoned by his elusive father, 'something-Bebb', who, in Sammy John's suggestive meteorological trope, 'came and vanished from Cymmer town like a piece of weather' (*SLHB*, 10).[14] In keeping with Raglan's pattern of heroic development, we are told virtually nothing of Hector's early childhood. He is taken in and fostered by Sammy and Sue John, who, in the text's final draft, have no children of their own. Sammy becomes not only Hector's surrogate father –who 'dotes on him' (*SLHB*, 104) – but also his mentor. Like the archetypal hero warrior figure, Hector is separated from female influence. Sue John's initially maternal concern for him withers until 'she'd have trampled over Hector in the gutter' (*SLHB*, 11). Relocated into the space of the boxing gymnasium by Sammy, and animated by its male values of competition, somatic power and aggression, Hector is distinguished from his fellows by his enthusiasm for the disciplines of training, preparation and contest. It quickly becomes evident to Sammy that he incarnates a remarkable form of potent masculinity: 'Pure single-mindedness, fighting his one and only love' (*SLHB*, 10).

Fundamental to Hector Bebb's pre-eminence is his fusion of ratiocination, intuition and utter self-belief. On an early visit to the White Hart gymnasium, he displays the innate proficiency marking out the hero figure when, after initially taking a beating, he knocks unconscious with two deadly blows the experienced Len Jules, who 'sat there like a man sleeping' (*SLHB*, 15). Almost concurrent with his greatest success, having won the British middleweight title through a feat of controlled aggression, Hector displays 'a vitiating excess', an unusual loss of control, in killing Emlyn Winton, his wife Millie's lover. A prey to chronic claustrophobia, he dreads prison and flees. His expulsion from an enclosed world in which he is pre-eminent echoes Raglan's paradigm that the hero 'loses favour with the Gods [. . .] and is driven from the throne and city'.[15]

Hector Bebb finally suffers an early death, not, as Raglan accords some heroes, 'at the top of a hill', but from a fatal fall down one, and like other heroes he is revered by men after his death.[16] While *So Long, Hector Bebb* secularises religious iconography, respect bordering on reverence is inflected through two differing though connected topologies.[17] The first, communicated through Bella Pearson's narrative, reveals the chasm existing between male and female evaluation of Hector. For Bella, with her aspirations to bourgeois respectability, Hector is unlamented in death. He was simply uncivilised: 'One of the lowest of the low' (*SLHB*, 241). Her husband, however, Hector's manager, the invariably unsentimental Abe, feels compelled to undertake a secular pilgrimage to 'take a last look' (*SLHB*, 241) at Hector's remarkable body. Gathering Hector's associates together, he visits Tosteg, views the body, weeps, and salutes Hector's memory by uncharacteristic generosity later in Tommy Wills's pub.

In the second topology, communicated through Sammy John, Prince Saddler, a disfigured war veteran devoted to Hector, insists that he and Sammy brave the bitter weather to visit the site where Hector died. Raglan notes that the dead hero 'has one or more holy sepulchres',[18] and Sammy's severely pragmatic approach to the visit contrasts with the quasi-religious experience it is for Prince. The text has already implied Prince's reverential attitude to Hector when he wagers generously on him to win a fight, with the simple words, 'I have faith' (*SLHB*, 75), and for Prince the visit becomes 'a pilgrimage' (*SLHB*, 259). Despite Sammy's feeling that it was the most 'futile trip I've ever undertaken' (*SLHB*, 259), even he resorts to religious discourse to express his own feelings. He believes that if the world ends and boxing begins again with strangely mutant contestants, 'some junior monk will tote [Hector's] credit' (*SLHB*, 259) by carrying a signed, mass-produced photograph of him as a relic that survived the conflagration. The final phrasing of this reflection is significant, for it underwent delicate honing in the novel's redrafting. The first draft offers the anaemic assurance that if, after a global calamity, boxing begins again 'from scratch [. . .] they'll still remember Hector Bebb'.[19] In a later draft, the photograph is added as an iconographic 'relic', and the vague pronoun 'they' is changed to a typewritten 'some fanatic'. Presumably because of its pejorative associations, 'fanatic' is later erased and the handwritten phrase 'junior monk' with its favourable connotations of homage and veneration inserted instead.[20] The eschatological breadth of the image, together with Sammy's view that Prince 'had the look of a man expecting to be saved [. . .] the look of a rigorous Christian' (*SLHB*, 259), combine to lodge Hector Bebb securely within the pantheon of heroic figures, the memory of whom carries a redemptive promise.

Within this broad architectural design of the fated hero, the text defines Hector through references to more specific *agonistic* iconographies. Varda Burstyn observes that sport bases itself in 'archaic residual values associated with the highly differentiated, ranked gender order of tribal male warrior culture'.[21] By having the veteran soldier Prince Saddler conceive Hector as both a reincarnated 'warrior' and a 'gladiator', someone who, like his own former comrades, 'relished war as the supreme existence' (*SLHB*, 60), the central sections of the novel create a symbolic and metaphoric pattern aligning him with a 'male warrior culture', where the lethal male body represents the apex of masculine definition. Hector Bebb is 'born for action' (*SLHB*, 9), a bellicose male for whom somatic passivity is a psychological itch that he can express only through a physiological figure: it 'hurts worse than a pasting' (*SLHB*, 9). Tommy Wills, by contrast, brings a distinct pragmatism to his career as a boxer. Shackled as he is into a pattern of patriarchal conformity, boxing for him is a means to an end; he fights in order to 'put up the bond' on a pub when he retires (*SLHB*, 81).

Joyce Carol Oates recognises the alluring but menacing status of the boxer, who inhabits a world where 'values are reversed, evaginated'. A boxer, she writes, is 'valued not for his humanity but for being a "killer"'.[22] The fictional Sammy John provides a similar insight into the boxer's ambiguous status. When he assesses the young Hector as 'a killer' (*SLHB*, 11), he is identifying his singular aptitude for conflict in a figurative compliment that becomes a proleptic truth connecting him to his mythical namesake. The veneration of the boxer as an exemplar of warrior manhood, as killer, exists in Western culture from antiquity. In Book V of the *Aeneid*, for instance, the Trojan Entellus 'showered volleys of blows, thick as the hailstones which storm-clouds send' on Dares, nearly killing him.[23] Similarly, in his championship fight with Jesse Markham, Hector is 'unloading as [Markham] tries to smother, over and under his arms, unloading my lot, everything right to the bell' (*SLHB*, 84–5). Even his gamesmanship against Mel Carpenter, when he responds to Carpenter's having a strip of wire in his glove by biting him on his shoulder, is legitimised by classical precedent. As Tom Winnifrith remarks, 'There is not in Homer the belief that behaving well somehow wins matches and battles.'[24]

However, Hector Bebb's mythical lineage extends beyond antiquity to interfuse with more recent incarnations of combative masculinity. As part of the novel's intertextual design, several characters, particularly Hector, have names that echo twentieth-century real life or fictional representations of the male as heroic combatant. Clearly, one has to be cautious connecting Hector of Cymmer with Hector of Troy, but in thus naming its protagonist the text incorporates Hector Bebb into the mythical literary tradition of the fated warrior hero, while also associating him through a phonic chiming with the real-life American boxing legend Harry Greb, the world middleweight champion between 1923 and 1926. While Hector Bebb suffers a damaging cut above his eye as the result of a foul blow, Harry Greb actually lost the sight in his right eye for a similar reason. As so often with those who are revered as heroes, Greb's early death, like Hector's, enhanced his iconic renown. A recent article on Greb, for instance, reaches quite naturally for the same combative noun that Prince employs for Hector, when it appraises Greb as 'the most formidable warrior in boxing history'.[25]

But suggestive nominal insinuations in the novel extend beyond Hector Bebb, although they all serve to burnish his reputation. Berry was well read in American fiction, and in Bernard Malamud's novel *The Natural* (1952), the hero Roy Hobbs ousts Bump Baily from his pre-eminent role as the baseball star of the New York Knights.[26] In a piece of intertextual legerdemain, in early drafts of *So Long, Hector Bebb* Berry introduces a parallel when a character called Jerome Wilkinson-Tanner acquires a name change into the middleweight champion boxer Bernard Bump Tanner, who is defeated by Hector. And, like Malamud's 'natural', Roy Hobbs, Ron Berry's Hector Bebb is both a fated hero and 'a natural' (*SLHB*, 12). More prosaic, but also indicative of the novel's intertextual apparatus, is the naming of Tommy Wills, a boxer also defeated by Hector, whose name echoes Harry Wills, the legendary American 'Black Panther'. Even a minor character, like the boxer Vic Crane, was originally called Soldier Crane, arguably after Ernest Hemingway's boxer Soldier Bartlett.[27] The cumulative significance of such resonances implies a subtle narrative strategy. The figures orbiting Hector Bebb in the novel secure his pre-eminence within a fictional constellation, but they also amplify his allure by their nominal connection to extra-textual embodiments of combative masculinity.

Freely sourcing mythic archetypes and paradigms in assembling Hector Bebb's distinctive alterity, the novel tantalisingly infuses a seemingly prosaic incident with an undercurrent of resonating extra-realism. In preparation for Hector's championship title contest, an odd-job builder, an 'old sioni craftsman, genuine as silver money' (*SLHB*, 73), assembles a practice ring for him. The builder, who is not named but is nonetheless endowed with unimpeachable integrity, does not appear in early drafts of the novel and when he does later, he does not address Hector. But as draft succeeded draft Berry's builder acquired a strangely seer-like presence, and a significant change in function. In Sammy John's account, the builder comments that Prince Saddler, who is present and of whom he has already heard, is 'something extra special', but he then turns to address Hector: '"though you got a touch of it in you too, boyo." He stroked his hand on Hector's chest then he went bobbing down the lane from Cwmbryn, toolbag humping his back. We never saw him again' (*SLHB*, 74). His ad hominem judgement and his stroking of Hector's chest – as though tactile contact confers a benediction and confirms an insight – contrasts the shrewdness of his perception with the clumsiness of his gait as he bobs down the lane, leaving without a farewell. The paragraph's closing sentence is at once factual and teasingly suggestive. There is no practical reason why the builder's departure should attract Sammy's comment, but in doing so it generates a suggestive frisson, where the realism of the occasion melds with the mythic paradigm of the stranger/seer who appears, impresses, pronounces and vanishes. It is appropriate that this incident is articulated by Sammy for he, too, recognises 'something extra special' in Hector. Speaking of himself and Sue, he acknowledges that: 'We're like a couple of adverts. No matter what, you've got to find the real, stick by whatever's real. Hector Bebb, he's real' (*SLHB*, 11–12).

Sammy's distinction between the ersatz and the authentic, and the jobbing builder's strangely resonating moment, both aid Berry's construction of Hector Bebb within the mythos of heroic masculinity, the warrior male living both inside and outside his time. But Berry goes further in substantiating Hector's distinctive alterity through two further attributes: his pre-eminent gifts as a combative male, and his attitude to women. As a boxer, Hector Bebb incorporates two cherished qualities of ultra-masculine definition: a physique and a psychology acutely suited to the rigours of extreme action and performance. A helpful distinction between this fictional representation of physical hegemony and a real-life equivalent is apparent in an interview R. W. Connell conducted with Steve Donoghue, an Australian champion surfer, whose 'job is to be an iron man and to market himself as a sports personality'.[28] Donoghue comments on the enormous personal sacrifices required to achieve and maintain such an exemplary 'iron man' status: 'it is a pretty disciplined sort of life. It's like being in jail'.[29]

So Long, Hector Bebb constructs Hector on a different model of hegemonic masculinity. Unlike Donoghue, who incarcerates himself in a job as an iron man in order to market himself as a product, Hector Bebb shows little interest in material self-advancement, though Bump Tanner is convinced that 'Hector's mug would sell shirts, socks, beer, anything. You name it, anything for men' (*SLHB*, 107). Significantly, it also places him outside a constraining system of patriarchal capitalism, for Donoghue's pragmatically functional incarceration contrasts radically with the liberation that boxing gives Hector Bebb for self-realisation. For him, a hard-fought contest is: 'A great fight. The inside of my smeller like a nutmeg grater. Two shiners. Ears like burnt cobs' (*SLHB*, 27). Christopher E. Forth writes that boxing 'foregrounds pain and violence as repressed male experiences that are at once cathartic, therapeutic and empowering'.[30] The complex psycho-physiological process Forth describes, where pain experienced through violent action is exhilarating, distinguishes Hector's masculinity from that of his more pedestrian colleagues, and enables the text to connect him once more to the elite masculinities of the warrior and the gladiator.

Hector's response to pain leads the prosaic Abe Pearson to regard him as a 'high grade machine' (*SLHB*, 22), an object to be utilised, but to do so is to mechanise his complex natural functioning. Sammy's observation that Hector is 'all fighter, pure and simple as a bird flying' (*SLHB*, 17), by contrast, emphasises Hector's unfettered integration of form, action and purpose. Virtually every action exhibits his self-actualising through preparation and performance. Millie complains, for example, that he even darted 'his fists across the table during meals, catching flies for boxing practice' (*SLHB*, 90).[31] In a text where bodily hexis is prominent, Hector's distinguishes him even from other boxers who train at the White Hart. Millie twice refers to him as a 'panther' (*SLHB*, 36, 37) in the ring, 'stalking', 'always on the go'. And when Prince Saddler first startles Hector on a training run, Hector 'jinked off like a surprised wolf' (*SLHB*, 58). The two references define key aspects of his predatory masculinity both in the ring and later on the hills: feline power, sinuous grace, and lupine associations with the untamed wilderness.

Dai Smith writes that 'the raw edge of boxing can never be completely overcome since it is this which lies at the heart of it', and it is in 'the raw edge' that Hector excels.[32] In a 'scrap' with Bump Tanner which Hector has subtly provoked:

> I'm out to put him away. Two short hooks sink in down below. Bump's feet widened for his right hand swinger. He'll never learn. I felt it dying like a flap of rag against my neck. Then Bump took four hard shots. Three lefts and a right, real hooks sent from the shoulder. (*SLHB*, 32)

In this compact passage, the text assembles a sequence of signifiers indicating Hector's particular combination of qualities: ruthless determination, technical proficiency, tactical awareness and contempt, as Bump's failed swinger leaves him exposed to the clinical finesse of 'four hard shots'. After the fight, Hector carries on training – 'medicine ball, speedball, skipping' (*SLHB*, 33). Bump, 'who doesn't look too dandy' (*SLHB*, 33) is off training for ten days. Hector's judgement of Bump – 'He can't ever go where I'm set on reaching in this game' (*SLHB*, 33) – reveals not only his own exceptional prowess – his *arete* – but a *hubris* that leads to the coming tragic peripeteia when he kills Emlyn Winton and becomes a fugitive.

Hector is also distinguished from his fellows by his attitude to women. Christopher E. Forth suggests that '[b]ravery, strength, endurance and sexual potency figure prominently in most lists of ideal male bodily attributes',[33] all of which the text confers on Hector Bebb, except for a strong libido. Indeed, the novel goes out of its way to make this clear. Abe Pearson believes him to be 'cool in the goolies' (*SLHB*, 23), and Millie compares her 'panther' in the ring to 'a little cock robin' (*SLHB*, 91) in bed. But in *So Long, Hector Bebb*, sexual potency becomes an attribute directed toward lesser characters, promiscuous users and abusers of women like Vic Crane, Emlyn Winton and Bump Tanner. Sarah Morse suggests that 'although Hector implies that his masculine energies are directed into his boxing career, the matter of his sexless nature is ambiguous'.[34] But it can also be argued that the text constructs in Hector Bebb a singular version of hegemonic masculinity which is largely detached from sexuality. And what Morse calls 'the question of [Hector's] sexual orientation',[35] is a means of defining rather than questioning this phenomenon. Sammy John's comment that before the fight with Jesse Markham, Hector 'slept like a saint' (*SLHB*, 74) makes a surprising but illuminating connection between two seemingly conflicting modes of being, the spiritually ordained and the physically embodied.

In this regard, Joyce Carol Oates makes the pertinent observation that boxing is 'a unique, closed self-referential world, obliquely akin to those severe religions, in which the individual is both "free" and "determined"'.[36] It is the paradox of freedom achieved through constraint that constructs Hector Bebb's singular mode of being. Obliquely akin to a saint, he, too, is engaged in the single-minded expression of unity of self through unity of purpose. It is, as even the severely pragmatic Abe Pearson recognises, 'a gift from on high', making Hector an elite example, one of those who 'don't come often' (*SLHB*, 24). Men like Emlyn Winton, the barman and Millie's lover, however, do come often. Commenting on his 'clucks and tishes' (*SLHB*, 45), and the way he 'wiggled his fingers through his gorgeous locks' (*SLHB*, 46), Sammy John dismisses him contemptuously as 'a genuine sack of lard' (*SLHB*, 45).

The novel, however, defines Hector Bebb not through success with women, but through the heroic conquest of men. Hector's marriage fails not because he abuses Millie, but because he is unable to appreciate her craving for a man who makes 'a girl melt like butter' (*SLHB*, 90). He recognises that 'she was left out in the cold a bit', but believes that she 'preferred herself that way' (*SLHB*, 7). She admits that 'at home there's no danger in him' (*SLHB*, 37), unlike Abe Pearson, who sadistically stubs out his cigar on his wife's thigh to demonstrate his dominance (*SLHB*, 134). Hector's difficulty in establishing intimate relationships with women recurs later when his liaison with Doreen Evass also fails. He realises that 'we were as different as salt and sugar. Me and Doreen were foreigners' (*SLHB*, 167). Within the larger context of the novel, this episode is less an observation of Hector's lukewarm sexuality than another instance of a problematic gender incompatibility that drives much of the narrative.

The intertextualities of the novel's mythic realism, then, enable a celebration of Hector Bebb as a representative of elite Welsh masculinity located within the pantheon of combative heroes. In its later sections, however, as the narrative accelerates him towards his tragic demise, it focuses more dramatically on what Christopher E. Forth calls the 'tensions between polish and primitivity, brawn and brain, and activity and sedentariness'.[37] It is these tensions, present in perceptions of Hector Bebb throughout the text, that are foregrounded in the final third of the novel where Hector as mythopoeic ultra-male becomes Hector as liminal fugitive, existing both physically and psychologically on the fringes of civilisation.

Structurally, the narrative progressively drives Hector Bebb from a social world limited to boxing to a narrower world with Prince Saddler at Bryn Farm (and later briefly with Doreen), to a male-defined domain on the hills above Tosteg. In this last space, the novel interrogates through Hector Bebb, what it is that remains of an elite manhood when the residual complications of social obligation fall away. This final trajectory of Hector Bebb's narrative is both actual and symbolic, and deeply personal to Berry himself. In an undated unpublished essay, he writes that: 'I felt drawn to the wilderness. Extremity manures the soul. The day by day imperatives of being civilised, are less significant when confronted by oneself under a weight of sky.'[38] Whereas in much Valleys fiction, green spaces afford recuperation and relaxation, *So Long, Hector Bebb* adopts a more ambivalent interpretation of Welsh pastoral, where the hills overlooking the valleys offer a threat as well as an embrace, an inhospitable otherness 'under a weight of sky' as well as a consoling return to nature. The dialogue with the self, generated by the extremity of the wilderness that Berry refers to, permeates the novel's examination of Hector Bebb's masculinity on the hills, and through it addresses some of the disturbing complications of the male as predator.

Prior to his forced exile, the amalgam of intertextual mythic archetypes underpinning his construction had been woven implicitly into the texture of the discourse, but these archetypes had not functioned as desired models of self-definition to which Hector Bebb himself aspired. As a peerless, primal male, Hector had required no external referents. When out shooting with Prince Saddler, for instance, he retrieves a mallard Prince has shot by plunging without hesitation into an icy lake too cold for the retriever. Overcome with admiration, Prince exults in this exemplary exhibition by 'a man matched to his environment' (*SLHB*, 151). However, when the novel removes Hector Bebb from virtually all human contact on the hills, and turns its lens unsentimentally on his unaccommodated masculinity, it dismisses Prince's easy elision of place and being. Instead, it provokes in Hector a direct confrontation not only with where he is, but who he is. Forced to re-evaluate his own ontological definition, the previously self-focalised Hector finds for the first time that he requires models of liminal masculinity through which to address his own new identity. Significantly, the two mythic models the novel gives him when *in extremis* are the American cowboy; and, as his prospects become yet more precarious, another liminal male, the wild man.

In an audio interview with Dai Smith, Ron Berry acknowledged that American cultural influences 'were an essential part of my growing up'.[39] It is perhaps no surprise, then, that the text uses the figure of the cowboy as a tool for shaping a subtle but significant modification in Hector Bebb's composition. References to Hector's enthusiasm for western novels, films and songs are strewn throughout the novel, and serve to align him by association with a culture that, as Jane Tompkins states, 'focuses exclusively on what men do'.[40] But when Hector is cast adrift on the hills, he is for the first time not entirely sure 'what men do'; or more specifically what a man would do in his position. From this point the novel moves into a new sphere of enquiry, where primal masculinity intersects with culturally influenced models. To provide himself with a new modus operandi, Hector actively and self-consciously constructs himself through the prism of western archetypes. And so, he imaginatively re-contextualises the hills above Pont Fawr as 'Bow and arrow country, [. . .] as pictured in Western stories' (*SLHB*, 190). When wet, chilled and disconsolate on his first night alone, he asks himself, 'What would a cowboy or a red Indian do on a night like this?' His response, 'Pull his slicker over himself and stick it out till daylight' (*SLHB*, 173), gratefully acknowledges not only the cowboy's stoicism, but illustrates the extent of his own imaginative immersion in a cowboy identity through his use of a western idiom for rainwear.[41] When the rain stops and he finds shelter, he builds a fire, enjoys a meal, and entertains himself with western tunes like 'Ghost Riders in the Sky' (*SLHB*, 173). Hector's masculinity is in no way impaired by this development, for as Jane Tomkins explains of the cowboy, while 'nature's wildness and hardness test his strength and will and intelligence, they also give him solace and repose'.[42]

Hector's identification with this liminal western figure offers the same solace and repose, and it marks a new development in someone previously 'born for action' (*SLHB*, 9). But in the novel's unsparing scrutiny of an elite masculinity thrust back entirely on its own resources, Berry introduces another, older and more problematic representation of liminal masculinity than the cowboy. Just as the hills in *So Long, Hector Bebb* project a tension between natural wildness, the depleted remains of an industrial past and an encroaching commercialised afforestation, so the novel positions Hector himself as occupying a transitional space between 'nature' and 'civilisation' in the ambiguous figure of the wild man.

When Tommy Wills sees a shabby Hector Bebb, whom he does not recognise, begging outside his pub, he associates him with 'the wild man of the woods [. . .] rotten, all hair, beard down to his chest' (*SLHB*, 179), hirsuteness being a signifier of the wild man's fallen state.[43] But a little later Tommy also sees him paradoxically as another kind of wild man, 'like a wanderer out of the Bible' (*SLHB*, 179–80). The dual optic through which Tommy views Hector both as degenerate subhuman and John-the-Baptist-like itinerant holy man identifies incompatible spheres of being represented by the wild man: the one traditionally a prey to ungovernable passion, the other a calibrated commitment to reflection and separation. Dorothy Yamamoto sees the wild man as a liminal figure who, 'Poised between two worlds, [. . .] brings to a head questions about the dividing line between animals and humans, and the distinctiveness of human identity'.[44] By utilising the manifold possibilities inherent in the wild man myth, the novel examines through Hector Bebb the complex amalgam of the human and the animal, intuition and intellect, frenzy and cognition, volition and reflection in a physically hegemonic subject when placed *in extremis*.

Throughout the novel, Hector has been 'poised between two worlds', between two incompatible, gendered perceptions by others of his manhood, as 'no more than a trained animal' (*SLHB*, 65) to Bella Pearson, and 'a single-minded genius' (*SLHB*, 213) to Sammy John. Having established through Tommy Wills how the wild man generates ambivalent responses to the 'other', the novel further confronts Hector Bebb's masculinity by aligning him with two equally incompatible, embodiments of this mythic archetype: the wild man as hunter-gatherer, and the warrior 'ape-man', Tarzan.[45] Both figures encode vastly influential, though differing perceptions of untrammelled masculinity through which Hector Bebb's final incarnation is represented. Yamamoto's 'dividing line between humans and animals' becomes a permeable tissue, through which the text interrogates Hector.

Both Jane Tompkins's writing on the cowboy and Roger Bartra's on the wild man reach similar conclusions on the relationship between these figures and the landscape they inhabit that connect them to Hector Bebb. Tompkins notes that although the cowboy's engagement with landscape initially involves fear and uncertainty, 'the landscape has ultimately a domesticating effect',[46] while Bartra contends that the mythical 'European wild man' is also 'the allegory of a domestic life in a wild context'.[47] Significantly, the wild man Bartra is referring to here is the hunter-gatherer Robinson Crusoe. While the hills above Tosteg have little in common with Crusoe's remote island, key aspects of Defoe's mythic archetype are apparent in Berry's novel, which point to a domesticating of Hector's virile masculinity. Like Crusoe, though in a lower acquisitive register, Hector makes calculated use of the products of civilisation, like a mandrel shaft, a shovel blade, stolen shoes and overcoats, so that the abandoned colliery winding-house on the hills becomes 'my home, funnily enough already my home' (*SLHB,* 196). Whereas Crusoe finds green limes 'very wholesome' and lays in quantities of grapes and lemons,[48] Hector, acutely aware of his physiological need for roughage, builds up 'a store of veg supplies from allotments' (*SLHB,* 219–20). Both figures find humour in their precarious positions. If Crusoe in his goatskin clothing 'could not but smile at the notion of my travelling through Yorkshire [. . .] in such a dress',[49] Hector in his wild-man beard 'felt tempted to laugh in [Tommy Wills's] face' (*SLHB,* 218) at being unrecognised outside Tommy's pub. And whereas Crusoe records salvaging 'bread, rice, three Dutch cheeses, five pieces of dried goat's flesh',[50] Hector, with an unmarked irony, refers to himself as 'concentrating like a housewife' (*SLHB,* 196) as he makes a shopping list of the essential goods he needs on a risky visit to Tosteg.

However, although Hector might domestically systematise his life on the hills, unrestrained violent action becomes a prerequisite of his very survival. Emma Smith suggests that 'incidents where Hector is at one with nature purposely romanticise such savagery',[51] but there is little romanticising when, weak with hunger, he drinks the hot blood of a sheep he has killed. This traumatic episode merits close examination, for it crystallises Berry's study of hypermasculine behaviour *in extremis.* As Hector prepares his assault on the unsuspecting creature, he once again requires a model of behaviour, and this time chooses Tarzan (*SLHB,* 193), a figure famous for his dauntingly impressive physical feats. Roger Bartra notes that the figure of Tarzan succeeds in popular culture because it displaces various 'uncomfortable aspects not readily adaptable to the requirements of imperialist culture'.[52] But the 'uncomfortable aspects' of male violence and their place in male identity, and therefore their interface with normative society, are exactly what Berry directly confronts as the novel progresses.

As Hector prepares for the attack, Berry, in a moment of textual brilliance, employs a taut figure that risks reducing the entire episode to bathos. Hector declares 'I [. . .] shoved Doreen's bread knife in my belt like Tarzan' (*SLHB*, 193). The conjunction is startling, for Tarzan's chosen weapon, we remember, is a long hunting-knife. Within its context, however, the image directs attention to the text's focus on the problematic intersection of violence and restraint, the primitive and the civilised, the hunting knife and the bread knife in shaping masculine definition.

Starving though Hector Bebb is when he sights the ewe and her lamb, he resists the temptation of a search for birds' eggs. The focus to begin with is on his monochromatic, cerebral self-objectification: '*Think*, Hector, use your wits', for the ewe means the deferred gratification of 'a big meal' (*SLHB*, 193). When the assault comes, however, Berry abruptly switches mode, internalising Hector's own experience to construct more radically how the human and the animal, the cognitive and the instinctive coalesce and conflict in moments of desperation. In a remarkable rhetorical sequence, Hector's discourse becomes impressionistic: it is allusive here, precise there, subjective and objective, graphic and mundane, a series of internalised sense impressions fusing with fleeting moments of objectified awareness, a blur of kaleidoscopic, ever-shifting data:

> I lost true sight, everything fuzzy and Roman candles firing inside my chest. Strength came in spasms, although I robbed myself, the lamb bleating, bleating, tormenting my mind. Blood splashed over my trousers. Heavy drops of rain began to fall. By and by dead lamb, unconscious ewe, me straddled over her, both of us quite still. She wiggled. I outed her again. (*SLHB*, 194)

Emma Davies judges this to be 'a fusion of the twin desires of sex and death, reconfigured by Berry as an orgasmic reclamation of (male) self'.[53] However, it is possible to see the experience less as a moment of ecstatic reclamation than as a loss of 'true sight', a moment of frightening self-erasure in a figure like Hector for whom self-discipline has been a defining characteristic. Freud reminds us that 'fright' is different from 'fear' because '[f]ear requires a definite object of which to be afraid. "Fright", however, is the name we give to the state a person gets into when he has run into danger without being prepared for it; it emphasises the factor of surprise.'[54] Throughout the novel Hector fears nothing, but here, for all his attempted modelling on Tarzan, the 'danger' he runs into is a frightening encounter with an aspect of himself rare in his previous experience. Desperate beyond measure as he is for food, the clinical control he displayed when he dispatched Bump Tanner with 'Three lefts and a right' (*SLHB*, 32) deserts him. His insight, 'although I robbed myself' becomes an aposiopesis, a curtailed self-evaluation referring not only to the strength he wasted, but to his horrified recognition that his violent paroxysms caused the lamb's terror. From being Prince Saddler's warrior figure, he becomes a contrite violator of innocence. In this critical instance, *So Long, Hector Bebb* distils the instantaneous and dynamic interaction between passion and conscience, action and self-scrutiny in moments of extreme mental activity. When his judgement returns, he feels that he has committed a transgressive act and buries the lamb – 'poor mite' (*SLHB*, 196) – in an act of reparation. As a boxer, Hector accepted the need to 'disregard sentiment' (*SLHB*, 9). As part of his narrative trajectory, he finds himself surprisingly susceptible to it, but also susceptible to 'fright', a very different 'factor of surprise'.[55]

In this final phase of Hector Bebb's construction, then, the novel inflects his masculinity through representations of the cowboy and the wild man. Together, they illustrate Hector Bebb exhibiting the problematical continuities of elite masculine definition more dramatically than the novel's earlier mythic prototypes had done. But through the figure of the wild man Berry goes much further, and pushes Hector Bebb to the very edge of a barely functioning cognitive manhood. When, later, he kills a dog for food '[u]nder some mad impulse' with 'two bangs against a rock' (*SLHB*, 219), and later still secretly visits Sammy John and Tommy Wills, the contrast between the celluloid figure of Tarzan and Berry's grimmer fictional reality is shocking. Hector, who 'jinked off like a surprised wolf' (*SLHB*, 58) in his prime, has now become 'a tired fox' (*SLHB*, 228). He is 'gnawed down in his spirit' (*SLHB*, 230). As a wanted man, and a wild man unable to reconcile the competing elements of his nature, there can be only one, fatal end to his trajectory. And so the manner of his going becomes crucial to cementing his tragic status.

Hector Bebb is both the agent and the victim of his own story, and he faces his death without complaint or fear. As he lies fatally injured from his fall over a sixty-foot cliff, his final monologue becomes a dialogue with himself expressed through stream of consciousness:

> It must have been instinct saying 'turn your head there's blood coming out from your mouth take it easy let go a bit at a time just let go slowly this is it this is it let go slowly this is it man let go for Christ's sake let go. Now let go'. (*SLHB*, 256–7)

The poet and critic Henri-Frédéric Amiel thought himself 'too much of a woman' and nursed a dream 'to be a man just once before death [. . .] to make my delicateness, my character, my style a bit more *brutal*, to *masculinize* myself and to *virilise* myself'.[56] Within the novel's strictly gendered dimorphism, Ron Berry creates in Hector Bebb a figure not needing to '*virilise*' himself. It is appropriate that the implication behind his final instruction, 'Now let go', asserts that it is he who will chose the moment when he commits himself to dying. As when he was a boxer, in confinement Hector finds freedom.

Ron Berry's achievement in so skilfully constructing a protagonist at once functioning within acceptable parameters of realism but enriched with mythic patterns and trajectories endows Hector Bebb with iconic status. In the manner of formal tragedy, the narrative ends not with the protagonist's death, but with a judgement upon him. When Sammy John and Prince Saddler visit the place where Hector died, it serves no purpose for the pragmatic Sammy: it is 'Useless offering so-long to Hector. He'll always be with me' (*SLHB*, 261). For Prince, however, an old warrior himself, only through physical proximity to the place of Hector's death can he express his reverence for and dependence on 'the old gladiator' (*SLHB*, 260). The novel closes with Sammy and Prince's mutual incomprehension. Either way, *So Long, Hector Bebb*, with its disarmingly colloquial but valedictory title, and its densely textured mythic echoes, serves as a requiem for and an enquiry into the passing of a cherished but problematical Valleys hypervirility. Cunningly wrought, linguistically dazzling, acutely perceptive and eight years in the writing, it is a novel, like Hector Bebb himself, of its time and for all time.

Notes

1. *Times Literary Supplement*, 3592 (1 January 1971), 5. Cited by Sarah Morse in '"Maimed Individuals": The Significance of the Body in *So Long, Hector Bebb* (1970)', in Katie Gramich (ed.), *Mapping the Territory: Critical Approaches to Welsh Fiction in English*, (Cardigan: Parthian, 2010), pp. 271–87 (p. 272).
2. Daniel. G Williams, *Wales Unchained: Literature, Politics and Identity in the American Century* (Cardiff: University of Wales Press, 2015), p. 45.
3. Craig Austin, 'Great Welsh Novels Revisited: *So Long, Hector Bebb*', in *Wales Arts Review* (10 November 2016). Available at www.walesartsreview.org/greatest-welsh-novel-6-so-long-hector-bebb-by-ron-berry. Accessed 18 November 2016.
4. Niall Griffiths, 'Foreword', Ron Berry, *So Long, Hector Bebb* (Cardigan: Parthian: 2006), p. xiii. All future references are to this edition.
5. Shlomith Rimmon-Kenan, *Narrative Fiction: Contemporary Poetics* (London: Routledge, 1994), p. 2–3.
6. John Pikoulis records that, 'As a young man Berry was what he calls a "Shoni Tarzan"', a nickname that could be anglicized to 'Johnny Tarzan'. John Pikoulis, 'Word-of-mouth cultures cease in cemeteries', *New Welsh Review*, 34 (Autumn 1996), 9–15 (p. 9).
7. Christopher E. Forth, *Masculinity in the Modern West: Gender, Civilisation and the Body* (Basingstoke: Palgrave Macmillan, 2008), p. 229.
8. Joyce Carol Oates, *On Boxing* (London: Bloomsbury, 1987), p. 75.
9. Austin, 'Great Welsh Novels Revisited: *So Long, Hector Bebb*'.
10. Ian Watt, *The Rise of the Novel* (Harmondsworth: Penguin, 1963), pp. 88–9.
11. Forth, *Masculinity in the Modern West*, p. 10.
12. A term M. Wynn Thomas uses when writing of Emyr Humphreys, in which myth enriches and suggests a deep-rooted continuity of human experience in an otherwise realistic text. In Berry's novel, the term indicates how Hector Bebb is at once a gifted Valleys boxer and a lineal descendant of heroic masculinities: M. Wynn Thomas, 'The Relentlessness of Emyr Humphreys', in *New Welsh Review*, 13 (1991), 37–40 (p. 39).
13. Lord Raglan, *The Hero: A Study in Tradition, Myth and Drama* (London: Methuen, 1936), p. 179.
14. Through Sammy's meteorological simile, the text teasingly hints at an extra-real agency fathering Hector. Zeus, we remember, came to Danaë as 'a piece of weather' – a golden rain shower – and fathered Perseus, the slayer of monsters, on her.
15. Raglan, *The Hero*, p. 180.
16. Raglan, *The Hero*, p. 180.
17. Barbara Prys Williams, 'History Is What You Live: Ron Berry's rumination on his life and conflicted times', pp. 13–28 (p. 15) in the present collection.
18. Raglan, *The Hero*, p. 180.
19. The Richard Burton Archives, Swansea University, Ron Berry Papers, WWE/1/1/3/1.
20. Ron Berry Papers, WWE/1/1/3/4.

[21] Varda Burstyn, *The Rites of Men: Manhood, Politics and the Culture of Sport* (Toronto and London: University of Toronto Press, 1999), p. 166.
[22] Oates, *On Boxing*, p. 74.
[23] Virgil, *The Aeneid*, Book V, trans. W. F. Jackson Knight (Harmondsworth: Penguin Classics, 1963), p. 133.
[24] Tom Winnifrith, 'Funeral Games in Homer and Virgil', in Michael Mallett (ed.), *Leisure in Art and Literature* (Basingstoke: Macmillan, 1992), pp. 14–26 (p. 16).
[25] Bob Mee, 'On This Day: Harry Greb dishes out one of boxing history's most savage beatings', in *Boxing News* (23 May 2019), n.p. Available at boxingnewsonline.net. Accessed 23 May 2019.
[26] Bernard Malamud, *The Natural* (California: Harcourt Brace and Company, 1952).
[27] See Ernest Hemingway's short story 'Fifty Grand', in *Men Without Women* (London: Jonathan Cape, 1975), pp. 114–56.
[28] R. W. Connell, 'An Iron Man: The Body and Some Contradictions of Hegemonic Masculinity', in Michael A. Messner and Donald F. Sabo (eds), *Sport, Men and the Gender Order* (Champaign, IL: Human Kinetic Books, 1990), pp. 83–95 (p. 85).
[29] Connell, 'An Iron Man', p. 85.
[30] Forth, *Masculinity in the Modern West*, p. 230.
[31] A likely reference to a scene from the western *The Magnificent Seven*, dir. John Sturges (1960), where the gunfighter Lee (Robert Vaughn) tests his reaction time by snatching at three flies on a table.
[32] Dai Smith, 'Focal Heroes: A Welsh Fighting Class', in Richard Holt (ed.), *Sport and the Working Class in Modern Britain* (Manchester: Manchester University Press, 1990), pp. 198–217 (p. 200).
[33] Forth, *Masculinity in the Modern West*, p. 8.
[34] Morse, 'Maimed Individuals', pp. 281–2.
[35] Morse, 'Maimed Individuals', p. 282.
[36] Oates, *On Boxing*, p. 13. Writing of the heavyweight boxer Rocky Marciano, she observes that he 'trained with the most monastic devotion', focusing unremittingly on his opponent 'as the cloistered monk or nun chooses by an act of fanatical will to "see" only God', pp. 28–9.
[37] Forth, *Masculinity in The Modern West*, p. 219.
[38] Ron Berry, 'A Necessary Kind of Love', an unpublished essay, a copy of which was given to me by his daughter, Dr Lesley Berry.
[39] Ron Berry, undated audiotape interview with Dai Smith: 'My influences were American authors, English authors', University of Swansea Miners' Library. My transcription. See also Mark Glancy, who suggests that it was through the western that 'generations of Britons became acquainted with American folklore, history and myth': *Hollywood and the Americanisation of Britain: From the 1920s to the Present* (London: I. B. Taurus, 2014), p. 212.
[40] Jane Tompkins, *West of Everything* (Oxford: Oxford University Press, 1992), p. 41.

[41] 'U.S., a waterproof coat, 1884'. *Shorter Oxford English Dictionary* (3rd edn), vol. 2, p. 2018.
[42] Tompkins, *West of Everything*, p. 81.
[43] Roger Bartra, *Wild Men in the Looking Glass*, trans. Carl T. Berrisford (Ann Arbor, MI: University of Michigan Press, 1994). Bartra sees the wild man as 'white, bearded, with an abundant head of hair', p. 88.
[44] Dorothy Yamamoto, *The Boundaries of the Human in Medieval English Literature* (Oxford: Oxford University Press, 2000), p. 144.
[45] Forth writes that Tarzan 'experienced a resurgence in popularity in the early 1960s', the decade when *So Long, Hector Bebb* was written: *Masculinity in the Modern West*, p. 219.
[46] Tompkins, *West of Everything*, p. 81.
[47] Roger Bartra, T*he Artificial Savage: Modern Myths of the Wild Man*, trans. Christopher Follett (Ann Arbor, MI: University of Michigan Press, 1997). Bartra distinguishes between the 'European wild man' and the 'savage': 'The former belongs to a Western myth with a long history; the latter is used to people "discovered" and colonised by modern Europe', pp. 164–5.
[48] Daniel Defoe, *Robinson Crusoe* [1729] (London: Penguin, 2012), p. 97.
[49] Defoe, *Robinson Crusoe*, p. 145.
[50] Defoe, *Robinson Crusoe*, p. 45.
[51] Emma Smith, *Masculinity in Welsh Writing in English* (Saarbrücken: Verlag Dr Müller, 2009), p. 143.
[52] Bartra, *The Artificial Savage*, p. 268.
[53] Emma Davies, '"Manufacturing Men": Literary Masculinities in Industrial Welsh Writing in English' (unpublished MA thesis, University of Wales, Swansea, 2001), p. 34.
[54] Sigmund Freud, 'Beyond the Pleasure Principle', in Angela Richards (ed.), *Penguin Freud Library*, trans. James Strachey (London: Penguin, 1984), vol. 11, pp. 275–338 (p. 282).
[55] Freud, 'Beyond the Pleasure Principle', p. 282.
[56] Henri-Frédéric Amiel (1821–81), cited by Forth, *Masculinity in the Modern West*, p. 141.

5

The Full-Time Amateur: Sport in Ron Berry's South Walian Imagination

Daryl Leeworthy

In the spring of 1959, Ron Berry was invited by the *Observer* newspaper to pen a series of match reports from Ninian Park, Cardiff, and Swansea's Vetch Field. Cardiff City and Swansea Town were both in the Second Division that year, playing against teams such as Fulham, Sheffield Wednesday, both Bristol clubs (City and Rovers), Liverpool and Huddersfield Town. He relished the opportunity, writing 'a goodish report, rather sociological, of that genre, the ninety minutes of football recorded as contingent stimuli'.[1] It proved to be 'a brief, abruptly terminated career in posh journalism' for Berry, who received five pounds plus expenses before being quietly dropped from the newspaper when a new sports editor was put in place. Some of what Berry submitted to the *Observer* has survived in his papers. Three short match reports from 1959, providing coverage of Cardiff City versus Fulham (4 April), Cardiff City versus Bristol City (5 September), and Swansea Town versus Liverpool (3 October), reveal a novelist's eye for character and place setting, as well as the sociological phraseology for which Berry is renowned. In his account of the Swansea game he described the 'Vetch' football field as 'ringed by cul-de-sacs and dog leg streets, and clearly laid down by pre-organisation man'. He concluded that Swansea beat Liverpool that day, 'because they were a better machine'. Yet it was Liverpool who delivered the better football:

> In the second half, [Ronnie] Moran of Liverpool scored a goal as perfect as anything deriving from mathematics and force. He took a free kick just outside the penalty box and shot past a barrier of five white jerseys,

finding a space gap like a science fiction hero [. . .] Of course, the spectacular is essential to soccer.²

Berry was no stranger to football or to the Vetch football ground, having played professionally for Swansea Town in the early 1940s. A severe injury in 1943 brought his footballing career to a sudden end, as it did his life as a 'man of action' who was then in his 'big-chested prime'.³

Invitations such as those made by the *Observer* at the end of the 1950s heralded the start of Berry's peak period of published productivity. The five novels which emerged at an average pace of one every two years between 1960 and 1970, together with television and radio work, presented a writer of tremendous ability, with a style perhaps best described as a Welsh twist on American beatnik or the British kitchen-sink drama. Yet strangely, Berry never achieved the lasting success that was warranted by the quality of his writing and, as Simon Baker has noted, 'it caused him "damage" to be so consistently and casually overlooked'.⁴ Berry's contemporary Gwyn Thomas made similar complaints about his own lack of commercial success, although he at least gained considerable renown as a raconteur, dramatist, playwright and commentator, becoming a full-time professional writer at the start of the 1960s. Berry, for all intents and purposes, remained a 'full-time amateur': always writing but never able to fully sustain himself, or his family, by his pen. Perhaps as much for this reason, as for distinctions of education and aesthetic enthusiasm, Ron Berry's Rhondda was no 'fucking-meadow-prospect' – the darkly humorous alternative world created by Thomas to critique contemporary life with sidling malicious obliquity.⁵

In their differing ways, Ron Berry and the Pontypridd-born writer Alun Richards rejected the operatic tone which Gwyn Thomas had employed in his novels of the 1940s and 1950s, and turned, instead, to masculinity, to nature, to sex and to sport. Thus, to borrow Dai Smith's apposite observation, Berry and Richards 'brought the relationship between a changing people and an enchanted, decaying history up to date. They found a way out of the dark forest of cliché and the deceptive maze of narrative History'⁶ and, perhaps, narrative biography.

Shrewd readers can immediately recognise the autobiographical quality of Berry's writing. Aspects of his life provided many of the narrative touchstones of his early novels –*Hunters and Hunted* (1960),

Travelling Loaded (1963) and *The Full-Time Amateur* (1966) – and his short stories, which 'smack[ed] sharply of the pains of personal experience'.[7] Having left school at fourteen and found work in the local pits of the upper Rhondda (an experience which he would explore in his last novel, *This Bygone* (1996)), Berry served briefly in the Merchant Navy and the Royal Ordnance Corps during the Second World War. Thereafter he found work as a peripatetic carpenter and fitter. The irregularity of that work was supplemented in the late 1950s by three seasons as assistant manager and teacher at the open-air swimming baths in Treherbert, and a period as a professional boxer. The latter added to the visceral realism of his most celebrated work, *So Long, Hector Bebb* (1970).

Although this range of employment had its advantages, not least a rich seam of experience to draw on for his writing, it failed to provide Berry with more than subsistence, and he and his family lived marginally for many years until a civil list pension was secured in the 1970s.[8] Yet life on the margins enabled Berry to remain *within* the community about which he was writing, whilst concerning himself with the decline of the Rhondda's old communal values – relocation to the Vale of Glamorgan or to the Mumbles was not for him. In his view, it was communal values which had suffered most from the relative prosperity of the Valleys in the post-war years, and also from the terminal decline of the coal mining industry. As Simon Baker records, Berry's 'aim was to lay down for posterity the life-experience and language of the Valleys' world he knew, even as it passed out of history into oblivion'.[9] Or in Berry's own words, taken from his posthumously published autobiography, *History Is What You Live*, 'Valley miners are genealogical all-sorts, socially unified by a short, delirious history, unity fragmenting as the industry died'.[10] The consequences of that fragmentation were increased individualism and the privatisation of social and cultural habits: the rise of the motor car over buses and trains, the replacement of cinemas with television sets, and so on.[11]

Economic and social change thus provided the central themes of Berry's work and the central features of his 'south Walian' imagination. In this regard, his Rhondda was little different from those of Rhys Davies and Gwyn Thomas, but he handled the consequences and meanings differently from his literary forebears and contemporaries. In Gwyn Thomas's 'Meadow Prospect', for instance, politics and society remained collective: the voters in the terraces lived lives which were often negatively impacted by external forces, but together they had to make the best of it, protesting forcefully when necessary. However, in Berry's Rhondda the focus was on the individual and the choices an individual makes in response to the odds – odds made by 'the detritus of industrial decay [and] the corruption of a consumer existence'.[12] As he explained to Dai Smith in 1992:

> Smith: You were growing up, you were a young man between the nineteen twenties, thirties and forties, that world which may be over-romanticised and the whole clichéd stuff, but nonetheless there were occasions in which great strikes took place, hundreds of thousands of people went on the march, there was a different kind of politics, a different kind of feel for it. Your world that you set out, there, in the fifties and sixties it's [. . .] [got] the individual core.
>
> Berry: Well, although I'd been involved in those upheavals they didn't leave a mark on me as a kind of [. . .] as a reason to do anything. I did what I wanted to do, that's the basic principle. I'm still trying to do it. It's the basic drive: you do what you want to do, take the consequences.[13]

And yet, for Berry, writing was always a conscious act of collective remembrance. Taken up in the early 1950s as a hobby, he honed his skills during a year's study at Coleg Harlech between 1954 and 1955, at a time when many of the leading practitioners of Anglo-Welsh literature, including Gwyn Thomas, Gwyn Jones and Glyn Jones, delivered lecture courses.[14] That collective remembrance irritated some metropolitan critics, such as E. D. O'Brien of the *Illustrated London News*, who wrote, following publication of *Hunters and Hunted* in August 1960, that,

> Ron Berry can write. Well, why doesn't he? He tells us the story of three young Welshmen; of their pursuit of women in one sector of their lives, and of their pursuit of hares and foxes (accompanied by dogs) in another [. . .] what Mr Berry seems to be trying to tell us is this: '*you've* never lived in a Welsh mining village. *You* wouldn't understand what I'm writing about. *You* would never have thought that someone like me would have read James Joyce'.[15]

One imagines an insouciant shrug of the shoulders, as if to say 'yes and *you* still don't understand'.

What follows in this chapter offers a means of understanding Berry's world by examining the strong relationship between various sporting activities and the 'south Wales' depicted in his writing.[16] Each of the works considered below, not least the novels *The Full-Time Amateur* and *So Long, Hector Bebb*, features a sportsman as the protagonist, although sport was not always the dominant feature of their lives. These characters were more Arthur Seaton than Frank Machin – yet sport was an ordinary facet of growing up in the Valleys. It sat alongside (for the majority of young men, at any rate) chasing girls, being cursed at in Welsh by your elders, and the challenge of finding work in a region where traditional industry was fast disappearing – a degree of apathy about the latter was sometimes depicted. In other words, sport conveyed the enthusiasms and masked the anxieties of young, working-class men whose lives had little of the certainty supposed either of a coalfield at the zenith of its economic power, or at its nadir. In this way, sport was central to Berry's remembrance of a south Walian imagination that was particular to him, but common to his generation. It was his – and our – inheritance. As he put it:

> Village kids are supposed to be doers. Too much chattering earned nicknames guaranteed to last a long time. Certain passions moved in families, modes handed down from father to son [. . .] My old man's interests were soccer, boxing and music. Other lads acquired rule of thumb about chickens, pigs, pigeons, billiards, gardening, rugby, the Bible, gambling, fashions, labour leaders.[17]

Clarion boys

Three sports dominated Berry's writing: boxing, association football (soccer) and cycling. Rugby, as he quipped in *History Is What You Live*, was the game of the establishment. 'Compulsory rugby in school', he wrote, 'soccer every Saturday' (*HWYL*, 49). The difference between freedom and insistence, conformity and individuality, was always plain in his mind. It was cycling which gave him the greatest amount of liberty, even though it did not feature significantly in his published novels.[18] Cycling introduced the young man and his friends to a world of international superstars. 'Every week we read *Cycling*', he wrote in an early draft of his autobiography, 'every issue [was] taken as gospel truth [. . .] Tour de France winners were heroes'.[19] If we look carefully at the unpublished writings, the final version of *History Is What You Live*, and several short stories, Berry's passion for cycling becomes self-evident. The most important of these, a novel as much about cycling as *So Long, Hector Bebb* was about boxing, was 'More Guts Than Sense', written in about 1959.[20] It bears all the classic hallmarks of a Berry story: young men, sport and masculinity.[21] The narrator is nineteen-year-old Dai Davies, a young man with little respect for authority.

> For the sake of decency, I'll begin with myself. Two years ago they put me on probation [. . .] This joker I hit, he had so much book learning he didn't know I was being victimised. He worked from the manager's book, the rule book, so he couldn't focus me, young Dai, in his picture. If you're seventeen, pretty roughish – although you may consider yourself sensitive as blue litmus – and you didn't *want* to be manager, nor a victim, and you muck through day after day with just being an employee so long as it isn't rubbed in, well, you *can't* avoid trouble. Why? Because it's dished out from the rule book by these modern managers.[22]

Sport provided Dai Davies with a means of escaping that suffocating environment; soccer was his imagined route to fame, and the bicycle a means of release. Like Arthur Seaton, who worked in the Raleigh factory in Nottingham, Dai owned an impressive bike, and his friend Joe Jones, 'five feet nine inches tall, cruiserweight, chin like a blunted wedge', encouraged him to make the most of it:

> How about you and me going for a run next Sunday?
> Where to?
> Abergavenny.
> Christ, no. I'm nowhere near fit enough and I'll be playing football the day before.
> Joe said, 'why bother to play football when you own a bike like this? You should be in training for next season'.[23]

Eventually, Dai and Joe joined the Maerdy branch of the Clarion Cycling Club, a group made up mostly of 'shoppies and tradesmen, with a sprinkling of miners. The girls were daughters of the same kind of people'. The incidents from the novel mirror, almost exactly, the autobiographical material laid out in *History Is What You Live*. Therein, Berry describes meeting Vernon Rees, a young man with as much of a serious appetite for cycling as he had:

> That your *London Streak?*
> Not paid for it yet, I said.
> Done any racing?
> No. You?
> I intend to, said Rees. How much is she costing you?
> Eleven quid just for the frame.
> Gem of a bike. Marvellous lugs on her. Mine's a short wheelbase Baines. I've done the same thing, built up from the frame.
> Fast looking bike, I said.
> She is, confirmed Rees, priestly solemn for an eighteen year old.
> [. . .]
> How about us doing a ride next Saturday?
> Where to? I said.
> Builth Wells.
> I said, I'm nowhere near fit enough for that distance.
> He says, Right, Brecon.

The scene concludes with Berry and Rees joining Pentre Clarion, whose clubhouse was near the Rhondda Urban District Council offices in the town (*HWYL*, 71–2).[24] The club had started in the mid-1930s amidst a flourish of cycling in the Rhondda (and elsewhere in the coalfield), particularly under the auspices of the National Clarion Cycling Club (NCCC). Until the early part of the decade, the NCCC had been conspicuously absent from the region for several years: there was no formal district union, and the handbooks produced each year for members elsewhere in the country made no mention of Welsh clubs. By 1938 there were over twenty clubs, stretching from Ammanford in the west to Newport in the east, and the South Wales Miners' Federation president, Arthur Horner, had been appointed as president of the NCCC's South Wales Union.[25] The Rhondda Valley Clarion Club, the first in the Rhondda, was founded at Porth in 1931, with the district committee (known as the South Wales Union) coming into existence the following year.[26] Both Pentre Clarion and Treorchy Clarion were up and racing by 1935.[27]

Although Berry found the Clarions to be 'nicely democratic', and he enjoyed being part of the racing section led by Percy Mantle,[28] he eventually felt stifled by the politics of some of the members, not least their desire to raise money for the international brigades, carry propaganda into the coalfield, and read Left Book Club volumes. So he, and his friends, (as he put it in 'More Guts Than Sense') 'paid our contributions, attended general meetings, and generally went our own way'.[29] Rather than involve himself greatly in the grassroots activism of the popular front, Berry yearned for escape and took the opportunity to do so. He recalled years later that he and his friends were 'coal face lads scruffed into mining', their 'tap roots starving in the rubble of *laissez faire* economics, so we fell for romantic gripe' (*HWYL*, 76). They stuck to the mountain roads like aspirant members of the Cyclists' Touring Club and competed in time trials. For these young men, freedom came from eating apples 'while riding home in the cool night, through Libanus and the Brecon Beacons, autumnal ripeness all around' (*HWYL*, 84). Berry competed in his last time trial for the Clarion in the summer of 1940. As his life was caught up in the Second World War, it was soccer, rather than cycling, which came to dominate his imagination.

The Fernhill soccer team

Of course, Berry had always played soccer. Like other boys he 'kicked sixpenny Felix balls in the schoolyard', and 'Christmas mornings always brought football boots off my old man'.[30] But soccer revolved around a duality, which demanded both team work and a kind of talented selfishness. This meant that 'there weren't any close friends among footballers' as there were among cyclists. Berry reasoned that at least league matches provided 'lessons in social ideas and geography'.[31] By his reckoning, the footballing experience lasted for a decade, from the age of thirteen (when his father taught him how to manufacture alternatives to studs, using iron strips, and how to make shin guards using horse-collar felt), to the accident which ended his playing career in 1943. At the time he was playing inside left for Swansea Town and for Blaenrhondda AFC, with whom he had won the local league cup in 1937, scoring the decisive penalty. He describes the fateful Saturday afternoon that 'Janus fate turned her head' on Llwyncelyn Field in Porth.[32] Hindsight led him 'to see the accident as predestined'.[33]

In Berry's autobiographical writing, soccer appears as both an inheritance and an artistic expression of the freedom for which he yearned. It was a sport played anywhere where vacant ground could be found: on coal tips, in the streets, at welfare grounds and in parks. At some of the 'recs', 'you had to be as jovially craggy as Sir Edmund Hillary to play football [there]', which must have contributed greatly to the spectacle.³⁴ However, poignantly, there was always the prospect of losing these sacred sporting spaces to those who wished to transform the economics of the Rhondda through industrial innovation. As Berry recalled, with an appropriate degree of sadness,

> Upper Rhondda Schoolboy rugby trials were played on Ynyswen tip, which disappeared under Polikoff's clothing factory in 1939 [. . .] Tynewydd Park, home ground for half a dozen teams in sequence, vanished when Rollo Hardy's factory was built on its storm-guttered clay [. . .] [a] naturally grassed field disappeared under Treherbert station engine sheds, since written off by Beeching [. . .] Pentre teams played on the Griffin field [. . .] Now a clothing factory occupies the Griffin. (*HWYL*, 49–50)

These memories, and the reality from which they were drawn, were fictionalised in Berry's third novel, *The Full-Time Amateur*, which appeared in 1966. It told the story of Hugh Davies, a young lad of fifteen, who left school and secured a job working in a mine in his native Rhondda. The year is 1964. Hugh had

> few inhibitions, and hardly any respect for established tradition. He takes what he wants *because* he wants it [. . .] He samples first love with Tegwyn, a hospital nurse; turns to Anne in delicious revenge after her brother beats him up; and meets his match finally in Jasmine, singer and actress, and wife of the secretary of the local football team.³⁵

In the opening chapter, Hugh is still in school, bored and causing trouble for his teacher, Mr Yeats, or Fella Yeats as he's called by the teenage boys. When they get the better of him, all Yeats can do is threaten to 'stop games', that is, the organised but chaotic spectacle of soccer played on the yard at dinnertime (*FTA*, 9). In the early chapters of the novel, before work and chasing women begins to drive them, the boys are obsessed with soccer. They sit around talking about it in Dom's Café, one of those typical Italian 'Bracchi' cafes which populated the Valleys in the early part of the twentieth century. Hugh describes the scene:

> Nothing ever happens in Dom's café. His jukebox's gone scrapey, all groan and rat squeals, and Dom himself is fifteen stones' worth of ignorance born in Wales from second generation Welsh-Italian parents.

> His wife's all right, lovely nature, a live Madonna. Can't imagine how she picked Dom. He's three parts mad. Contaminates all his customers. Most of us are partially mad though; when you poke into the core we all get mad ideas. (*FTA*, 14–15)

The conversation between the boys turns to the league match which they are due to play at the weekend, as well as to the fate and form of Manchester United, and contemporary stars such as Denis Law. Hugh is about to trial for Swansea Town but is unsuccessful in his efforts. He keeps plugging away regardless of the failure, until his father remarks, whilst standing in front of the shaving mirror, 'you had your chance with Swansea, boy. You might make the Welsh League' (*FTA*, 127). Hugh doesn't, and thereby fails to follow in his father's footsteps. Real life begins to get in the way, most notably the affair with Jasmine. When her husband finds out, he declares condemningly that Hugh 'won't ever play for Albion All-Stars again, not while I'm on the committee' (*FTA*, 198). At this point the threat has little impact – Hugh has moved on to a new game. His is a refusal to be the big fish in the small pond, a star of the very-local leagues, always playing at what he truly wished to be. As Hugh explains, with more than a little self-righteousness, 'The Rhondda's loaded with amateurs [. . .] Rugger players, soccer players, cricketers, card sharps, singers, artists, all amateurs, every sodding one of 'em. Senseless as sheep' (*FTA*, 101).

Hugh Davies is the youngest of Berry's protagonists in his novels (apart from Dewi Joshua in *This Bygone*), and is the most overt expression of the author's sense of working-class male displacement in the 1960s. As the sociologist Pierre Bourdieu put it, having successfully wriggled free of the benevolence of the 'left hand' of the state – counsellors, youth leaders, magistrates and teachers – working-class young men soon discovered that society had little regard for them and for the things in which they happened to be interested.[36] As a consequence, they became alienated from both traditional and contemporary efforts at imposing 'order' on a society that was rapidly losing its sense of unity. Writing about Thunder Bay, on the north-west shore of Lake Superior in southern Ontario, the Canadian sociologist Thomas Dunk usefully observed that 'working-class men actively construct sets of meanings and values in opposition to what they see as the dominant culture'. He concludes that 'the celebration of the local, the ordinary, of mass culture by the white male working class in Thunder Bay is itself a form of class resistance to their subordination'.[37]

Parallel practices of resistance can be observed in the behaviour of Hugh Davies and many of the other male characters in Berry's novels.

Focal hero?

The exception to the relative norm of masculine alienation ought to have been Berry's Hector Bebb, the character at the heart of his brutal boxing novel of 1970. After all, boxers are supposed to be hyper-masculine figures unbowed by the power of others – aren't they? Bebb seems to be the fulfilment of Berry's concerns about society, about masculinity and about being thrown on various scrapheaps.[38] Writing in the *Independent* a few years ago, the novelist Niall Griffiths summed up *So Long, Hector Bebb* as an 'extraordinary novel [. . .] Unmawkish, unjudging, it can only have come from the pen of one completely unafraid to write from the centre of his own culture'.[39] Hector Bebb was not the first fictional boxer to come from Wales, but he is perhaps the greatest. There were vivid passages on the manly art of boxing in Jack Jones's *Rhondda Roundabout* (1934) and in Richard Llewellyn's *How Green Was My Valley* (1939). Even Rhys Davies, who recoiled at the hypermasculinity of the Rhondda, with its groups of 'half-envied, drunken, football-match colliers', nevertheless included numerous passages about boxing in his short stories and novels.[40] Boxing is there, too, in the works of contemporary American authors as various as Jack London (with his *Abysmal Brute*), Ernest Hemingway, Norman Mailer, Saul Bellow and Joyce Carol Oates. The multitude of readings, both of these novels and the sport itself, whether in a Geertzian mode or otherwise, makes boxing a compelling window into working-class culture and, also, the careful limits placed on that culture.[41]

Told through a Brechtian chorus of fourteen separate voices, *So Long, Hector Bebb* is one of the most complex literary portraits of south Wales. When it was first published, reviewers wildly misjudged it and complained, to borrow the words of the *Times Literary Supplement*, that 'one had the impression of a confusion of voices, where one might have provided [. . .] a clear and credible narrative line'.[42] Except the novel would not work that way – it could not work that way. The feral descent of Hector Bebb from local hero to outcast is remarkable in its revelation of the flimsy character of modern civilisation and the sporting enthusiasms which provided for stage-managed violence, otherwise regarded as beyond the pale.[43] How easy to train someone to fight, and fight well, and to bind their prowess by the civilising limit of a pair of padded gloves and a padded headguard. Remove the gloves, and that skill can quickly turn away from socially acceptable sport into something rather more brutal. 'I would rather not be reminded about Hector Bebb', remarks one of the female protagonists, 'He's beyond control. He's uncivilised' (*SLHB*, 39). Another put it caustically, 'he's no more than a trained animal' (*SLHB*, 65).These women fear the pugilist for his uncouth behaviour in the pub, rather than admiring him for his skill in the ring.[44]

Berry uses female voices to incorporate into the narrative the perspective of those who questioned the existence of boxing in modern society. 'Boxing', writes Sam Toperoff, 'is a throwback, a vestige of our dark, irrational past. That's one reason it is usually under sharp attack in a society that likes to believe it has evolved very different and superior values'.[45] But to focus on the (false) distinction between a 'peaceful society' and the violence of the boxing ring is to miss the point: as Lucia Trimbur has persuasively demonstrated in her study of Gleeson's Gym in New York City, boxing is a form of labour – the gymnasium a place to find the kind of masculine socialisation once found in factories or coal mines. It is therefore a means of rescuing personal value for working-class men otherwise cast aside by deindustrialisation.[46] Hector Bebb has no other means of earning money than the prize belts he can win each week, something which Millie, his wife, casually disregards: 'Every evening you'll find him in the White Hart', she complains, 'Training. Boxing. Sammy John this, Sammy John that, training, boxing, Sammy this and Sammy that' (*SLHB*, 91). But if one was to think of that passage as about mining, not fighting, then the hollow essence of that barb becomes apparent: 'Every evening you'll find him in the pit. Working. Hewing. Nye Bevan this, Nye Bevan that, working, hewing, Nye this and Bevan that.' Of course, Millie Bebb has other reasons to lambast her husband for his commitment to the boxing gym. She seeks to justify, to herself and to her friends, her affair with Emlyn. As she explains:

> Emlyn reckons he's [Hector] a semi-eunuch. Em swears I married a near enough eunuch six years ago [. . .] Panther inside the ring, bash-bash-bash, and shivering finick as a little cock robin once in a blue moon, I mean under the sheets. Any pathetic wife who watches the moon from her bedroom window night after night has my full sympathy. It makes a woman feel out and out sick. (*SLHB*, 91)

Ironically, despite her accusations that he is acting 'contrary to nature' by failing to satisfy her sexual appetites, Bebb dotes upon on his wife and spends his boxing prize money buying presents for her. On returning to Cymmer after a championship fight, for instance, he carries a solid silver locket and chain purchased from a jeweller's shop in Manchester (*SLHB*, 36, 88). Such romantic presentations of love are not expected of a man who is a panther in the ring; rather, Hector Bebb is expected to carry that masculine prowess into the bedroom. His failure to do so leads to accusations that he is gay. 'Dear oh dear, 'ere's a little fairy', taunts one opponent, and the local promoter Abe Pearson, whom Sarah Morse usefully identifies as occupying 'a position analogous to that of the exploitative colliery owner', bluntly demands to know whether Bebb is 'a poof or something' (*SLHB*, 15–16).[47] He is not. Rather, he is a man bound by a code of honour; in the words of Loïc Wacquant, 'the specific honor of the pugilist, like that of the ancient gladiator, consists in refusing to concede and kneel down'.[48] He is capable of both caring for the injured, as evident in his Billy Casper-esque empathy for the animals he finds on the mountain tops, and responding vigorously to injuries inflicted on him by others. Thus, when Bebb returns home from his championship bout and learns of Millie Bebb's dalliances, he cannot simply forget about it. He must answer the blow, which he does by killing Emlyn.

In crossing the line between 'civilised' pugilism and 'uncivilised' violence, Hector Bebb becomes like David Morrell's John Rambo, rather than remaining a working-class hero in the model of Rocky Balboa (although this is never entirely Hector Bebb's fate).[49] By using his skills to murder, Hector Bebb loses control of his ability to, in the words of Joyce Carol Oates, 'exert his "will" over his merely human and animal impulses', which served as the line between civilised and uncivilised forms of violence.[50] Thereafter, Bebb becomes a different kind of man – one forced to live in a feral manner, outcast from society but subject, still, to the social violence imposed on men like him.[51] Forced, eventually, to flee to the mountaintops, he has to survive by his wits, hunting for food in a society that has been completely converted to buying from shops, unaware of the violence involved in its production. This is not, as Daniel G. Williams has argued, a transformation wherein 'the prizefighter becomes a yokel', nor does it evoke the noble 'return to the land' supposed in a reading of Hector Bebb as a quasi-cowboy (something akin to Kirk Douglas's character in his 1962 classic *Lonely Are The Brave*, perhaps), but something rather more viscerally violent.[52] That violence reveals itself in Hector Bebb's killing of a ewe which he spots grazing with her lamb in the fields near an abandoned colliery. Once he would have left the animals alone, but in his new state he merely sees the food which he needs to survive.

> I heard her hooves on the fallen stones. As her black nose came level I hit her one CLUNK, like wood on wood. Flinging out to full length I grabbed her hind legs. She was trapped. But I lost true sight, everything fuzzy and Roman candles firing inside my chest. Strength came in spasms, although I robbed myself, the lamb bleating, bleating, tormenting my mind. Blood splashed over my trousers. Heavy drops of rain began to fall. By and by, dead lamb, unconscious ewe, me straddled over her, both of us quite still. (*SLHB*, 192)

It is a genuinely horrific moment, indicative of just how far Bebb has travelled from 'civilisation'; or, rather, how far his skill as a fighter could take him outside of the boxing ring. He drags the ewe down to a nearby stream, slits her throat and watches the blood flow into the water. He takes some of the bloody liquid in a baked-bean tin and drinks, 'sicked it up, swigged some more and washed the taste away with water'. He then moves on to eat the raw 'heart, liver and kidneys. Ideal nourishment for a man with hundred and seventy-eight fights behind him'. He is not fully feral, though, and buries the remains of the animals with dignity. 'Her lamb went under some stones', he reflects, 'only bits left of him, poor mite' (*SLHB*, 194–6).

What, then, prompts Hector Bebb's descent into killing? Is it the training he received in the 'forge which creates the pugilist', as Wacquant describes the gymnasium?[53] Is it really a descent at all? That, it seems to me, is what Ron Berry is asking of his audience. Who is more of an animal? The 'panther' who reacts in the way that he has been trained? The woman who plays behind her husband's back with another man? The boxing promoter who fiddles with prize money? The citizens who happily watch Hector Bebb beat another man with gloves on (or get beaten himself), but recoil in horror when the gloves come off and the same level of violence occurs? Or the society which kills that which it cannot contain? It is hard to imagine another sport which allows for such ruminative depth as boxing, but, it should be noted that rugby and soccer also contain certain elements within them that are 'legitimate [and] socially sanctioned forms of violence'.[54] *So Long, Hector Bebb* was an overt exploration of the issues which Ron Berry had been examining all along in his novels – what happens to young men conditioned to act and think in certain ways, when the opportunities for such actions and thoughts disappear?[55] How does a society refashion itself but not lose sight of that which makes it distinctive?

Playing out of position

In 1950, the medical officer of health for Rhondda Urban District, Dr D. J. Thomas, recorded in his annual report that

> The district is entirely industrial in character, the principal industry being coal mining. Though the larger portion of the male employed persons are engaged in the mining industry, a large number of men residing in the district are employed in factories or constructional works in adjoining or neighbouring areas. During recent years a number of light industries have also been established in the district and these industries have absorbed a considerable amount of female labour as well as male labour.[56]

The first factories and light industrial units had opened at the end of the 1930s, and by the 1950s the Rhondda Trading Estate in Porth and Alfred Polikoff's clothing factory in Treorchy were significant employment alternatives to domestic service or work underground. To Berry, that new workforce seemed to lack the same spirit as the miners of an earlier generation (his father's generation, for example), and he was concerned about the attraction to cars and television sets, bingo halls and foreign holidays. These concerns were shared by Berry's contemporaries including Gwyn Thomas, who memorably reflected on the transformation of the Rhondda's many chapels from places of worship into 'a kind of pleasure dome, not of Kubla Khan but of people with far less taste'.[57] For Gwyn Thomas, the question was a social one; for Berry, it was a question of individual reaction to real, faced conditions. The results were the same.

Berry's writing was simultaneously about the decade in which it was published and the decade in which he grew up, a point underscored by a very early attempt at writing his autobiography: 'Sing a Song of Ego, Boy'.[58] Dated to March 1964, this manuscript adds far more to the relationship between Berry and Vernon Rees, to the sporting enthusiasms which they shared, and to the author's contemplations on masculinity. Early in the piece, Berry remarks on the youthful tussle between the boys and their parents:

> We were both having a real disciple's run of trouble with our parents. It used to be the norm in the Rhondda, pre-war. The valid squabble, from leaving school to leaving home. Fight the good fight, typical of our industrialised Celt country. It used to be quite a lousy, criminal environment, fairly desperate for adolescents. I'm duty bound to thrash this obvious horse. Dull work, but it's typical. If you can't be desperate inside the lasso of sex-stretch and earn your bread and butter, you go under.[59]

The conflict, as so often, was that of freedom versus conformity. As Berry observed later in the draft, his mother

> was still thinking about the pits, naturally, coal and hymns, football and boxing, politics and the wit of cornered citizens; these were the assets available in the Rhondda pre-war. Unless you were a bookie or a teacher or a librarian or anything else along those lines.[60]

A writer, perhaps?

Sport provided a temporary way out of that conflict and for two years, at the end of the 1930s, 'Vernon and I lived like commandos [. . .] exercising our obsessions, the old bone and muscle'.[61] Even though that Berry, in the 1930s and early 1940s, was in his 'big-chested prime', he was outdone in every physical respect by his friend. 'This Vernon Rees was massive. Massive thighs and calves, chest like a water butt. He trained as a weightlifter from the age of fourteen until he bought his all-chrome Baines.'[62] But Rees was also different, 'he was touchy in his attitude towards girls' and 'enjoyed singing quietly to himself'.[63] He was not the hypermasculine figure which his training suggested. Berry frequently sought to bring the subject back to girls but Rees was single-minded, 'serious as a tree [. . .] and incapable of giving in'.[64] Sport rather than sex occupied his attentions: 'If Vernon had known a girl like Dorcas, he mightn't have been so attached to his hungry looking Baines short wheelbase'.[65] The echo of Hector Bebb is distinct, perhaps deliberately so, although Berry later remarked that he had 'manufactured Hector Bebb from half a dozen boxers' whom he knew. The similarities are, however, compelling.

No other Welsh writer, in either language, with the singular exception of Alun Richards, used sport as frequently, or as effectively, to convey the experience of coalfield masculinity. Ron Berry was, in this respect, utterly unique. It is what gives his work its most enduring quality. For him, sport, and in particular soccer, provided a means of marking the passage of time: a childhood and adolescence rich in physical activity, and in the friends made by being part of such activity, and then the loss and absence of 'the team', in old age. Hence, the poignancy of the ending of *History Is What You Live*: 'Mark [. . .] the Fernhill soccer team, cup winners, on Caemawr field, Treorchy, 1937. Ten are long dead, destroyed by pneumoconiosis, injuries, heart attacks and disease. The inside left who scored the winning penalty goal, he's spending words on paper' (*HWYL*, 147). That he concluded the story of his life that way ought to have alerted readers, all along, to the centrality of sport to Berry's south Walian imagination. He was the last of his team to die, but not before he had committed their memory to paper and ensured that subsequent generations could remember them. 'What a way to come to an end', reflects Hugh Davies in the last passage of *The Full-Time Amateur*, 'we're in training to go the distance and win. We can't be beaten' (*FTA*, 198). He may have been right.

Notes

[1] Richard Burton Archives, Swansea University, Ron Berry Papers, WWE/1/7/1/3: 'Splinters Off A Square Peg', p. 141.
[2] Richard Burton Archives, Swansea University, Ron Berry Papers, WWE/1/7/3/12: 'Swansea Versus Liverpool, 3 October 1959'. The final score was five goals to four in Swansea's favour. Moran's goal came in the seventieth minute.
[3] The phrase 'man of action' derives from Berry's interview with Dai Smith filmed as part of the Writers of Wales series by the Polytechnic of Wales in 1992; 'big-chested prime' can be found in Ron Berry, *Hunters and Hunted* (London: Hutchinson, 1960), p. 9.
[4] Simon Baker, 'Introduction', in Simon Baker (ed.), *Ron Berry: Collected Stories* (Llandysul: Gomer, 2000), p. xii.
[5] The phrase is Alun Richards's. Letter from Alun Richards to Ron Berry, 29 March 1963. Published in Dai Smith, *In the Frame* (Cardigan: Parthian, 2010), p. 192.
[6] Dai Smith, *Aneurin Bevan and the World of South Wales* (Cardiff: University of Wales Press, 1993), p. 133.
[7] *The Times*, 24 July 1997.
[8] Financial difficulties had also foreshortened a period of study at Shoreditch College in London, where Berry undertook teacher training.
[9] Baker, 'Introduction', p. xii–xiii.
[10] Berry, *History Is What You Live* (Llandysul: Gomer, 1998), p. 97. All further references will be made within the body of the text (*HWYL*).

11. On these themes see Daryl Leeworthy, *Labour Country: Political Radicalism and Social Democracy in South Wales, 1831–1985* (Cardigan: Parthian, 2018).
12. Dai Smith, 'Introduction', in Ron Berry, *History Is What You Live*, p. 8.
13. This transcript is taken from 'Ron Berry Reading His Work and Talking to Professor Dai Smith', produced by the Centre for the Study of Welsh Writing in English at the Polytechnic of Wales in 1992 for their Writers of Wales series. The recording can be found at the University of South Wales in Treforest. Readers of *HWYL* will note that Berry observes his parents reading the *Daily Herald*, the newspaper of the Labour Party, and he went along to talks given by various figures, including the Communist Party leader Harry Pollitt (*HWYL*, pp. 32, 50). In later years Berry read the *Freedom Bulletin*, an anarchist newspaper (*HWYL*, p. 106).
14. Coleg Harlech, *Twenty-Eighth Annual Report, 1954–5* (Harlech, 1955).
15. E. D. O'Brien, 'A Literary Lounger', *Illustrated London News*, 13 August 1960.
16. A theme previously examined, albeit with differing points of emphasis, by Gareth Williams, '"The Dramatic Turbulence of some Irrecoverable Football Game": Sport, Literature and Welsh Identity', in Grant Jarvie (ed.), *Sport in the Making of Celtic Cultures* (London: Leicester University Press, 1999), pp. 55–70.
17. Richard Burton Archives, Swansea University, Ron Berry Papers, WWE/1/7/1/3: 'Splinters Off A Square Peg (Autobiography)', p. 34.
18. The exception lies in the short story 'Clarion Boys', published in *Collected Stories*, pp. 145–9.
19. Richard Burton Archives, Swansea University, Ron Berry Papers, WWE/1/7/1/3: 'Splinters Off A Square Peg (Autobiography)', p. 98.
20. Richard Burton Archives, Swansea University, Ron Berry Papers, WWE/1/2/7/1: 'More Guts Than Sense (1959)'. All references hereafter are to this manuscript.
21. The novel contained a few hints at a queer character, too. In his 'camera estimate' of one of the principal characters, the narrator, Dai Davies, remarks that the young man (his friend, Joe Jones) 'does outlandish Greek things once in a while'. Joe was also one of those who 'never combs his hair, he brushes it as if it's a nuisance'. This was regarded as unusual, since 'very few youngsters in the prime of adolescence neglect their hair. It's always groom, groom, preparing for the mating stakes'. For a sense of these themes in Welsh society, see Daryl Leeworthy, *A Little Gay History of Wales* (Cardiff: University of Wales Press, 2019).
22. Berry, 'More Guts Than Sense', p. 1.
23. Berry, 'More Guts Than Sense', p. 4.
24. The 'London Streak' was manufactured by F. H. Grubb, the bicycle business owned by the Olympic road-racing cyclist Frederick Henry Grubb (1887–1949) and based in London. It was advertised as 'the machine you can win on'. The Baines bicycle, probably their VS37 'Flying Gate', was manufactured by W. and R. Baines in Bradford. The art of 'building up from the frame' was illustrated regularly in the pages of *Cycling*. See, for instance, *Cycling*, 25 November 1936.

25 National Clarion Cycling Club, *Handbook 1938*, pp. 157–61.
26 National Clarion Cycling Club, *Handbook 1932*, p. 154. This, and other Clarion material cited below, was consulted at the Greater Manchester County Record Office: O16/5/1. A wider sense of the history of the National Clarion Cycling Club is given in Daryl Leeworthy, 'Partisan Players: Sport, Working-Class Culture and the Labour Movement in South Wales, 1918–1939', *Labor History*, 55/5 (2014), 580–93.
27 *Western Mail*, 9 October 1934, 1 July 1935.
28 Percival Holmes Mantle (1909–78). Described by Berry as having worked behind the counter in the local Co-operative store. 'A tall, stooped man devoted to Pentre Clarion, something broke in Percy during the war. He served in the RAF [. . .] we trusted him. Percy was reliable. [He] arranged cheques instead of medals, small cheques which bought equipment and racing shoes. Percy had a greyish authority for making deals' (*HWYL*, p. 76).
29 Or, as Berry put it: 'sometimes we stood critically on the fringe of Clarion gatherings. It was awkward trying to be sociable cyclists' (*HWYL*, p. 76). For a sense of the politics of the Clarion in this period see *Clarion Cyclist*, 1/10 (April 1937), 150; 1/11 (May 1937), 171.
30 Berry refers to this both in 'Splinters Off A Square Peg', p. 21, and in *History Is What You Live*, p. 49.
31 'Splinters Off A Square Peg', p. 56.
32 'Splinters Off A Square Peg', p. 140.
33 'Splinters Off A Square Peg', p. 140.
34 'More Guts Than Sense', p. 61.
35 The description is taken from the flyleaf blurb for *The Full-Time Amateur*.
36 Pierre Bourdieu, *Acts of Resistance* (Cambridge: Polity, 1998), pp. 1–10.
37 Thomas W. Dunk, *It's a Working Man's Town: Male Working-Class Culture* (Kingston and Montreal: McGill-Queens University Press, 2003), pp. 3–4.
38 Berry had also intended to write a biography of Tommy Farr. His working title was 'Bred in the Bone'. His collected notes and sketches can be found at Richard Burton Archives, Swansea University, Ron Berry Papers, WWE/1/7/3/8. See also the letter from Ron Berry to Dai Smith in Smith, *In the Frame*, pp. 233–4, which discusses his efforts.
39 *Independent*, 17 December 2010.
40 Huw Edwin Osborne, *Rhys Davies* (Cardiff: University of Wales Press, 2009), p. 12. Boxing features, for instance, in *Count Your Blessings* (London: Putnam, 1932); *Jubilee Blues* (London: William Heinemann, 1938); *A Finger in Every Pie* (London: William Heinemann, 1942); and *Marianne* (London: William Heinemann, 1951). See also Meic Stephens (ed.), *Rhys Davies: Collected Stories, Volume I* (Llandysul: Gomer, 1996) and his *Rhys Davies: A Writer's Life* (Cardigan: Parthian, 2013). The relationship between boxing and Welsh literature is fully explored in Dai Smith's 'Focal Heroes: A Welsh Fighting Class', in Richard Holt (ed.), *Sport and the Working Class in Modern Britain* (Manchester: Manchester University Press, 1990), pp. 198–217.

41. Clifford Geertz, 'Deep Play: Notes on the Balinese Cockfight', *Daedalus*, 101/1 (1972), 1–37; Kasia Boddy, *Boxing: A Cultural History* (London: Reaktion, 2009).
42. David A. Harsent, 'Other New Novels', *Times Literary Supplement*, 3592 (1 January 1971), 5.
43. The following discussion draws partly on Sarah Morse, '"Maimed Individuals": The Significance of the Body in *So Long, Hector Bebb*', in Katie Gramich (ed.), *Mapping the Territory: Critical Approaches to Welsh Fiction in English* (Cardigan: Parthian, 2010), pp. 271–88, although the final conclusions are my own.
44. Conversely, in Rhys Davies's work, the female gaze is from the audience at a boxing match. They look upon the fighters with a degree of admiration for their skill, and with obvious lust; for instance, Davies, *Marianne*, pp. 127–8.
45. Sam Toperoff, *Sugar Ray Leonard and Other Noble Warriors* (New York: McGraw-Hill, 1987), p. 185; see also Kasia Boddy, who observes that 'to evoke boxing is always to dissociate oneself from the sentimental, the refined, the feminine'. Kasia Boddy, *Boxing* (London: Reaktion Books, 2009), p. 391.
46. Lucia Trimbur, '"Tough Love": Mediation and Articulation in the Urban Boxing Gym', *Ethnography*, 12/3 (2011), 334–55; Lucia Trimbur, *Come Out Swinging: The Changing World of Boxing in Gleason's Gym* (Princeton: Princeton University Press, 2013). See also Loïc Wacquant, 'The Prize Fighter's Three Bodies', *Ethnos: Journal of Anthropology*, 63/3–4 (1998), 325–52; Loïc Wacquant, 'Pugs at Work: Bodily Capital and Bodily Labour Among Professional Boxers', *Body and Society*, 1/1 (1995), 65–93; Loïc Wacquant, *Body and Soul: Notebooks of an Apprentice Boxer* (New York: Oxford University Press, 2006).
47. Morse, 'Maimed Individuals', p. 276.
48. Loïc Wacquant, 'The Pugilistic Point of View: How Boxers Think and Feel About Their Trade', *Theory and Society*, 24/4 (1995), 489–535 (p. 496).
49. David Morrell, *First Blood* (London: Barrie and Jenkins, 1972).
50. Joyce Carol Oates, *On Boxing* (New York: Ecco Press, 1995), p. 15.
51. Here I have in mind the social violence examined by Edouard Louis in his novel, *Qui a tué mon père* (Paris: Editions Seuil, 2018). The English-language edition is *Who Killed My Father* (London: Harvill-Secker, 2019). The ideas of social violence derive from Bourdieu, notably his concept of 'symbolic power'. As Bourdieu put it, this is a form of violence 'which is exercised upon a social agent with his or her complicity'. Pierre Bourdieu and Loïc Wacquant, *An Invitation to Reflexive Sociology* (Cambridge: Polity Press, 1992), p. 167.
52. Daniel G. Williams, *Wales Unchained: Literature, Politics and Identity in the American Century* (Cardiff: University of Wales Press, 2015), p. 46; Emma Smith, *Masculinity in Welsh Writing in English: The Cases of Lewis Jones, Glyn Jones, Gwyn Thomas and Ron Berry* (Saarbrücken: Verlag Dr Müller, 2009), p. 143.
53. Loïc Wacquant, 'Protection, discipline et honneur: une salle de boxe dans le ghetto américain', *Sociologie et Sociétés*, 27/1 (1995), 76. My translation. The original reads: 'Le *gym* est cette forge où se façonne le pugiliste.'

54. Allen Guttmann, *From Ritual to Record: The Nature of Modern Sports* (New York: Columbia University Press, 1978), p. 120.
55. The theme continued to be explored in Berry's plays, notably 'But Now They Are Fled', broadcast on the BBC in 1971, and 'Uncle Rollo', which followed in 1972. As the programme notes for the former record, 'Dai and Cissie court and tease each other and talk of marriage, but the teasing becomes aggressive and at times savage'.
56. D. J. Thomas, *Report of the Medical Officer of Health for Rhondda Urban District for the Year 1950* (Ferndale: W. T. Maddock, 1950), p. 17.
57. Gwyn Thomas, 'One Pair of Eyes' (BBC TV, 1968).
58. Richard Burton Archives, Swansea University, Ron Berry Papers, WWE/1/7/1/1: 'Sing a Song of Ego, Boy' (9 March 1964).
59. 'Sing a Song of Ego, Boy', p. 2.
60. 'Sing a Song of Ego, Boy', p. 160.
61. 'Sing a Song of Ego, Boy', p. 28.
62. 'Sing a Song of Ego, Boy', p. 4.
63. 'Sing a Song of Ego, Boy', p. 4.
64. 'Sing a Song of Ego, Boy', p. 6.
65. 'Sing a Song of Ego, Boy', p. 6.

6

'THE INADEQUATES': RON BERRY AND DISABILITY

Georgia Burdett

Within Wales, heavy industry has left a sinister legacy in the form of psychological scarring and permanent physical disability. Indeed disability has been the subject matter of many contemporary Welsh anglophone writers from the former coalfield and beyond, such as Desmond Barry, Lloyd Jones, and Niall Griffiths. But the work of one of their most significant predecessors has been largely ignored. The fiction of Ron Berry embodies the values of a Wales where political systems, industries and bodies are damaged and impaired. Until the 1950s disability was accepted as a natural accompaniment to the mining profession, a gradually developing phenomenon for men working underground, that would progressively worsen until it caused them to finish work or to die – whichever happened first. There were many evils waiting at work for the miners: quick death by crushing, slow death by dust inhalation, quick paralysis by rock falls, slow paralysis through rheumatism and arthritis.

Remarkably astute, Ron Berry's novels, short stories and autobiography portray his multiple attempts at finding a 'workable' place for disability in a highly physical mining world, where bodies are socially and materially valued according to their physical output. The chronological span of Berry's oeuvre is such that it chronicles the emergence of a post-industrial Welsh landscape, inhabited by literary successors like Niall Griffiths. Literary depictions of disability in the context of de- and post-industrialisation chronicle and perhaps even create new categories of disabled persons.

But even though disability, injury and accidental death were part and parcel of pit life, both the number and complexity of Berry's disabled protagonists is surprising. Crucial, to our understanding, is the fact that Berry was a disabled writer himself. There is the sense that his relationship to these disabled protagonists is more than straightforward empathy – he *becomes* them. Berry's work shows the complexities of an all-too-common problem in industrial Wales: employment causing disability, and disability causing unemployment. Consequently, his work often presents characters caught in the midst of this transition, the 'moochers', 'cripples' and 'lungers' (*CS*, 6) made useless and uncivilised by their removal from the labour market. Consequently, it must be pointed out that Berry's fiction is very much focused on instances of 'the work-limiting disabled'.[1]

Berry was born in 1920 in Blaencwm (or Blaen-y-cwm) at the top of the Rhondda valley. Hating institutions and social conditioning in any form, Berry's individualist nature became apparent at a very early age. His attendance at school was enforced and sporadic. He was often a 'mitcher' or truant, preferring to roam the distinctive Rhondda landscape; the formidable peaks of Pen Pych and Cefn Nant y Gwais were to be a continuing source of inspiration to him in his writing, to which he did not turn until middle age. His idiosyncratic viewpoints, of which there are many, are reflected in his fiction; many of his characters appear isolationists who deliberately shun the normal or disparage any form of collectivity. In an audio-recorded interview with Dai Smith, Berry admits that in his youth, without money and education he lived 'in a very narrow, circumscribed world'.[2] He left school at the first opportunity, and followed his father and grandfather before him down the pit, where he remained brooding and unsatisfied until the outbreak of the Second World War. When asked about his time underground during interview, he stated matter-of-factly: 'I wanted to get out pretty soon after I got in.'[3]

Destiny for Berry merely meant choosing your own sort of hell. He recalls male bodies 'smashed'; colleagues with broken legs, backs or worse (referring on one occasion to human remains being brought to the surface in a pit pony's feedbag). Welsh industrial fiction tends to depict examples of protagonists *becoming* disabled more frequently than those who are *born* disabled, in order to creatively charter this loss of concordant identity.[4] This undoubtedly contributes to dramatic effect; the plight of a crippled miner is made more acute when he is socially, culturally and geographically located. The reader is forced to consider how disability will intersect with a host of other normative social 'givens', considering that these people are of a certain generation, occupation and political disposition.

A keen sportsman, Berry cycled marathon distances and played football for Swansea Town until a nasty tackle serrated his knee joint. He was an avid walker, and this at first seemingly minor injury marked the beginning of Berry's torturous struggle with mobility issues. He was only too aware of the financial hardship that disabled men could face in communities that were built on relentless, hard, physical labour. The effects of this knee injury, combined with general restlessness, led Berry to rack up a catalogue of jobs, many of which the protagonists in his short stories share. He totalled at least fifteen different occupations, giving the impression of being somewhat of a 'Jack of all trades'. Writing, his true master-trade, often imposed poverty on his family, and, unfortunately, gave him very little economic profit during his lifetime. He was unable to finish a teacher training course on economic grounds.

Berry vehemently denied that he was an Anglo-Welsh writer of the common sort; he insisted that his writing was not contaminated by the likes of Jack Jones and Lewis Jones in any way, as he simply had not read them. He believed that his work had, 'no precedent, no touch, no contact' with this heritage.[5] He accused such writers of having been on the periphery of Valley life; not in the 'broil', in the 'muck' of it.[6] For Berry, these other writers from the same writing background were unconvincing and unreal, knowing nothing of the environment that they were attempting to portray. Instead, he devoured works by important American authors: Faulkner, Fitzgerald, Nathanael West and Henry Miller, cultivating a style similar to theirs: hard, grounded, firmly located writing that undermined all expectations and just dared his readers to see things from any alternative perspective. Berry rejected Dai Smith's labelling of him as a 'maverick'[7] of Welsh writing in English, saying that such terms were just 'tabs', and that if he had *wanted* to belong intrinsically to the tradition, he would have. Berry believed that people needed only very limited experience in life to be able to write: 'angels and saints and devils and idiots'[8] were all equally capable. He recognised that in order to paint a true picture you needed to paint things from all possible perspectives and vantage points. Perhaps surprisingly, Berry admired the work of the aesthete Gwyn Thomas, whom he described as skilfully transmuting 'gold out of dross'.[9] Yet, Berry ultimately felt that the dross, dust and detritus itself was much more important, and in need of truthful recording as it threatened to fade from living memory.

The onset of disability was arguably the catalyst of Berry's writing career. The frequent references to other accidents and near misses lead me to believe that he saw disability as a seemingly natural part of the life course. In *History Is What You Live*,[10] Berry relates his 'first accident' (*HWYL*, 57) to the reader, when, while working down the mine in his supervisor Jimmy's stall, the 'thin end of a roof scaling' (*HWYL*, 57) collapsed on to his back and shoulders. He describes struggling for breath until it was levered away. Berry believed that fate dealt him a fair hand that day. He says, matter-of-factly, 'had the thickest end fallen on my back, the rest of my life would have been spent in a ward' (*HWYL*, 57). Such comments reiterate the fact that severe impairment and even death were everyday occurrences in Berry's original line of work. He noticed that in their over-confidence and naivety, the young were particularly vulnerable to physical harm, believing that 'in industry and war, civilised nations have a flair for damaging adolescents' (*HWYL*, 28).

As a historically industrial region, it is unsurprising that Wales should have a major rate of physical impairment. In 2001, the Labour Force Survey calculated that almost one-fifth (19.85 per cent) of the Welsh working-age population could be classified as disabled.[11] Viewed comparatively with the rest of the United Kingdom, Wales's disability statistics come second only very marginally to those of the north of England (21.11 per cent), another geographic area with a heavy industrial heritage. As McIvor and Johnston state, 'there is no doubt that occupation-induced respiratory disease (primarily pneumoconiosis, bronchitis and emphysema) in coal mining represented the largest occupational health disaster in British history'.[12] Wales's historical role as the coal-mining capital of the world meant that a large percentage of the country's disabled population was made up of elderly men. In 2001 the disability and gender difference was still more apparent in Wales than in anywhere else in the United Kingdom.[13]

Labour Force Surveys have established that the types of disability and health problems show some divergence by region. The most common disabilities amongst the UK's general population were those affecting limbs, skin and breathing. Unsurprisingly, these disabilities were shown to be even more common in Wales, coalescing with the previous prevalence of industrial injury and disease in the country.

Until very recently breathing disabilities in Wales were frighteningly common; however, the visibility of pneumoconiosis and silicosis in mining communities is increasingly rare, as the last generations of miners suffering from these horrendous life-limiting afflictions pass away.[14] In 2002, Smith and Twomey suggested that regional variation in disabilities was largely associated with 'the distribution of injuries, the availability of and access to healthcare and adequate housing; lifestyle and dietary behaviour, levels of education and the age distribution of the population'.[15] The Rhondda of Berry's depiction fares unfavourably under all of these headings. Berry also pre-imagines contemporary theorists of disability's interest in how disability intersects with other significant factors, such as gender, age, and ethnicity.

The Disabled Persons Employment Act of 1944 was perceived as bestowing on disabled people the right to engage with the labour market and consequently achieve full citizenship. However, as Anne Borsay notices, the Act 'embodied the division between "normal" and "abnormal" workers'.[16] Disability was irrecoverably associated with unskilled work, with employment rehabilitation centres being orientated towards settling people in manual jobs. Policy concentrated on finding fitting individuals to carry out jobs and compensating employers for taking them on. Consequently, rehabilitation across the full occupational range was unsuccessful.

Many found their job options to be limited by their disability, or that they were forced to take jobs where their skills or qualifications were not used. In Berry's last novel, *This Bygone*, Dewi comments on the existence of compulsory light work for disabled miners, jobs 'for the crocked and battered so long as their guts isn't spewing giblets'. His mate Irfon replies, 'Picked by fucken office blokes you wouldn't trust to fill a sack of horseshit' (*TB*, 177). The Minister for Labour in 1945, Ernest Bevin, was adamant that: 'This country will not be able for the next fifty years to afford an unemployed man or to allow a man to be kept away from industry because he is (un)fit or injured'.[17] However, positive attitudes to the employment of disabled people faded as the wartime labour shortage abated.

In reality, the prospect of securing alternative employment for a disabled miner in mid-twentieth-century Wales was slim. Where such opportunities could be found, the productivity of disabled miners was closely monitored. Studies were commissioned by the government in order to ascertain the efficiency of groups of ex-miners disabled by pneumoconiosis, who were then employed in the very few 'light labour' industries in South Wales. It was hoped that the findings would encourage more employers to provide work for these afflicted men. In 1949 Treasure found that such studies were difficult to conduct, because the efficiency of most types of labour (including coal mining) is measured most directly by output. But as most of the disabled men employed were employed on light labour, store-keeping and the like, they were only 'indirectly productive'.[18] Consequently, his study revolved largely around less obvious quantitative measures of 'efficiency', including absence from work, labour turnover and accident rate.[19] Treasure issued a questionnaire to various employers of disabled ex-miners in south and west Wales inviting them to comment on any aspect of their employees' performance. The comments are remarkable in their divergence.

The manager of a factory in Porth employing three certified disabled men provided pleasantly surprising feedback: 'We would like to say most emphatically that these men show, in our opinion, a greater amount of keenness and interest in their work than normal men, and are most satisfactory employees in all respects.'[20] The employers in this study are shown to be particularly concerned at measurements of 'lost time' accumulated by their disabled employees. A factory in Treforest said that 'The time lost is practically nil', whereas one in Carmarthen reported: 'The tendency is definitely more, for these men do lose more time than a normal healthy person as far as this factory is concerned.'[21] Most employers commented that overall in terms of performance there was no noticeable difference from the nondisabled workers, with 'No wanton absenteeism. Average late-coming and sickness'.[22] One employer stated that 'if *they* do fall ill with ordinary colds, influenza etc., they are absent from work for a much longer period than normal workers'.[23] However, perhaps the most telling remark was made by an employer of twelve 'certified' and eight 'uncertified' disabled men on general labouring duties at a factory in Carmarthen, who declared: 'Some appear to work satisfactorily in all kinds of conditions, whereas others cannot, or will not, put themselves out. I believe a number could be more gainfully employed if they could get over the fact that they are permanently ill.'[24] The men concerned in the study were said to have been 'very reluctant' to reveal their disability because they believed that they would be dismissed if identified as cases of pneumoconiosis. This is interesting, in that it shows an alternative attitude to those discussed in texts like Berry's 'Natives' (*CS*, 78), where 'dust cases' boasted of the extent of damage done to their lungs through work. Removed from the mining environment these men appear to have been at greater risk of social stigma and shunning by non-disabled non-mining men (pen-pushing managers), who viewed them as slovenly, damaged and potentially contagious.

The provisions made for the alternative employment of disabled miner were wholly unsatisfactory. Between the years of 1938 and 1953 no fewer than 26,000 miners became disabled, yet re-employment rehabilitation statistics from this period are laughable:

> the total of such disabled men who have been accommodated in the ten special Grenfell factories by 1952 was just one hundred and forty-eight. On the other hand, between July 1948 and 1952, 5,500 certified cases (the vast majority of new cases)had elected to remain in the pits. This process continues, and the numbers of these disabled men have been increased also by the return to the mines of men previously suspended under the Workmen's Compensation Act.[25]

The increasing employment of women in factories and other industries since the war was sometimes resented by men who struggled to find work due to ill-health.[26] Johnes comments that 'there was indignity among some miners who discovered that they were earning less than their wives or daughters'.[27] The 1952 Socialist Medical Association conference went on to deal with these critical questions of alternative employment for pneumoconiosis victims, calling for more Remploy factories, sheltered workshops and retraining centres for these men. They also demanded that their pay be made up to the minimum union rate from public funds. Sadly, in reality, attempts to secure justice for those left disabled by this industrial evil were found to be wanting.

The danger of dust inhalation to men working underground is documented in Berry's short story 'Time Spent'. Lewis Rimmer's lungs are certified as being 'one hundred per cent dust' (*CS*, 92). In utter disbelief, 'Lew' complains to himself:

> By Jesus, Men are pegging out with fifty per cent. I'm miles from that state. Rough chest first thing in the morning, short of breath until the circulation starts moving. Good Christ almighty, fifty-seven, packing it in at my age. Doesn't make sense. Bloody hell. There's colliers in Fawr close on pension time, old plodders clearing their yardage every shift. Me, bloody scrap-heap. (*CS*, 94)

Berry soon makes it apparent that Lew's disabilities are in fact multiple: 'A six foot man in his prime, the curvature of his spine lowered him six inches, the curve prominent hard packed under the shiny serge of his long, double breasted jacket' (*CS*, 94). Life in the pit has led to an enforced scoliosis, but Lew is strangely proud of this outward evidence of the extent of his physical toil: 'he raised his head, breathed deeply, held himself firm, striding, but ache from his shoulder-blades, his ribs so he relaxed, hands in his pockets, chin out-thrust, sight fixed on the coming and going of his toecaps' (*CS*, 94). He is told by Doctor Gammon, 'The Coal Board dare not employ you after serving fourteen days' notice' (*CS*, 94).[28] Lew takes the blow incredibly hard. The story chronicles his last days in the pit and the reactions of his workmates and wife to the news.

In his depiction of Lew, Berry considers the 'damaged pride' (*CS*, 101) and reputation of the dust-victim. Lew's young 'butty' hears the news rumoured in the local club and says, 'So you're going on compo, Lew' (*CS*, 100). Lew snaps at his 'butty' to get the dram filled. Not satisfied with the validity of the doctor's condemnation, he embarks on one further mission of self-harm. Pneumoconiosis and scoliosis aside, Lew does not feel 'broken' enough to be written off from work. Feeling the need to acquire one further outward sign of impairment (and thus ineptitude to work), Lew proceeds to break his own arm in an accident underground:

> Pride again, remorse, smothered grunts, his spoiled self-esteem turned vicious, aiming the pick, his body angled away by instinct, teetering, the soft-jointed stone   sliding soundlessly out from the side where he'd been ripping, falling edge-wise on his outflung forearm, breaking the bone. (*CS*, 101)

With this injury, Lew's employment is terminated instantly. Berry leads the reader to believe the accident to be deliberate, the physical pain no comparison to the emotional torment Lew endures working his notice. With his diagnosis, Lew is relegated from being a good role model to the younger, fitter men. Instead he becomes a terrible warning of what could still happen to them.[29]

In Berry's fiction, women are dangerous. Many are curiously endowed with the power to inflict various disabilities upon their men. Mothers are presented as the most damaging of all women. Emma Smith notices Berry's penchant for portraying these 'mother-messed' men. She notices in one of Berry's novels, *The Full-Time Amateur*, that the main protagonist, Huw, 'is set against minor characters who are "shaped" like men, but bear none of the masculine attributes privileged by Berry. If men, mostly in these positions of power, are repressed, "messed with", then it is the fault of their mothers.'[30] Dogged by unemployment and ill health after a mining accident, Huw Davies, the 'full-time amateur', is chided by his mother: 'Your father had a war to go to, you've got nothing' (*FTA*, 91). Huw's generation is lacking a heroic cause, and everything goes against his quest to attain a meaningful masculine role in the ways his father did.

In an unpublished short story, 'The Disabled', of which there are three drafts held at the Richard Burton Archives at Swansea University, Berry clearly struggled with politically correct phraseology surrounding impairment. Indeed, the first draft (written in 1988) shows the story title to have been crossed out not once, but twice. The first title is illegible, having been scribbled out beyond all recognition; the second is, rather provocatively, 'The Inadequates' – a title that emphasises Berry's apparent fixation with impairment, productivity and performance. He finally settles on 'The Disabled', but throughout the text returns to this need to classify and categorise his protagonists: 'Low on hope yet proud, they belonged to a catchword norm. They were classified, sanctioned, ungovernable citizens the side of blind faith.'[31] From the scribblings on the first draft, Berry had evidently struggled with but gave in to using the catchword of 'disabled'. By this point in the 1980s it was a well-known and politically loaded term, suggestive of stereotype from the outset.

One of 'the disabled' is Haydn Roper, a one-time man of action before his 'blackouts'; he was 'fated, unfulfilled, his 8 O-levels "Gone to waste", vowed his mother'.[32] The other is Sydney Tremain, who 'had the deliberacy of a wizened pensioner', maimed by childhood polio, 'his shrunken, white skinned hand' always 'pouched in his jacket pocket',[33] and whose mother carps at mealtimes: 'Trust the devil to find work for idle hands',[34] amongst other statements indicative of her resentment of his sedentary lifestyle. In Berry's *Hunter and Hunted* another disappointed and embittered mother says: 'Son, it's normal for men and women to get married. Your father was normal, I'm definitely normal. Bill is normal', and her son replies, 'I'm not normal!' (*HH*, 42). Berry's disabled men are presented as subdued, temporarily reprieved and then shamed by their mothers and wives, exonerated from clocking in and clocking out.

Berry dwells on the familial consequences of a pneumoconiosis diagnosis in 'Time Spent'. On hearing of her husband's certification, Bessie, Lew's wife, 'pouting resentment', (*CS*, 95) complains over the garden wall to his one-time lover, Esther, about his physical arrogance: 'My Lewis won't be told. Always out to prove himself diff'rent, nothing at all like anybody else God ever put breath into. From now on he'll have to knuckle down, stands to reason with one hundred per cent dust' (*CS*, 95).[35] Bessie's comment that as a consequence of his disability Lew will now have to 'knuckle down' is a loaded one. It is perhaps rather better reinterpreted as her hope that the medical confirmation of Lew's impairment will make him 'back down' and give her more free rein to do as she pleases. During an argument she has a sly dig at his increasing debility, saying: 'You can't frighten me no more' (*CS*, 96). Such remarks are indicative of the common belief that the onset or existence of disability in heteronormative men is inevitably emasculating.

Berry seems to be very interested in women's reactions and responses to men who become sick or disabled. In 'Time Spent', Bessie's first reaction on hearing of Lew's diagnosis is to scold him in an 'I told you so' manner for his uselessness, before asking: 'D'you ask Doctor Gammon about a fortnight in that convalescent place on Gower? Don't suppose you did' (*CS*, 95).[36] Women like Bessie are shown to be excessively materialistic in the face of their husband's physical tragedies: '"How much is full compo these days?" she inquired, friendly now, leaning towards him' (*CS*, 97). Bessie takes it upon herself to ensure that they receive every material benefit that they are now entitled to.[37] She says that she will go on an errand 'down his surg'ry' to find out the 'facilities laid on' for the 'likes of' Lew, who paid the NUM for years and years, 'without so much as a pint of beer off of 'em' (*CS*, 96). In Berry's last novel, *This Bygone* (1996), Dewi's mother worries about the reaction of Mrs Kitchener to Mr Kitchener's becoming disabled: 'Lew Kitchener had a stroke. Finished he is. She'll be in a pickle. God knows how she'll take this, sick man on her hands' (*CS*, 12). In these texts, the onset of disability is presented as a personal affront to the woman of the house, whose workload will surely increase as a result of it. In the short story 'Blood Money', two sisters Brenda and Olive resent having to provide personal care for their elderly father, Abe, whom they are desperate to have admitted to hospital, since he has been 'a burden right throughout', with 'No consideration for anybody 'cept hisself!' (*CS*, 212).

However, despite this, further reading seems to suggest Berry's quiet reverence for female fortitude, particularly in the face of deprivation and its physical consequences. He admits to a puzzling curiosity around women's behaviour and motivations. Women are complicated for Berry, but he is not as obliquely anti-feminist as one might think. Rather, his male characters treat women warily and with a great deal of wonderment: 'Girls, women: I'd throw away a few years to learn how they *are*. A man can't know' (*FTA*, 136).

Decreased mobility was a personal tragedy for Berry in later life, and he uses 'Time Spent' as a mouthpiece for these feelings: 'It's well over twenty years since I climbed Pen Arglwydd. Can't manage it now. Finished. Christ, aye, I'm finished' (*CS*, 99). With no more drams to fill and no more mountains to climb, men like Lew are mourning the loss of physical feats by which to measure their human worth. Indeed, McIvor and Johnson comment on the 'persistence of a machismo, high-risk work culture'[38] as factors that contributed enormously to the damage accrued to coal worker's bodies. Berry's short stories are elegies not just for a specific time and place, but for a specific male body. His understanding of the economic and social damage being inflicted upon his comrades is communicated partly by the poor physical condition of his protagonists, so that disability functions partly in his fiction as a means of dramatising industrial masculinity in crisis, a prominent theme in Welsh writing in English. In Lewis Jones's *Cwmardy* (1937), for example, implicit in the contrast between powerful Big Jim and his puny son Len, successive generations of miners, is an elegy for the passing of the era of physical prowess.

In addition, Berry's male characters are living through disintegration of several kinds. They are no longer strong or virile but depleted, lacking, and mourning their combined loss of strength. He shows an acute awareness of how 'manly' identities impinged upon the body, as well as community evaluations of the dust, accidents and injuries that wrecked so many lives. However, Berry shows that it is Lew's inability to cope with unemployment rather than the debilitating effects of pneumoconiosis that ultimately kills him. He takes his own life in his pigeon loft: 'Stooped in the aisle, cursing, his broken arm hanging, clenching the mouth of the double barrel between his teeth, Lewis gagged curses as the trigger slicked back under his thumb' (*CS*, 103). While there is no statistical evidence of increased suicide rates in disabled miners, 'Time Spent' is a rumination on the stark and sudden social ostracism that could accompany disabled status, not simply through prejudice but, more commonly, through resulting unemployment. In these texts it is difficult to see whether it is the men's physical disabilities or their damaged gender roles that most compromises the validity of their citizenship. For Berry, all bodies that are unable to engage in the physically demanding occupations and processes that are expected of them, due to impairment, injury or unemployment, are incapable of performing conventional gender roles, and therefore disabled.

The working-class disabled?

Disability is shown to do strange things to class perception and categorisation. While his writing is free from middle-class moralising and false sentimentality, Berry is concerned with the idea that disabled people cannot (at least literally), be considered part of the traditional *working* class. In 'Before Forever After', the experience of becoming disabled is shown to be economically profitable, and actually enables upward class mobility for the protagonist in question. This is the only time this happens in Berry's body of work; it is particularly interesting in that he seems to have anticipated very current controversial ideas around the economic over-privileging of disabled people.

In this story, the narrative focus is on a group of men who are seven weeks behind schedule on a building site. They are in no rush to finish the job; they joke, play pontoon and discuss Big 'Strapper' Cullen's beautiful, middle-class girlfriend, Rebecca. Friendly Strapper is introduced as the 'most favoured character on the building site. A wide open man, generous, brotherly. Everybody loved him' (*CS*, 31). He is handsome, athletic, and the epitome of male youth and strength. Disaster strikes when he has an accident at work 'deflecting off a RSJ, falling all-shapes, the visible bounce of his body on the ground floor concrete' (*CS*, 41). Berry's portrayal of the accident coincides with the increase of 'visible accidents' in contemporary culture. Anne Borsay comments on this trend:

> No longer regarded as more or less private (individualized) happenings, accidents became public events, affecting or concerning the whole of society. The re-conceptualization of employment, acting in concord with the newly visible accident, served to stimulate additional segregated employment for disabled people.[39]

In Berry's story, the other men stand stunned as they witness the tragedy unfold. Time momentarily stands still: 'seconds ticked out, glacial, then frenzy' as men raced down ladders and scaffolding 'like monkeys' (*CS*, 41) in their eagerness to help their workmate. A character called Chris, who was Rebecca's childhood admirer, and suitably jealous of Strapper, takes charge of the emergency, delegating tasks to the other men. Pete, who feels responsible, is in tears. Chris asserts that 'This isn't a case of negligence. Act of God' (*CS*, 41). The rest of the group take his word for it, and no more blame is cast. Strapper looks to be a 'goner': 'Skull fracture, fractured spine, pelvis crushed. He fell on his spanners and podger' (*CS*, 41).

The narrative then accelerates a year, and on the anniversary of the event Big Strapper returns to the site to thank Chris for 'looking after' him when he took his 'big tumble' (*CS*, 43). Strapper stands 'hunched over a pair of alloyed crutches', with 'one of those three-wheelers for disabled persons parked on the kerb behind him' (*CS*, 43). Since the group last met Rebecca and Strapper have married, he boasts, while he was 'still in my plaster cast' (*CS*, 42). Rebecca is 'facially harder', 'untidy', having lost her girl-shape under 'a black PVC windcheater' (*CS*, 42). She defends Strapper's remaining physical capabilities to the non-disabled men at every opportunity, asserting that '"John swims every afternoon in the sea"' (*CS*, 43). The men acknowledge this achievement and Strapper jokes that he swims like a 'drunken crab' until he gets into his 'crawl stroke' (*CS*, 43). The jovial content of the dialogue does little to mask the discomfort that every character feels towards Strapper's new disabled identity, apart from perhaps the man himself.

After various comments on how remarkably well he is coping, Strapper announces that he has 'bought this six roomed bungalow down in Pembroke' (*CS*, 44). On departure, he urges them to 'Pay us a visit. Stay a couple of weeks. Any time.' Suddenly, the whole tone of the narrative changes as the real social and economic differences between the friends are revealed; non-disabled protagonists 'don't know what to say' as the couple leave them with this slightly tainted picture of marital solidarity and affluence. Strapper now has time and money to spend, but his body is already spent. It is left obvious to the reader that his old friends will never visit. The story ends in a curious way, with an intentionally righteous dialogue on the 'guts' of the couple, and a strange concluding statement by a character called Chris: 'Chris squared his shoulders, ground out his feelings like dogma,

"Yes, boy, they do make a man feel small, they definitely do'" (*CS*, 44). This idea of 'smallness' must in some way relate to this new assertion of class distinction, the economic differences between friends being laid bare. Berry shows material difference to be even more detrimental to the protagonists' relationships than their new-found physical differences. Berry's work successfully predicts that perceived economic privileging will indeed threaten disabled and non-disabled relations, particularly within the traditional working class. Acquiring money seems to distance Strapper from his colleagues much more than the acquiring of physical disability does. Berry's work thus anticipates current debates about disability benefits by raising questions about how much physical and intellectual ability is materially worth to the individual and the state.

The main benefits available under the Industrial Injuries system at the time of Berry's writing were disablement benefit, special hardship allowance and industrial death benefit. Berry's texts reveal the tendency for some miners and ex-miners to abuse the benefit system, having learned how to 'fiddle' it to their advantage. In *This Bygone* the men undertake a planned benefit strategy, having been given fourteen days' notice from their pit:

> Men went sick instead of registering as unemployed. Lumbar and stomach pains recurred, old injuries or ailments guaranteeing minimum weekly income until they were laid off Benefit and had to register. Then they were compelled to take one of three job offers, invariably away from home, labouring for low money. Eight young colliers joined the army. (*TB*, 110)

Many men, resentful of their treatment during the Depression, saw the war as an opportunity to escape the dirty and dangerous world of the pit. While Berry's work looks back on the laying-off of thousands of unwanted miners in the 1930s, there is less narrative interest in the resulting labour shortage during the war years, with 25,000 men having left the industry between 1938 and 1941.[40] However, he does briefly mention the 'partially disabled' men who were recruited as hush-hush temporary labourers 'widening the parish track for 6/- a day. Bribes, bartering and promises remained word of mouth' (*TB*, 153).

In his unpublished story 'The Disabled', Berry presents being in receipt of benefits as actually preferable to employment: 'Occasionally they went hitch-hiking on their Invalidity Benefit, as tourists. They weren't anxious for a better lifestyle. When cash ran out they returned to the tolerable humdrum of Pengwaelod village.'[41] Time and again, Berry's novels reveal the general sentiment among coalfield workers and their families that if the employers were made to pay compensation directly (full pay for six months after the initial discovery of disease) to their workers, it would not only give people economic security in the early stages of treatment but would make employers more interested in the prevention of disease and injury. The cost of disability was twofold. Physical and sensory impairment generated extra expenses, not just for aids and adaptations but also for additional heating, food, laundry, travel and recreation. Income deprivation was thus aggravated by the additional costs associated with impairment.

However, occasionally, Berry also shows shared disabilities to induce solidarity between men. In the short story 'July Saturday in 1940', he refers to the 'shared fragility' of shaky Charlie, 'who contracted rheumatic fever as a kid', and 'hunch-backed' Billy, who carried 'desperation in his tiny bones' (*CS*, 48).The pair are debating the legitimacy of a story told by Mr Everett's young son, Isaac (who is by their accounts 'a bit backward'), that he saw German parachutists landing in Cefn Nant-y-Bwlch. This is an interesting scene in that it reveals an apparent hierarchy of disabilities, the physically disabled assuming precedence over those with intellectual difficulties. Berry's work is inherently concerned with issues of male camaraderie explored in his works by way of a paradox. His 'heroes', presented as inherently and essentially individualistic, are normally both at peace with and yet distinctly apart from the normative fellowship of men. This 'apartness' does not necessarily translate as 'better than'. Berry discusses the importance of 'sameness' for men in his interview with Dai Smith:

> And although some, boys, a lot of boys, were treated abysmally . . . grafting on diets of beggars, died young as a consequence, at least boys grew up with the same environment, the same [. . .] exactly the same things, spoke in the same language. I think when you share a bond like that, like being in trench warfare, or being aboard a ship, you know it is crisis and extremity, they bond people.[42]

Indeed, crises of extreme poverty and warfare have traditionally seemed to bond people. Yet, despite the above words, Berry's writing often seems to explore the opposite. The deciding factor in terms of human solidarity, particularly involving men, seems to have been the condition of physical capability. Disability is shown to be thoroughly capable of both binding and severing ties between men.

This grouping of physically disabled men together is explored further in other short stories like 'Natives': '"We are the immovables, financially deprived, dauntless, capable of social sweetness, murder by degrees, slow suicide, humility, even visions. Anything at all on the graph of human behaviour." "Bar earning a living wage," grumbled Felix. "King Coal, the rotten waster"' (*CS*, 77). The narrative is a rambling booze-filled discussion between three disabled men on an unspecified 'Modern disease' (*CS*, 77). Levi, Martin and Felix are propping up the bar in their local 'Institute' complaining about the severity of their financial situation and the falsehoods of socialist politics: 'There's too much yap about balance of payments, productivity, mobility of labour, royal commissions examining this and that, it's a disease of the soul' (*CS*, 77). Martin, who functions as the group's reality checker, complains of living in a 'ghetto' and of feeling 'politically powerless' (*CS*, 77). He ends his lament with one further sorry statement: 'we're well past middle age, we're on compo and hardship allowance' (*CS*, 78).

Berry's protagonists attempt to make light of these damning facts. The idea of having a shared, legitimate and written classification of their disability seems important to the men, as Martin reminds them: 'Being disabled, the three of us on the books in Hobart House, London S.W.1.' (*CS*, 78). This proof and verification of disability seems to succeed in making certain behaviours accepted and permissible; the 'compo and hardship allowance trio' are greeted warmly by the community. 'Knocking back scrumpy five nights a week, beer on Fridays and Saturdays' (*CS*, 78) might otherwise have been frowned upon if they were working men. The men are careful to exhibit the expected signs of their illness at the appropriate times. They resort to 'controlled bout(s) of coughing' (*CS*, 78) and tongue-in-cheek competitiveness over which of them has the greatest percentage of dust in his lungs.

Berry does seem to favour certain leitmotifs when portraying disabled protagonists. They are often very well read: Workingmen's Institute librarians, book-stealers, and just plain know-alls. In one of Berry's unpublished short stories, 'The Disabled', Sydney and Haydn are partners in crime, the first disabled in youth by polio and the second by epilepsy (caused by a rugby injury). The narrative reveals what activities fill their purposeless days, being unemployable and verging on middle age. Berry reveals that 'Sydney "lifts" books' and has a particular penchant for Nietzsche. Haydn admits that 'He's heavy, I can barely follow him.' Leniently disgusted by his friend's ignorance, Sydney squeaks: 'Take time then!' Discussion follows, on there being 'plenty of time about', at least for men like them. Haydn asks: 'What are we here for anyhow?' Sydney replies that it's a 'fluke', but '[it's a] damn sight better than being a shovel-full of gravel'. Berry shows his disabled protagonists' questioning of their human 'condition' to be significantly more uplifting than that of the non-disabled others. An almost identical bookish disabled protagonist appears in 'Natives', where Levi aggravates his friends with his alienating waffle: 'I'm one of your stall and heading ex-miners who filled out coal on a diet of Spinoza, Immanuel Kant, Nietzsche, Voltaire and Charles Darwin, with Walter Whitman and Johnny Keats for afters' (*CS*, 79). Unsurprisingly, these are the writers that Berry himself considered most appealing.

The men in these texts are shown to turn to self-education following impairment or accident. This becomes apparent when Martin reveals Levi to have 'dropped in clover after his kneecap was busted' and consequently to have spent the next 'twenty years in the Institute library, franking the date on Westerns, Thrillers' (*CS*, 79). Felix vows that such behaviour is both incompatible and discordant with their original literary-oblivious, macho occupation: 'Some fuckin' collier' he remarks bitterly and adds, 'As from tonight universal literacy is a curse, a cancer spread by Fleet Street' (*CS*, 79). The self-education of disabled miners in Berry's world is not presented in any way as even potentially economically advantageous. Rather, it is presented as an alternative pastime to 'real' work; these men acknowledge that intellectual strength cannot compensate for their lack of physical strength. Considering the large number of miners who were disabled, it is surprisingly rare to see presentations of a disabled 'collective' in this fiction. The trend appears to be for the afflicted to be diagnosed, removed from work and, in their isolation, to fade quickly from memory.

Disabled protagonists are frequently portrayed as being politically astute. Berry presents them as keen social observers, remarking upon their surroundings and prophesying in a way reminiscent of, but significantly less dignified than, the blind seers of old: 'By the year two thousand and eight, every infant will slot-fit instant social service before he's off the breast, his poop conduited to manufacture manna, his water processed corpse will magic blossoms from gravel!' (*CS*, 79).

Berry's protagonists do not mince their words in registering the bodily reality of the human condition, but the effect is rarely, with one or two notable exceptions, grotesque. The impression given by the physically disabled is that they are static watchers, perfectly positioned as Levi, Martin and Felix are to argue relentlessly about 'the rising and falling histories of Upper Coed-Coch' (*CS*, 85).

Berry has a great deal of knowledge regarding industrial hazards in the productionist environment of Welsh coal mining, and sheds light on a heavily camouflaged process of disablement. In a tribute to Berry, Robert Minhinnick composed a highly effective poem made up from their correspondence, where he describes him as having 'fashioned each page/ As a rune against mendacity'.[43] In this line Minhinnick reiterates Berry's belief that 'mendacity' or lying was the 'Unlovely spirit of the age'. Complicatedly, Berry uses disability as a diversionary and shock tactic, 'Willing us to see as [he] had seen'. Ultimately, and probably intentionally, he encourages the reader to pull away from fiction, in both life and literature.[44] Having actually experienced disability, Berry did not overplay its creative function as a metaphor, being primarily concerned in his fiction with promoting a more truthful way of regarding it.

In her seminal work *Illness as Metaphor* Susan Sontag trenchantly observes that: 'the attraction of disability to a writer must be that its metaphors seem to affirm the value of being more conscious, more complex psychologically. In this way, health can seem banal, and even vulgar.'[45] While Berry hardly depicts health as vulgar in these texts, he certainly does not treat able-bodiedness complacently, being aware at first hand of its often fleeting nature. Given the complexity and poignancy of Berry's portraits of disability, M. L. Jenkins's critique of his writing as clinically cynical seems unfair: 'there is a wryness and refusal to take either pleasure or pain seriously which lends an air of lost confidence to much of the work. That, at least, is how it may seem to minds trained on more refined fare.'[46] Pain is a more frequent occurrence than pleasure in Berry's world; the muscle-tight concision of his texture stabs home one insight after other. From this compression a unique kind of lyricism emerges. John Pikoulis writes of Berry's short story collection that '[r]arely has English prose managed to sound so physical',[47] and certainly, the physicality he is referring to is far less to do with human flesh than it is with the bare bones and sinew of his honed writing style. However, Berry's work is at its most frightening when it lays down what the human body is capable of doing or becoming, when it is damaged or when it malfunctions. For Berry, the correlation between writing and disability is multifaceted. It is presented simultaneously as therapeutic, truth-telling, but also illustrative of the potential for misunderstanding.

Berry did not receive the critical acclaim he deserved in his lifetime. Dai Smith published early pieces championing his work, and, later, so did John Pikoulis. It was not until the emergence of Simon Baker's edited collection of Berry's short stories (published in 2000, three years after Berry's death) that his honed skill as a short-story writer began to be widely acknowledged and the texts made readily available.[48] Such neglect served only to underline the peculiarity of his case. For someone of Berry's social class and background, to be a writer was itself a disability. It made him 'queer', and set him apart. The connection between writing and disability would therefore seem to be much more complex than a single, causal one, and to involve a psychological nexus of profound significance.

From its first emergence during the 1920s and 1930s, Welsh industrial fiction has always been centrally concerned with registering economic, social and political disadvantage. Berry's fiction represents a new departure in this tradition. Differently from the majority of anglophone Welsh writing in this period, it does not seek to function as a product or shaper of the ideal or normal; instead, it uses disability to convincingly present a complex process of social critique, and as a site of alternative reality and even value. It is difficult to establish whether Berry actually goes so far as to envisage social or creative potentiality as issuing from such damaged protagonists and landscapes. However, I would argue that this revolutionising of relationships between texts and ideology that results from Berry's shaping of disability as a majority presence in everyday life produces a more real depiction of his and our continuing reality.

Novelist Niall Griffiths states that Berry's work gave him a 'seismic' revelation that the way people truly *were* was 'important and valuable and uniquely expressive and possessed of a huge communicative power'.[49] Ordinary people were disabled, and they could be the subject of books, they mattered. Their lives were worthy of exploring in literature. From the 1990s onwards, Griffiths takes up Berry's mission to present voices perfectly captured without caricature or condescension, and we finally hear those who, although we know they have been here all along, have been neglected most by literature. Glyn Jones summarises Berry's late stylistic tendencies in *The Dragon Has Two Tongues*:

the valleys man of the future, of a degutted South Wales, without coal and without pits, whose people never met together for political action, or singing, or worship, who are songless apart from their pop records and solitary apart from strip-tease clubs and bingo halls.[50]

While Berry was one of the first to describe the places left discarded after the working guts were ripped from these post-industrial communities, it is Griffiths who takes a closer look at the inhabitants of the carcass. His 'potchers' and drug-addled 'zombies' are the racier descendants of Berry's 'dry weather cripples, lungers, and ailing moochers' (*CS*, 6). Even in the 1990s and 2000s, these predominantly male protagonists remain absolved of everything through the ancient familiar crises of health, work and money.

Notes

[1] The term 'work-limiting disabled' is interesting as many contemporary surveys and questionnaires indicated that if the rate of working output is not affected by disability, then the individuals in question were not regarded as disabled.

[2] Dai Smith, 'An interview with Ron Berry', audio recording, undated. Held at the South Wales Miner's Library, Swansea University. Transcribed by this author.

[3] Smith, 'An interview with Ron Berry'.

[4] Disabled, injured and ill miners can be found in Lewis Jones's *Cwmardy* (1937), Menna Gallie's *The Small Mine* (1962) and Gwyn Thomas's *Sorrow For Thy Sons* (considered 'too bleak' for publication in 1937, and remaining so until 1986), and in many others.

[5] Smith, 'An interview with Ron Berry'.

[6] Smith, 'An interview with Ron Berry.

[7] Smith, 'An interview with Ron Berry.

[8] Smith, 'An interview with Ron Berry'.

[9] Smith, 'An interview with Ron Berry'.

[10] Ron Berry, *History Is What You Live* (Llandysul: Gomer, 1998). All further references made are to this edition and will be within the body of the text.

[11] Office for National Statistics (ONS), Department for Work and Pensions (DWP), Department for Education and Skills (DfES) and National Assembly for Wales (2002), *Annual Local Area Labour Force Survey (LLFS) – Summary Publication 2001/02*. This survey uses a broad definition of disability that includes individuals with a long-term (twelve months or more) health problem covered by the Disability Discrimination Act and/or that limits the kind or amount of work an individual can do. It is important to emphasise that this survey also considers disability to be the mental incapacity to perform certain tasks.

[12] Arthur McIvor and Ronald Johnston, *Miners' Lung: A History of Dust Disease in British Coal Mining* (Hampshire: Ashgate, 2007), p. 2.

[13] *Annual Local Area Labour Force Survey 2001/02*. In 2001 there was still a divergence of disability and gender in Wales of almost 3 per cent (21.25 per cent males and 18.42 per cent females, respectively).

[14] While the exact number of miners disabled by lung disease will never be known, some sense of the impact can be gauged from the fact that at the 2004 deadline for miners and their families to register for compensation under the 1998 bronchitis and emphysema litigation against British Coal, a staggering 570,000 claims had been made. See McIvor and Johnston, *Miners' Lung*, p. 58.

[15] A. Smith and B. Twomey, 'Labour Market Experience of People with Disabilities', *Labour Market Trends* (August 2002), 415–27 (p. 418).

[16] Anne Borsay, *Disability and Social Policy in Britain Since 1750* (Hampshire: Palgrave Macmillan, 2005), p. 14.

[17] Ernest Bevin, cited in Martin Johnes, *Wales Since 1939* (Manchester: Manchester University Press, 2012), p. 83.

[18] J.A.P. Treasure, 'A study of the efficiency of groups of ex-miners disabled by Pneumoconiosis employed in light labour industries in South Wales', *The British Journal of Medicine* (1949), no. 3, 127–38.

[19] There is, of course, no necessary correlation between absence and efficiency on the job, but the two are probably inversely related.

[20] Treasure, 'A study of the efficiency of groups of ex-miners disabled by Pneumoconiosis employed in light labour industries in South Wales', 136.

[21] Treasure, 'A study of the efficiency of groups of ex-miners disabled by Pneumoconiosis employed in light labour industries in South Wales', 136.

[22] Treasure, 'A study of the efficiency of groups of ex-miners disabled by Pneumoconiosis employed in light labour industries in South Wales', 136.

[23] Treasure, 'A study of the efficiency of groups of ex-miners disabled by Pneumoconiosis employed in light labour industries in South Wales', 136.

[24] Treasure, 'A study of the efficiency of groups of ex-miners disabled by Pneumoconiosis employed in light labour industries in South Wales', 136.

[25] T. Francis Jarman, 'Industrial Dust Disease: By the South Wales Medical Correspondent of *Medicine Today & Tomorrow*' (1939), 7. Available at the SWCC pamphlet collection, South Wales Miners' Library, Swansea University.

[26] Deirdre Beddoe's *Out of the Shadows: A History of Women in Twentieth-Century Wales* (Cardiff: University of Wales Press, 2001) and Mari A. Williams's *Forgotten Army: The Female Munitions Workers of South Wales, 1939–1945* (Cardiff: University of Wales Press, 2002) discuss the expansion of female work opportunities in south Wales during the war years.

[27] Johnes, *Wales Since 1939*, p. 14.

[28] Prior to 27 November 1974, the Medical Board had power to issue a certificate suspending a man suffering from pneumoconiosis or tuberculosis from further employment in occupations known to cause and exacerbate the disease. Such a certificate was regarded as sufficient proof for claiming 'Special Hardship Allowance'. The power of suspension was withdrawn from the Medical Board

by virtue of the National Insurance (Industrial Injuries/Prescribed Diseases) Amendment No. 2, 1974. Suspensions already in force at this time continued to have effect.

[29] In their examination of the oral histories of disabled miners, McIvor and Johnston noticed that peer pressure operated to induce workers to eschew safety measures, a culture which, accompanied by 'a fossilisation of attitudes and stagnation in health and safety measures', tells us much about the real effect of state regulation on health and safety in the workplace. See McIvor and Johnston, *Miners' Lung*, p. 14.

[30] Emma Smith, 'Masculinity in Welsh Writing in English: the cases of Lewis Jones, Glyn Jones, Gwyn Thomas, and Ron Berry' (unpublished PhD thesis, Swansea University, 2006), p. 165.

[31] Ron Berry, 'The Disabled', unpublished short story available in three editions. The Ron Berry Papers are held at the Richard Burton Archives, Swansea University. MS 2, p. 1.

[32] Berry, 'The Disabled', MS 1, p. 1.

[33] Berry, 'The Disabled', MS 1, p. 1.

[34] Berry, 'The Disabled', MS 1, p. 4.

[35] Berry frequently refers to physical arrogance as a collier-specific trait. For example, when Lew imagines what the other colliers' verdict of him will be as they sup beer in the workingmen's club: 'Lew Rimmer's finished. All the slashers travel the same road to Coed-coch cemetery. Pig-headed Lew, never wears a mask when he's boring holes. Tight-fisted money grabber, won't wait for the dust to clear after shot firing. Big Lew, he's packing muck in the gob walls when you can't see your hand in front of your eyes. Typical slasher, They all go the same way. Silicosis or pneumo. Loaf around on street corners until they're only skin and bones. Nothing but skeletons by the time the undertaker comes to measure them' (*CS*, 101).

[36] This reference is potentially to the large Miners' Convalescent Centre that existed in Langland, Gower. The centre was a dominant building, built in Scottish baronial style by the Merthyr Tydfil ironmasters, the Crawshay family. After a period of closure it has been renamed Langland Bay Manor and converted into twenty-seven luxury apartments.

[37] According to a report on 'Slate-Quarrymen and Silicosis' by J. Emrys Jones, secretary of Labour Party Wales in 1978, once a man was certified as suffering from silicosis or pneumoconiosis he became eligible for disablement benefit. The benefit was not compensation for loss of earnings but was based upon an assessment of the extent of disablement. The assessment was expressed as a percentage, representing the extent to which the man was handicapped by the disease in comparison with a normal healthy person of the same age. For men who were incapable of working, sickness benefit or invalidity benefit could be paid in addition to disablement benefit. In 1974 a man categorised as having 10 per cent disablement was entitled to £2.86 disablement benefit per week, rising incrementally to £28.60 for 100 per cent disablement. A report on silicosis by the Labour Party in 1978 revealed that one man seeking disablement benefit

had been turned down by the Medical Board on twenty-seven occasions (a remarkable statistic, considering that it was not possible to take a case to the Board more than twice in any year.) When his trade union representative appealed for him to be seen by the Central Pneumoconiosis Panel, largely considered to be the more generous, he was instantly assessed as being entitled to 20 per cent disablement benefit. Both reports available at the South Wales Miner's Library, Swansea University. Accessed June 2011.

[38] McIvor and Johnston, *Miner's Lung*, p. 3.
[39] Borsay, *Disability and Social Policy*, p. 127.
[40] Hywel Francis and Dai Smith, *The Fed: A History of the South Wales Miners*, 2nd edn (Cardiff: University of Wales Press, 1998), p. 396.
[41] Berry, 'The Disabled', MS 3, p. 2.
[42] Smith, 'An interview with Ron Berry'.
[43] Robert Minhinnick, 'A Rune Against Mendacity: At the Cremation of Ron Berry 22.07.97', *New Welsh Review*, 38 (Autumn 1997), p. 15.
[44] This awareness of fictionality can be seen as typically post-modern. Berry exposes grand narratives for what they really are: other people's stories. Protagonists in Berry's *Flame and Slag* (1968) challenge the way in which language is used as an instrument by the strong against the weak, for example lines are given as punishment by the teachers, and Rees's word-play is seen as excessive and dangerous by his psychiatrist.
[45] Susan Sontag, *Illness as Metaphor* (London: Penguin Books, 1983), p. 26.
[46] M. L. Jenkins's review of Robert Nisbet's anthology of short stories, *Pieces of Eight* (Llandysul: Gomer, 1982), in which Berry had three short stories, describes his work as 'rough and ready' at best.
[47] John Pikoulis comments on Berry's style on the back cover of Simon Baker (ed.), *Ron Berry: Collected Stories* (Llandysul: Gomer, 2000)
[48] At present an extensive number of Berry's unpublished short stories are held at the Richard Burton Archives, Swansea University.
[49] Niall Griffiths, 'Book of a lifetime: Ron Berry, *So Long, Hector Bebb*', *Independent*, 17 December 2010. Available at: *https://www.independent.co.uk/arts-entertainment/books/reviews/book-of-a-lifetime-so-long-hector-bebb-by-ron-berry-2162262.html*. Accessed 12 November 2013.
[50] Glyn Jones, *The Dragon Has Two Tongues: Essays on Anglo-Welsh Writers and Writing*, ed. Tony Brown (Cardiff: University of Wales Press, 2001), p. 58.

7

'GREEN ALWAYS COMES BACK':
RON BERRY'S ECOCENTRIC WRITING

Sarah Morse

It may at first seem curious to describe Ron Berry, a writer firmly aligned with the experience of coal mining, as an environmentally engaged writer, but his short and novel-length fiction (including the unpublished novel 'Below Lord's Head Mountain'),[1] his autobiography, *History Is What You Live*, and his natural history text, *Peregrine Watching*, all feature an underlying environmental and ecological concern.[2] His archived papers reveal an active engagement with environmental issues, recording his protests against a Forestry Commission and Rhondda Borough Council recreation park scheme, and, intriguingly, a letter in which Berry describes himself as a 'long-time, rather disillusioned campaigner'.[3] This environmentalist aspect of his activities beyond his writing, invites a consideration of Berry as an ecocentric writer.

Drawing on the frameworks of Terry Gifford's 'post-pastoral' literature and Lawrence Buell's definition of 'environmental writing', there are two distinct elements of ecocentric writing: the long interaction of human and natural histories; and environmental conscience, responsibility and accountability: inhabiting, reinhabiting and respecting the natural world.[4] Both of these approaches are informed by the understanding of nature and the environment as a whole system, an ever-changing process, with humanity as part of it. It is an anthropogenic awareness of how human and societal interactions with the natural environment are actions that change it, that shape the space and our understanding of it. It is these approaches that will frame my analysis of the ecocentric features of Berry's writing, through a consideration of habitat, reinhabitation and the industrial forest of the upper Rhondda Fawr.

Habitat and histories

Berry's writing is rooted in a strong sense of belonging to the upper Rhondda Fawr valley; it is an expression of his habitat, or *cynefin*. *Cynefin*, the Welsh concept of how a sense of place, is created, disseminated and maintained, renders 'the physicality of the Welsh environment as a vitally human space', as Matthew Jarvis has observed.[5] It is how we come to feel a sense of belonging in a landscape through engagement with the histories, cultural practices and traditions that come to define a place: we inscribe the landscape with our actions, and thus it reflects the stories we tell. By fixing his various narratives in the Blaencwm locale, Berry is able to reinforce his identity and locate his self. The closing lines of *This Bygone*, his last published novel, conclude that the protagonist is '[b]oy inseparable from man in his time, in his place', reflecting the Berry's own situation (*TB*, 202). As Barbara Prys Williams has observed of his writing, 'there is a feeling that, whatever he knows himself to be [. . .] it is because, with his genetic endowment, in his particular historic time and environment, he can be no other'.[6]

Before examining how Berry understands habitat it is necessary to outline how he transfers his understanding of the centrality of place in his fiction. In his novels and short stories he imagines a geography strongly influenced by the upper Rhondda Fawr. The settlements of Blaenddu and Tosteg in particular recur in Berry's work, which seem to be versions of Blaencwm and the nearby Treorchy.[7] Berry worked in Blaencwm's Graig level drift mine, a version of which appears in *Hunters and Hunted* as the Gwynt level, that 'ran directly into the Graig mountain' (*HH*, 21), and as the Druid level, which 'runs into Graig Ddu mountain' in *A Full Time Amateur* (*FTA*, 24). Blaencwm's pit, the Tydraw colliery appears variously as Blaenddu's Bobbin pit and as the Vivian.[8] Pen Pych mountain appears in his fictional work as Pen Arglwydd mountain, in both Berry's novel-length and short fiction; a literal translation of the name provides the title of the unpublished novel-length manuscript, 'Below Lord's Head Mountain'.[9] In *The Full-Time Amateur*, the same mountain appears 'far off under moon glow', through the windows of a new house on a building site (*FTA*, 135), and as a 'green and granite temple to Rameses I' (*FTA*,

130). In the short story 'Time Spent', the mountain is a signifier of freedom, as the pneumoconiotic miner watches carrion crows 'winging down below [its] high level rim' (*CS*, 99).

In his autobiography, *History Is What You Live*, Berry reflects on the significance of his sense of *cynefin*. From the summit of Pen Pych mountain at the head of the Rhondda Fawr valley, Berry observes 'Blaenycwm village [lying] outstretched, panoramically sideways, matchboxed by distance, locale interregnum between first squall and last gasp' (*HWYL*, 29). The scene meditates on the inherent in the interrelation of time, space and place. But the phrase 'locale interregnum' is ambiguous. It suggests the significance of location during one's life, but also the apparent brevity of this authority, limited as it is to between the 'first squall and last gasp' of life. The locale possesses more potential than is typically acknowledged, at once a repository of the past and an inheritance of the future, inscribed with the evidence of each passing generation. The autobiography opens with Berry's earliest recollection, an upland picnic, which grounds his sense of self in Blaencwm:

> Maiden memory, summer of 1921, striking miners and their families gathered on a green field. Still frocked and napkined on Mary Ann's lap, lost and found next to my unborn sister Marian [. . .] Before the next long strike of 1926, the field lay beneath acres of slag. Now (1996) it's green again, two pitshafts filled in, my Uncle Glyn's life's blood (1927) buried two hundred years [*sic*] deep for all time this side of eternity, that packaged mystique of religions.[10]

The 'maiden memory' reveals Berry's rootedness in the context of both the Blaencwm landscape and its history. As a character reflects in *The Full-Time Amateur*, Berry lived 'to see the wheel turn full circle' (*FTA*, 193). His lifetime spanned the expansion of the first pit in Blaencwm to the closure of the last colliery in the Rhondda, and his own story is embedded in the land. He traces the changes to the landscape from green field to slag tip, to 'landscaped' greenery, signifying the shift from industrialisation to de-industrialisation.

In his introduction to *History Is What You Live*, Dai Smith observes of Berry's work that 'no writer has so dissected a world living [. . .] inside the husk of its own history' (*HWYL*, 9). This sense of a deep locatedness in both place and history is borne out by the title of the autobiography, which underscores the significance of the lived – and historical – consciousness of the area to Berry. His archive reveals how he viewed the landscape and environment of the Rhondda as his (and his family's) 'inheritance' and his autobiography inscribes this perspective. Indeed, the writing of his experience of his habitat transmits and continues the legacy.[11] Berry's writing enacts and expresses Simon Schama's observation in *Landscape and Memory* that 'before it can ever be a repose for the senses landscape is the work of the mind. Its scenery is built up as much from strata of memory as from layers of rock'.[12] We are accustomed, Schama notes, 'to separate nature and human perception into two realms, [although] they are, in fact, indivisible'.[13] The 'maiden memory' evokes this sense of the indivisible connection between the human and the non-human, world; it is a non-dualistic perspective.

Barbara Prys Williams recognised that conceptually, the village and the mountains of Blaencwm provide the 'organising framework' of *History Is What You Live*.[14] Much of the text, is a guided walk through the upper Rhondda Fawr landscape. In the text, Berry recreates his own experience of his immediate surroundings; he 'wanders in memory the mountain tops of Blaen-y-cwm [sic]' vacillating between the past and the present' (*HWYL*, 81). The narrative is punctuated with dense descriptions of the landscape that excavate the history of the geographical features of the area and, as Barbara Prys Williams observes, Berry 'interprets his habitat [. . .] so that we can see its value through his eyes' (*HWYL*, 81). His gaze extends beyond the surface of the landscape to consider the narratives embedded in it. His accounts of the landscape negotiate the pre-historic, the pre-industrial, the 'gloran', the industrial and the de-industrial phases and aspects of this area.[15] The following passage reveals how Berry uncovers the 'strata of memory' of Pen Pych mountain:

> Two streams, Selsig and Blaenrhondda, converge at the foot of Pen Pych, becoming Rhondda River for 12 miles down to Pontypridd. On Blaenrhondda's flank of Pen Pych, scattered hardwoods older than Cardiff city. Above the trees, whinberry ledges, ivied buttresses, shale slips, raven territory up and over the flat summit. Around towards Blaenycwm, descending belts of bracken, patches of scree, gale-shaped hawthorns, and a lateral row of holes entering Pen Pych's breast, scars left by Depression miners who burrowed for coal and shouldered hundredweight bags down sheep tracks like vassals of the Dark Ages. (*HWYL*, 28)

The scene is located: the streams and river are named, reminding the reader of the origin of the name Rhondda and of the geological processes which formed the valley. The native hardwood trees are described and their growth rings are metaphorically counted ('older than Cardiff city'), and the other natural features of the mountainside are also recorded (shale, whinberry ledges, windblown hawthorn bushes). Finally, Berry draws the reader's attention to the 'lateral row of holes entering Pen Pych's breast', a feature that a more casual observer would overlook. We learn that the holes are evidence of the hardships endured by miners during the Depression, who improvised and adapted their typical industrial activity by burrowing into the hillside to find coal.

It is the processes of coal mining that reveal to Berry the 'strata of memory' of the Rhondda, or, as Gwyn Thomas had earlier remarked, its 'geology of remembrance'.[16] The experience of working underground, and witnessing the geological strata seems to imbue Berry with the ability to perceive the depth of history of his habitat, and he explores this understanding in this fiction. The conclusion of *Flame and Slag* sees Berry consider the 'earthbound past' of Daren:

> Always the past, the mortifying past. John Vaughan's past, past time out of mind, all Daren's earthbound past putrefying from uncountable sweats, worshipful feasts, January-nights, dried lungs, broken backs, burnt blood, lucifered Christs, ghetto dreams, shanty chapels, tombstone chapels, the first shovelful of muck multiplying into Caib tip-slide, and farther away still those Hunter and Fisher Folk (our first ever) chipping flint arrowheads with the surety, precision of monocled watch repairers. The Folk curled like badgers in mountainside holes, sniffing dawns millions of years after the last pterodactyls sparred fanged mating bouts in humid glades beside hydrolytic swamps, the Coal Board's property virginally seamed down beneath Waunwen, awaiting, awaiting royal protocol, £164,000,000 to the coal-owners and His Majesty's sanction on 12th July 1946. (*FS*, 166–7)

Berry undertakes a textual excavation to expose the processual features of landscape. The resultant perspective extends beyond the industrial community, past the *gloran*, or native, pre-industrial inhabitants of what was then the Ystradfadwg parish to a Neolithic people; it is a deepening of time. One of the most striking aspects of this extract is the image of the 'folk curled like badgers in mountainside holes, sniffing dawns millions of years after the last pterodactyls'.[17]

This image functions in three ways. It first conjures the flint-using 'Hunter and Fisher Folk' living in their subterranean homes; furthermore, it alludes to their entombed bodies deep in the mountainside.[18] The act of 'sniffing dawns millions of years after' can also be seen to suggest the miners extracting the carbonised residue of the hydrolytic swamps in the drift mines that pockmark the hillside, and later in the coal pits. Berry also explores the long history of the area in the character Charlie Page. On his enforced retirement due to ill health – specifically a dust level of fifty per cent in his lungs – Charlie, who worked underground for thirty-four years, takes up archaeology and becomes 'the doppelgänger of a Hunter and Fisher Folk shaman' (*FS*, 72). He spends his days excavating the tip, collecting the flint-scrapers and arrowheads of the Neolithic communities, and also fossils from the pre-human era. Berry's autobiography suggests that this character is grounded in reality. On walking up Pen Pych he recalls the slag tips that once littered the mountains opposite:

> Bigger than Cadbury mounds once bulged along the silhouette of Graig y Ddelw and Mynydd Ty Isaf, slag heaps from defunct Tydraw colliery, landscaped now, contoured and conifered. Attractively quaint, petrified mussels from 250,000,000 BC are sprinkled within like Absolute currants. Some of these are in Cardiff Museum. (*HWYL*, 30)

For Berry, the slag tips form part of the 'grammar of the landscape'.[19] They reflect the industrial and post-industrial narratives of the south Wales coalfield in their creation and remodelling; their unearthing of what lies beneath the surface lays bare the buried history of the area. The incongruity of the 'petrified mussels' in the uplands echoes a similar discovery in the novel *Flame and Slag*. Charlie Page's 'clutch of small fossilized mussels' reveals to the characters how once there was 'salt water everywhere over Daren. No mountains, no woods, no coal' (*FS*, 73). A similar perspective is also presented in Berry's fictional accounts of industrial accidents. In *The Full-Time Amateur* the injured narrator reflects how the rock that injured him 'waited about two hundred and fifty million years' to fall (*FTA*, 57), and in the short story 'Left Behind', a rock which falls, killing a miner, is described as 'slamming down out of millions of lightless years', exposing the prehistoric context of the product of the earth (*CS*, 82). It is as if the glimpse of human mortality offered by the chance industrial accidents prompts a profound realisation of the seeming permanence of the land.

Reinhabitation and reclamation: recovering the natural and narratives of place

Berry's excavation and dissemination of the historical narratives embedded in the 'geology of remembrance' of the landscape seem to enact the process of reinhabitation. Berry's affinity with his local environment, and his expression of this connection, gives rise to the sense that he is a 'specimen' of his *cynefin*. He is 'native born slot fit' (*HWYL*, 64).

Reinhabitation involves a reconciliation with a habitat, as the prefix suggests. Originally conceived by Peter Berg and Raymond Dasmann, as the process of 'applying for membership in a biotic community and ceasing to be its exploiter',[20] reinhabitation is a 'specific method of committing oneself to a place'.[21] Lawrence Buell provides a valuable definition of the concept:

> Advocates and practitioners of reinhabitation, whether or not they use the term, start from the premise that not only has the environment been abused, aspiring reinhabitors have themselves been wounded by displacement and ecological illiteracy so they must (re)learn what it means to be 'native' to a place. Moreover, the reorientation process cannot simply be a solitary quest but must also involve participation in community both with fellow inhabitants in the present and with past generations through absorption of history and legend. In short, reinhabitation presupposes long-term reciprocal engagement with a place's human and nonhuman environments and welcomes the prospect of one's identity being molded [*sic*] by this encounter.[22]

Berry's writing aspires to reconnect with the Blaencwm habitat in numerous ways. It offers a return to the land, engaging with the social, historical and natural surfaces of the landscape, as well as the subterranean plane. He remains a conscious inhabitant of his locality, but is aware of the metaphoric displacement experienced by others in his community. His papers indicate that, despite the sense of dislocation in the community, the people of the Upper Rhondda area remain the 'inheritors of natural and industrial history', although they may not be conscious of this inheritance.[23] This sense of rupture has been caused by the economic shifts in the area, primarily the decline, and continuing legacy, of heavy industry, the wide-ranging social effects of which have been outlined elsewhere.[24]

At the forefront of Berry's concern is the disturbed interaction with the landscape, the narratives it contains and the natural environment it sustains. His act of reinhabitation emphasises a concurrent rehabilitation: the recovery of the narratives of industry, the re-establishment of what he terms 'the dialectic of man and his environment', and a restoration of the community and *cynefin* he inhabits. In *History Is What You Live* he outlines how the process of deindustrialisation has changed the Blaencwm landscape:

> See where the NCB has demolished (1966) Glenrhondda colliery, leaving blackened wasteland. Two collieries razed, Glenrhondda and Gorllwyn, the same old Hook and Eye pit where Bill Brunker and Pricey Jones were killed, where Tom Walters lost his leg and Will Deane his arm and part of his face. Across the valley, climbing from Selsigriver, see Hendrewen inclines ballasted for dumper traffic, the adjoining mountainside herring-boned with huge drainage ditches since Aberfan's tragedy shook the bowels of absent experts. (*HWYL*, 29–30)

He reads the scars of the land, explaining the 'blackened wasteland' left by the demolition of a colliery in the 1960s, the significance of the drainage ditches and the 'conifered' hillsides. It is a landscape defined by an absence, as much of the industrial history has been erased, the rest obscured. But Berry is able to restore a sense of this lost narrative.

The Hook and Eye pit (the local name for the Glenrhondda colliery) is remembered as a place where men were injured, maimed and killed, emphasising that it is more than a place of work. Berry recovers the narrative of the specific industrial history and experience of Blaencwm from the 'naked facts and figures' published in the records of the mining surveyors, Whitaker's (*FS*, 44). Deaths and pit-related injuries may have been recorded, but the long-term effects of the industry are overlooked. Indeed, as he notes in *Flame and Slag* when his voice briefly emerges in the narrative, stating that the first-person narrator 'Rees Stevens doesn't have to blurb this piece', records of men incapacitated by mining were concealed (*FS*, 44). He remarks that 'There are no publicized records of men (numbers, when and where) suffering from dust, no how, when and where record of the disabled, but the NCB statement of accounts does publish the *total* amount of money paid to disabled miners and ex-miners' (*FS*, 45). Personal experiences are made indistinct by the national authority and Berry would later challenge this in his autobiography, reinscribing the names of those whose suffering is overlooked.

Part of Berry's rehabilitation of the area's industrial history is the revelation of the continuing 'dialectic of man and his environment', a relationship which he believes has been damaged in the Upper Rhondda by institutionalised interpretations of industry. His descriptions of working underground challenge this perception, re-emphasising that coal mining can be an intimate interaction with the earth. Of his first working day in the Graig level, Berry recalls filling his water bottle from a mountain stream, and noticing the 'fungus on double timbers' just inside the entrance of the mine (*HWYL*, 55). Such observations reveal the proximity of the industry to the natural world. Berry had earlier described coal as the 'insanest natural phenomenon' (*FTA*, 132), and in the later short story 'Left Behind' he revisited this sentiment: 'if there is some time out of mind Lord God, he undoubtedly said *Let there be carbonised vegetable matter* – to prove how poxy Nature is' (*CS*, 88). The narrator continues:

> Peace on earthers spout delusions, drool about rapport with the birds and the bees, but Nature herself has to be manhandled, forced, controlled, exploited, and coal-getting's the essence of it, less than a short spit away from deep sea trawling. Human nature takes some forcing too, else we'd still be scratching fleas off each other's backs. (*CS*, 81)

The need to manhandle, control and exploit nature is here ventriloquised by Berry, whose own interaction with the environment was more sympathetic. The scene is located in the non-dualistic natural sphere, as human nature too is seen as in need of 'some forcing'; innate human nature is rendered indivisible from the wildness of the natural world, in another expression of Berry's awareness of the dialectic of man and environment.

Writing decades before scientific discourse turned to consider the Anthropocene epoch, Berry is nonetheless concerned by humanity's detrimental impact on the environment. In particular, he expresses concern about the pollution of the natural world in industrial societies: 'Old mining, steel, railway and dock communities accepted environmental pollution as integral to themselves, just as generations of city folk persist without horizons of grass or trees' (*HWYL*, 54). In the draft of his 'Objections to Rhondda Forest Recreation Project', Berry argues:

> Our rivers should be clean, but they aren't. Citizens should respect their environment [. . .] but they seldom consider the matter as a moral issue. More middle aged and pensioner natives of Rhondda, than children and youths, throw domestic rubbish into our rivers, understandably too, pollution being intrinsic to their birthright, their habitual dumping a fly-speck compared to the endless, massive pollutions of industry. Walk up the brooks in Blaenrhondda, Blaenycwm and Cwmparc; from each brook one sees slag tips, NCB and British Railways dereliction, and shanty backyards.[25]

Berry believes that the continuing exposure to neglect and exploitation of the environment has conditioned the Rhondda inhabitants to also despoil their habitat. He outlines how generations of people have been conditioned to accept without question the 'massive pollutions of industry' that surround their homes, and they also enact similar actions on a micro-scale: pollution is a given, 'intrinsic to their birthright'. Terry Gifford argued that environmental exploitation paralleled social exploitation, and a similar concept is in evidence here as Berry suggests that environmental neglect is symptomatic of social neglect.[26] He reflected in the novel *The Full-Time Amateur* on the socio-environmental projects that seem to offer a means of a community reinhabitation of the landscape, suggesting that they 'merely niggle' at the social problems of the area:[27] 'Currently, they're publicly discussing ways and means of clearing up, beautifying the valley and edifying the citizens. Aeonian prospect' (*FTA*, 193). Berry's papers recount a 1975 effort to 'rehabilitat[e] Graig Fawr corrie'. He describes how:

> It was agreed on professional and local advice to landscape the waste spoil, obliterate access roads, plant native grasses and some trees i.e. hawthorns, alder, willow, birch. Lower slopes of the corrie are already landscape and seeded. Approximately 380 trees were planted; approximately 140 remain alive. The others were destroyed by ponies, sheep and vandals.[28]

He argues that villagers should have been given 'an intensive continuing programme of education' to teach them the importance of the preservation of the natural world in order to make the project sustainable. But most significantly, Berry exposes the scheme as a superficial effort to rehabilitate a deprived and socially fragmented community which requires a far more sustained programme of social and economic rehabilitation. Indeed, his protest once again returns to the sense of a non-dualistic natural sphere and the symbiosis of social and ecological justice.

Berry is also concerned with the reinhabitation of his habitat, both the communal social history and the environment. Indeed, *History Is What You Live* is a manual for the practice of reinscribing the social, industrial and natural histories of the Blaencwm locality. Barbara Prys Williams observes that by the end of Berry's autobiography, the reader 'has a sense of a memory bank overflowing with intense recall, a human personality unusually endowed in recording, being nurtured by and finding meaning in, what he sees'.[29] Whilst it is undeniable that Berry's autobiography is an attempt to record his self and his personal history, I would propose that the text is also an expression of a shared history which he feels compelled to disseminate in order to maintain. The text is a guide, a shared map and route, as the narrative signals his – and his reader's – position in the landscape, and in time:

> now we're up here on Cefn Nant y Gwair. Robens and Beeching are elsewhere, honing themselves for hatchet-work. The pits are producing coal and its steam engines blowing up valley, through the tunnel to Swansea. Blaenycwm football field hasn't yet been levelled at the base of Pen Pych mountain. Gorllwyn tip behind Hendrewen Road is black. About 70 years will moss, lichen and grass it green. Over on the left, across the ravine, another slag tip had grown since 1859. (*HWYL*, 41)

This passage negotiates a time span of over one hundred years. The scene opens in a time before 1961, as the National Coal Board Chairman, Alfred Robens, and the British Railways Board Chairman, Dr Richard Beeching, seem yet to be appointed, and the Rhondda railway tunnel is open. After describing the bustling coal industry of the mid-twentieth century, Berry shifts to the future, considering how in seventy years, 'moss, lichen and grass' will green the Gorllwyn tip, a perspective which extends beyond his own lifetime. The final remark of the passage once more vacillates between his present and the past, precisely dating the development of the other slag tip. In unearthing and recounting this history, Berry traces and disseminates the narratives of place, the text offering a manual to facilitate a reconnection, and reinhabitation, of the locality.

Berry's unpublished novel, 'Below Lord's Head Mountain', also records a similar process of reinhabitation, as Shad Beynon returns to the environment of his youth and finds it changed. Shad has to re-learn his once familiar environment, changed both by the dismantling of the coal industry and the establishment of the Forestry Commission plantations. He is aided in his efforts by his partner, Lottie, who is also keen to connect Blaenddu and its environment:

> We left the car at the edge of Spiller's wood. Markie Spiller shared a grave with his wife in Golau Nos cemetery. The farmhouse was a shop selling craft-work and health foods, having failed as a pony trekking centre. There weren't any sheep among the sitkas on Pen Arglwydd. We climbed the mountain of my boyhood, Lottie questioning what I had never seen before, the green shallow mound above the village, where once four pits sent coal to Cardiff and Swansea docks. Endlessly pouring out steam coal.[30]

For Lottie, Blaenddu is an alien landscape. She questions 'what [Shad] had never seen before', capturing the new landscape features created by de-industrialisation, but also the older features of the habitat that Shad once taken for granted. As Shad comes to reinhabit the area, he shares his knowledge with Lottie, and she begins to appreciate the 'wild grandeur' of Blaenddu's uplands.[31] Indeed, soon we see that Shad's shared experience of his reconciliation of his memory of Blaenddu and the contemporary actuality has enabled Lottie to identify and name the surrounding mountains.[32] Her familiarisation with Blaenddu, shadows his reinhabitation. Towards the conclusion of the narrative Lottie recounts how embedded in the habitat she has become:

> Every evening driving up from Tosteg, I see Pen Arglwydd mountain looming. It's so huge, dominating, rising steeply from the verge as you approach Blaenddu, then veering away to the north, to Wion waterfall, and curving back towards the village, the white foam of Ychain glaring, and then the nakedness of Theo's quarry, I prefer Blaenddu to Tosteg. I like the timeless atmosphere. It's our home.[33]

Echoing her partner's account of the hills and waterfalls at the beginning of the test, Lottie maps the natural landmarks of Blaenddu.

Shad has exposed the 'strata of memory' of the area, and is now their shared cynefin.

It is the same 'timeless atmosphere' that defines the Blaencwm landscape for Berry: 'hills, brooks, natural phenomena and wildlife are [. . .] here, have been in varying degrees since time immemorial'.[34] Identifying himself as a 'naturalist by instinct', he outlines in his private papers his own efforts to maintain his local ecosystems:

> I introduced the first trout to Llyn Fach, 220, caught in Rhondda brooks and transported illegally, strictly speaking, on Forestry Commission roads, myself riding pillion with large containers hanging from the ends of my arms. Two years ago, I placed 20 minnows in LlynFach. [. . .] Originally barren water, deficient by my own pH readings, but not *totally* barren. In season, the water teems with frogs and newts, and there is a fertile population of water beetles. I have counted carapaces in heron droppings. While on this subject, many years ago when Rhondda river ran black as ink to join the equally black Taff at Pontypridd, I introduced small native trout to the headwaters of Nant Selsig, Blaenrhondda river, Nant Orchwy and Cwmsaerbren dam.[35]

He describes the way in which he assumed responsibility for populating a once barren lake on the Rhigos with native trout. In *Peregrine Watching*, Berry later meditated on the distinction between the conservation and the management of the natural environment, reflecting that conservation 'means leaving be, stepping out of the skin of monomania, shedding nationhood and dogmas from on high, the huffs and puffs of consciousness buggered by realities' (*PW*, 87). For Berry, therefore, conservation is an act which transcends the self and the anthropocentric instinct; it returns to the more beneficial 'dialectic of man and his environment'. His preoccupation with conservation is motivated by his wonder at the endurance of the natural environment of Blaencwm, despite the best efforts of heavy industry. He explains how 'since time out of mind, stocks of fish in our two main rivers have been sustained, despite pollution from heavy industry, by the natural hatchery waters above colliery pit-heads'[36] and describes how areas of the landscape have 'survived exploitation' despite industrial activity.[37] Indeed, he appears to share the conviction of the character of Ellen in *Flame and Slag* that 'green always comes back' (*FS*, 47).

The industrial forest: de-naturing the natural

Berry's published work suggests his disapproval of the policies, actions and authority of the Forestry Commission in Wales, but it is his private archive which reveals his long protest against the activities of the public body. The archive includes numerous letters of objection to the environmental regeneration work of the Forestry Commission, and in particular, a series of letters arguing against the plans of Rhondda Borough Council to develop (in conjunction with the local authority and the Forestry Commission) an 'area of informal countryside recreation', the Rhondda Forest Recreation Project.[38]

Before examining Berry's writing on the issues surrounding the Forestry Commission plantations and activities, it is useful to consider the history of the south Wales coniferous forests. The Forestry Commission's forested area in the former south Wales coalfield, known as the 'Valleys forest', constitutes 23 per cent of their estate in Wales, and covers an area of 27,261 hectares. Although planting began in the area in the 1920s, only half of the trees in the plantation are over thirty years old; as such, the process of plantation remains a recent experience and memory for much of the local population. One study of the coniferous forest outlines its characteristics as follows:

> The forest is not a single discrete area of trees. Rather it consists of blocks of trees interspersed with communities, open country, farm land, derelict mine workings and mountain areas. Forest blocks are largest around the Neath, Afan and Rhondda valleys. The Valleys forest is unique in its proximity to populations and is the largest urban forest in Western Europe, with approximately 1.7 million people living in the forest area.[39]

The scale of the woodland reveals that it is an industrialised forest; indeed, as some have described it, a 'wood factory'.[40] To Berry and others who protested against the policies and activities of the Forestry Commission, the afforestation of the south Wales coalfield is the persisting (and persistent) invasion of the garden by the machine. As Leo Marx remarked, increased ecological and environmental awareness imbued the 'archetypal nineteenth-century image of the machine invading the landscape [. . .] with a new, more literal meaning and credibility'.[41] As Berry described the situation, 'King coal is dying, along with free range Welsh mutton and wool. Long live King conifer marching the crammed landscape, reaching for sunlight above ground where no grass will grow.'[42]

Various studies have outlined and analysed the processes of land acquisition employed by the Commission.[43] In particular, Kirsti Bohata's framing of the afforestation debate in a post-colonial theoretical context provides new insights, considering the construction of the Commission and the plantations as 'an alien, colonizing force' by writers in Wales.[44] Bohata's study considers the way in which Welsh writers record the process of the 'erasure of place' that the afforested communities of west Wales experience, a process which, as suggested above, Berry also witnesses in Blaencwm.[45] His papers emphasise that fences and forest surround 'Cwmsaerbren Basin, Graig y Ddelw, Mynydd Tŷ Isaf, and all around to the villages of Nantymoel, Blaengwynfi and Glyncorrwg, over to Pen Pych mountain [. . .] and above Blaenrhondda, Tŷnewydd and Treherbert, extending over to Maerdy and down almost to the entire length of Rhondda Fach'.[46] The toponymic memory which Berry has inscribed in his habitat is obscured by a tide of conifers. The unpublished manuscript narrative of 'Below Lord's Head Mountain' is also inflected by the alienation and sense of exile felt by the community as their surrounding landscape is remodelled:

> The old incline had greened over, a sunken track between thousands of larches.
> Smaller pines blobbed every square yard of turf among acres of scree below Theo's quarry.
> I felt destructive.
> Lottie warned, 'Stop it, you sound like a degenerate.'
> 'Coal face language,' I said. 'They've ruined everything. You wouldn't understand.'[47]

The returning Shad Beynon feels a visceral sense of loss when he is faced with the afforested landscape. It echoes Berry's own reaction to the development: 'the operation of the Forestry Commission sickens my heart'.[48] His papers reveal that the last remaining evidence of the pre-industrial *gloran* communities was erased when historic dry-stone wall boundaries were bulldozed in order to erect Forestry Commission fences.[49] Berry also stresses how the local population is prevented from accessing the hillsides, a practice which, as the introduction to his autobiography describes, has been a part of Upper Rhondda landscape interaction for generations. He disputes the Commission's claim that there is 'unrestricted public access *on foot* throughout land in its ownership', arguing that 'walkers are compelled to walk on FC roads' ('Working Party Report', 6), and that 'the land is ploughed deep, [making it] ankle-wrenching to traverse on foot, and when trees are up to canopy, only a dwarf with a torch can move at ground level'.[50]

Berry later explored this often-overlooked impact of the forestry plantations in the short story 'Natives'. The story follows the experience of a group of retired miners, 'well past middle age, [. . .] on compo and hardship allowance [. . .] sacrificial victims to the old black diamonds' (*CS*, 78). Sitting in a pub, they discuss the influence of afforestation:

> 'Aye, Upper Coed-coch has been renamed Isolated Area by our county planning experts. Consequently, the Forestry commission has taken over. Surface pillage succeeding subterranean rape.'
> 'Mountains around here,' said Martin, 'they'll be like the Western Front when these trees are cropped.'
> [. . .]
> 'We shan't witness the millennium,' promised Levi.
> Martin looked angry. 'Nor roam the mountains on Sunday mornings. You need a can-lamp and knee-pads to crawl under the bloody Christmas trees.'
> Levi dipped a finger in his beer, swam it humming around the rim of the glass. 'Economics, the name of the game.' (*CS*, 78)

The description of crawling under the trees, using a lamp and knee pads to negotiate the dark forest floor, is inflected with the miners' experience; the image recalls the subterranean activities of mining. In this subtle analogy, Berry once more highlights the origins of the fossil fuel and the dialectic between the coal industry and nature. In doing so, Berry also reveals the irony of the re-afforestation of the Rhondda; as the British Coal Authority publication, *The Environment*, remarked: 'It is paradoxical that coal is derived from trees and that the finest cover for reshaped coal spoil tips is that self-same source'.[51]

Timber has long been associated with the industrial activity of south Wales. Before the extraction of coal in the area, plantations were necessitated by the expansion of the coal industry, as pitwood was needed to reinforce and support the tunnels of mines.[52] As the industry declined, it was argued that forestry offered a convenient and suitable means to ameliorate the scars of industrial activity in the coalfield.[53] The apparent ideological shift to a concern for environmental aesthetics was reflected in the 1956 text *Tomorrow's Landscape*, where it was argued that a 'landscape cluttered by industry' can be improved by the introduction of woodland. Giving the example of the view from above the Rhymney valley, it is noted:

> In the valley are a station, a railway, its attendant posts, wires and buildings, a string of reservoirs, some pleasant, some appalling, but all having the taint of artificiality. All these elements between them destroy the magic of the hills and worry the eye with a restless disorganized litter. A great sweep of forestry here would absorb the jarring elements and restore a feeling of peace.[54]

But the Forestry Commission afforestation of the coalfield landscape has done little to 'restore a feeling of peace'; instead, the 'geometrized landscape' of the plantations covertly continue the industrialisation of the area (*FS*,173). A letter to the *Sunday Times* outlines Berry's despair at the remodelled landscape of Blaencwm. The Forestry Commission, he states, has

> compounded a real and aesthetic blasphemy upon myself, my children and my grandchildren [. . .] We have been robbed of our natural ecology of space, simple geography, vistas, landmarks, besides ground nesting birds: pipits, lark, wheatears, whinchats. Crows, magpies, pigeons, jays and foxes are thriving. [The Forestry Commission] has contributed to the ruination of my inheritance. Midway into the next century, the village where I was born will be drowned in conifers.[55]

The word 'drown' is particularly significant here, as Berry aligns the forest plantation with the appropriation of land for the construction of reservoirs, another instance of the 'perceived disregard, or undervaluation, by the London government of the rural Welsh and their culture'.[56] The plantations have defamiliarised and alienated the known 'natural ecology of space', and the narratives inscribed in the land. Berry's writing on the subject reveals that he is motivated to expose the industrialised ideology of the Forestry Commission operations in reaction to the public body's 'annual PR stunts', the attempts to reposition the conifer plantations as a natural feature of the landscape (*PW*, 53). He asserts in his non-fiction writing that the Commission's activities are primarily concerned with profit, rather than the environment and local community, a sentiment also expressed in his fictional writing: 'The Forestry Commission just fenced and planted. It's still going on. Nobody can stop them. They're worse bastards than private coal owners but it's less obvious. They press on quietly like a dose of pox'.[57] In *Peregrine Watching* he suggests that the Authority is analogous with 'righteous gangsters', making 'enemies in the gospel name of Economics' (*PW*, 53). Berry was to return to this theme in his autobiography, asserting that the afforestation of the Rhondda signifies 'pre-history sacrificed to Mammon masked as a quango' (*HWYL*, 31).

The continuing exploitation of the Rhondda environment also causes Berry to reflect on the impact of the forests on the natural ecology of Blaencwm. His papers draw attention to the 'planned vandalism', or environmental disregard, exhibited by the Forestry Commission. He reflects:

> More and more, planned vandalism becomes apparent to us all. The Forestry Commission has left fencing materials, mechanical and human litter all over our hills. Across the skyline where water pours from two of the loveliest waterfalls in the County, [. . .] the Commission has strung fences. Men with the aesthetic nous of Neanderthals [. . .] The NCB, British Railways, local authority departments and manufacturing industries supply examples of vandalism / dereliction too common-place to itemise.[58]

He suggests that society's increased environmental conscience prompts an awareness of the 'planned vandalism' enacted in the landscape. This narrative of environmental vandalism is analogous to Lawrence Buell's concept of 'toxic discourse', the 'expressed anxiety arising from perceived threat of environmental hazard due to chemical modification by human agency'.[59] Berry's concern is not the threat of toxic pollution in the natural world (though his archives reveal an awareness of the dangers of the development of new chemical pesticides), but the apparent reckless remodelling of the deindustrialised landscape.[60] Berry argues that the Forestry Commission, although positioned as conservators of the landscape, are contaminating the new coniferous forests with industrial debris ('mechanical and human litter'), and fences which recall the eighteenth and nineteenth-century enclosure acts.

The authoritative aspect of the Commission also extends to influence people's interaction with the environment: it reinforces the perceived distinction between humanity and the environment, a distinction which Berry transcends in his non-dualistic, anthropogenic approach. He asks:

> Why not become a bona fide naturalist under the aegis of the Forestry Commission? Stride eyes front (what else?) along its drives; better still, count birds (not species) on a Forestry Commission bursary. Do not cavil with district officers; they are merely doing a job of work, acquiring Public Record Office awareness during these times of emergency. Do not question the book-keeping of the commission. Walk patiently outside a fence until you come to a stile which is guaranteed to lead you to a drive surfaced with stone chippings. Condition your grandchildren to loss of song-birds, bare skylines, profiled, accessible mountain streams, the footloose ways of your own childhood.[61]

Fences restrict access and cross time-worn paths, leading those who walk in the forest to 'walk patiently outside a fence' until they find a stile. The very action of investigating the (once) wild landscape is now controlled and there is little opportunity for exploration. The wild landscape is reduced to the sum of its parts, to the mechanics of a land-based ecosystem. The conifer forests, as Berry reflected elsewhere, have 'de-nature[d] [the] physical environment'.[62] The natural has been rendered unnatural and uniform, and furthermore, the concept of a natural forest itself is distorted, as it is used to define and describe an industrialised wood factory. Berry's description of the forest emphasises the manmade aspect of the plantations, paralleling conventional descriptions of cityscapes as the restricted horizons of the gravel roads evoke anonymous streets: 'Stride eyes front [. . .] along its drives'. Berry goes on to reflect further on the behaviour the Forestry Commission encourages through the planning and development of the area's conifer plantations:

> In the Year of the Tree, litter bins and rustic seats accompany every lay-by carved by the Commission. Sit and look, munch and drink etc, and throw wrappings, bottles and condoms into the bins. Mother Nature, that great mindless Mom of life and death, now delivered to us all by courtesy of the Forestry Commission.[63]

The features added to make the natural environment more comfortable for its consumption by the visitors (faux 'rustic seats' and litter bins) domesticate, and therefore de-nature, the forest landscape.

The post-industrial forest project enacts Jean Baudrillard's simulacrum, the simulation of the real.[64] The 'geometrized landscape' of conifer reconstitute the wooded hillsides of the pre-industrial Rhondda valleys, but in a form that is planned, regimented and unnatural. The coniferous manmade forest cannot replace the indigenous deciduous woodland of the area that was harvested during the nineteenth century, to provide fuel for the furnaces of the ironworks, and pitwood for the collieries. Although this broadleaf forest is not a landscape feature that twentieth-century inhabitants of the Rhondda valleys were ever familiar with, it exists in a collective myth: the frequently retold (and idealised) story of how before the industrialisation of the south Wales steam coalfield, a red squirrel could journey from Cardiff to the upper Rhondda through the tree-tops. Furthermore, the alien ecology imposed by the coniferous forest masks the landscape and ecosystem established in the area since the clearing of the first forests, thus concealing the upland environment familiar to the twentieth-century inhabitants of the upper Rhondda.

As considered above, this imposed (un)natural environment has also been landscaped and modelled for the benefit of leisure participants, a process which further removes the forestry from the natural and the wild. It offers a sanitised, safe representation of the natural and wild. The fantasy offered by the manmade forest also conceals the long-term cycle of the forestry plantation: planting, maturation, harvesting, fallow land, replanting, a process that Berry is keen to expose. In *Peregrine Watching* Berry reflects that when 'the conifers are harvested in the next century, areas of ancient Gwalia will look like the Western Front, reeking of diesel and cordite' (*PW*, 7): it will be a spoiled, post-industrial landscape once again. In his papers, he outlines the plans for the leisure development of the upper Rhondda, noting that they fail to mention 'harvesting those vast plantations surrounding the historically industrialised populations of Glamorgan. Imagine this ravaged ecology, our grandchildren's inheritance. Derelict hills comparable to slag heaps, until the next crops are planted.'[65] In the marginalia Berry added to the working party papers of the project, he remarked that the public consultation material should include 'illustrations of felled forests, showing over-all dereliction, cite ruined ecology, relate Rhondda Forest Recreation Project to this inevitable end. Be honest.'⁶⁶ This was later redrafted as part of his response to the project, when he reminded the borough council that harvesting will cause 'visible desolation on a greater scale than that created by the coal industry'.⁶⁷ Berry's concern is that the Rhondda Forest Recreation Project can be neither a long-term nor sustainable scheme, given that the forest it inhabits will be harvested – it will repeat the pattern of the original deciduous woodland of the Upper Rhondda.

Berry's papers also suggest his awareness of the simulation at play in the establishment of country parks. Reflecting on the probable impact of the Rhondda Forest Recreation Project, he draws on the example of Aberdare Country Park :

> Designate these places [Cwmsaerbren Basin, Blaencwm, Blaenrhondda] publicise them as beauty spots, and they perish. Perish in themselves, change, become vulgarised. Witness such abortions as Aberdare Country Park, its dozens of fences criss-crossing the landscape, the plethora of signposts, the utterly frivolous artificial cascade (how long has it been dry?) the [unreadable word] ponds, the over-all atmosphere of purpose-built despoilment.⁶⁸

In this succinct description, Berry captures the way in which simulacra of country parks function. In allocating such a label, the designated spaces 'perish in themselves, change, become vulgarised'; they are no longer what it was intended to protected and celebrate. The 'purpose-built despoilment' that has been introduced to the area in order to make the landscape conform to the expectations of a country park has destroyed the natural beauty of the place. The idea of natural beauty is subsumed by the manipulated beauty presented by the manmade country park. Berry reflects that an 'utterly frivolous artificial cascade' was installed in the park, presumably because there was an absence of natural waterfalls, or that the waterfalls that already existed were not suitable; this addition simulates the landscape, and only the lack of water running down it signals that it is not a natural environmental feature. On reflecting on publicity events for the Rhondda Forest Recreation Project, Berry reflects on how the simulation of landscape – in this case through the optic of a Land Rover safari tour of the Cwmsaerbren Basin – influences people's reaction to the landscape. He considers the irony that a member of the Recreation Project Committee did not 'realise the total beauty and isolated splendour of our mountain tops and forest walks; until transported by Land

Rover'.[69] Only once the landscape is packaged as an attraction does the participant (a lifelong resident of the Rhondda) appreciate its importance and beauty: only once the real natural landscape has been simulated through the image offered by a 'safari'-style tour is it accepted and celebrated.[70] Baudrillard observed that 'when the real is no longer what it used to be, nostalgia assumes its full meaning', and Berry's writing exposes this aspect of simulation.[71] As noted above, he reflects in his papers that only the memories of the freedom of his childhood, and those of his peers, remain to express the experience of the natural near-wilderness of the upper Rhondda Fawr valley.

Berry's evocation of, and deep engagement with, his habitat reveals that he is a writer of place. His writing on landscape moves beyond the aesthetic and cultural resonances of rural imagery and reveals a concern for society's engagement with the natural environment, placing him, if unexpectedly, as an often ecocentric writer. The locatedness of his writing creates sustained consideration of the social, economic and environmental issues of the Upper Rhondda Fawr valley and, indeed, the wider south Wales coalfield. In reading the narratives inscribed in the landscape, he reasserts the importance of land and the environment in the history of the area, but his ability to perceive the 'deepening of time' that the landscape signifies also allows for a longer perspective, stretching into prehistory. This awareness of, and appreciation for, the long history of this *cynefin* informs Berry's wonder at the natural world. He does not discount the visceral and emotional responses that nature can prompt, indeed in his non-fiction writing such responses are central to his interaction with the environment, and this is also reflected in his fiction. It is his sense of awe that triggers his attempts to recapture the non-dualistic engagement with nature he experienced as a child, but as an adult he is aware of the risks of becoming lost in nature; he does not place himself at the centre of the natural world, but rather sees himself as a constituent of it.

In his liminal position moving between nature and community, the wild and civilised, in both his life and his work he does become a mediator in the two spheres. It is in this role of mediator that Berry explores the process of reinhabitation. Seeking to reconnect his community with its environment, he became an environmental activist of sorts. His work also challenges conventional perceptions of the coal industry, as he deconstructs the actions of coal mining and reconstructing the practices as an interaction with natural resources.

Perceiving place and the narrative of place as inseparable, in addition to advocating a reconnection with the natural environment, Berry urges re-engagement with the history of a place. His elegiac recounting of the narrative of Blaencwm reflects how distant the industrial past of the area now seems. But in reinscribing the industrial history of the Upper Rhondda valley, which was obscured when the coal industry was dismantled, and further overwritten by the re-greening of the landscape, Berry offers the opportunity to access the lived experience of the historical narrative. His work, both fiction and non-fiction, captures his *cynefin*, and offers his readers a means to inhabit, or re-inhabit, the history, landscape and environment of the Upper Rhondda Fawr.

Notes

1. Ron Berry, 'Below Lord's Head Mountain', Richard Burton Archives, Swansea University, Ron Berry Papers, WWE/1/2/1/.
2. Ron Berry, *History Is What you Live* (Llandysul: Gomer, 1998); *Peregrine Watching* (Llandysul: Gomer, 1987).
3. Ron Berry, letter to *Western Mail*, 20 September 1977, Richard Burton Archives, Swansea University, Ron Berry Papers, WWE/1/10/14.
4. See Terry Gifford, *Pastoral* (London: Routledge, 1999), pp. 146–74, and Lawrence Buell, *The Environmental Imagination: Thoreau, Nature Writing and the Formation of American Culture* (Cambridge, MA: Belknap Press of Harvard University Press, 1995), p. 7.
5. Matthew Jarvis, *Environments in Contemporary Welsh Poetry* (Cardiff: University of Wales Press, 2008), p. 141.
6. Barbara Prys Williams, 'History Is What You Live: Ron Berry's rumination on his life and conflicted times', pp. 13–28 (p. 14) in the present collection.
7. Like Blaenddu, Blaencwm is a mining village comprising one pit and a drift mine, as Berry outlines in the introduction to *History Is What You Live* (p. 13). Blaenddu is the setting of *Hunters and Hunted* (1960) and Berry's unpublished novel 'Below Lord's Head Mountain'; Tosteg is a nearby village further down the valley. The villages are also referred to in *So Long, Hector Bebb* (1970). Tosteg is mentioned in *Flame and Slag* (1968) and Blaen-du features in the short story 'Comrades in Arms' (*Collected Stories*, pp. 57–63). The novel *The Full-Time Amateur* (1966) seems to be set in Tŷ Mawr (there is no explicit location, but the club the principal character frequents is the Tŷ Mawr Con Club).
8. Berry, *Hunter and Hunted*, p. 21, *The Full-Time Amateur*, p. 128.
9. Drafts indicate that the text was originally titled 'Under Pen Arglwydd' or 'Colours of Saying', Ron Berry papers, Richard Burton Archives, Swansea University, Ron Berry Papers, WWE/1/2/1/2.
10. Berry, *History Is What You Live*, p. 13. The word 'years' is a misprint in *History Is What You Live*. In the BBC Wales documentary *Read All About Us*, Berry

reads from the draft of his autobiography, confirming that the correct text read 'two hundred *yards* deep'. Dai Smith (executive producer), *Read All About Us: Ron Berry* (BBC Wales, 1996).

[11] The notion of landscape as personal inheritance features in the draft document 'Objections to Rhondda Forest Recreation Project' (1 July 1975), a letter to the *Sunday Times*, 4 October 1976, and a letter to the *Western Mail*, 20 September 1977. Richard Burton Archives, Swansea University, Ron Berry Papers (Rhondda Forest Recreation Project Papers), WWE/1/10/14.

[12] Simon Schama, *Landscape and Memory* (London: Fontana, 1996), pp. 6–7.

[13] Schama, *Landscape and Memory*, p. 7.

[14] Prys Williams, p. 14.

[15] *Gloran* is a term used by Berry to describe the 'original Rhondda bloodstock' and as such provides a useful term to succinctly describe the pre-industrial agricultural history of the area. Berry, *History Is What You Live*, p. 23.

[16] Gwyn Thomas, *A Welsh Eye* (London: Hutchinson, 1964), p. 18.

[17] Berry was to revisit this image in the unpublished novel-length manuscript 'Below Lord's Head Mountain'. The narrator reflects on a former miner's 'subterranean ethos' and sees how he is a 'cameo of a Celtic mole, a troglodyte under Pen Arglwydd'. Berry, 'Below Lord's Head Mountain', p. 77.

[18] Many Mesolithic artefacts have been discovered in the Rhondda valleys, predominantly in the upper areas around Blaenrhondda, Blaencwm and Maerdy. The mainly Stone Age items relate to hunting, fishing and foraging, which suggests seasonal nomadic activity. See Glamorgan-Gwent Archaeological Trust, 'Historic Landscape Characterisation: The Rhondda. 029 Rhondda Fawr: Enclosed Valley Sides'. Available at *http://www.ggat.org.uk/cadw/historic_ landscape/Rhondda/English/Rhondda_029.htm* Accessed 20 January 2019.

[19] Anne Whiston Spirn, *The Language of Landscape* (New Haven, CT: Yale University Press, 1998), cited in Jim Perrin, 'Land and Freedom', *New Welsh Review*, 74, 8–18 (p. 12).

[20] Peter Berg and R. Dasmann, 'Reinhabiting California', *The Ecologist*, 7/10, 399–401 (p. 399).

[21] Jarvis, *Environments in Contemporary Welsh Poetry*, p. 71.

[22] Lawrence Buell, *Writing for an Endangered World* (Cambridge, MA: Belknap Press of Harvard University Press, 2001), p. 84.

[23] Berry, 'Objections to Rhondda Forest Recreation Project', p. 1. Richard Burton Archives, Swansea University, Ron Berry Papers, WWE/1/10/14. The collection relating to the Rhondda Forest Recreation Project dates from 1973–7.

[24] See K. Bennett, H. Beynon and R. Hudson, *Coalfields Regeneration: Dealing with the Consequences of Industrial Decline* (Abingdon: Joseph Rowntree Foundation, Policy Press, 2000), and John Sewel, *Colliery Closure and Social Change: A Study of a South Wales Mining Valley* (Cardiff: University of Wales Press, 1975).

[25] Berry, 'Objections to Rhondda Forest Recreation Project', p. 2.

[26] Gifford, *Pastoral*, p. 165.

[27] Berry, 'Objections to Rhondda Forest Recreation Project', p. 4.

[28] Berry, 'Objections to Rhondda Forest Recreation Project', p. 2.

[29] Prys Williams, p. 16.

30 Berry, 'Below Lord's Head Mountain', p. 15.
31 Berry, 'Below Lord's Head Mountain', p. 55.
32 Berry, 'Below Lord's Head Mountain', p. 135.
33 Berry, 'Below Lord's Head Mountain', p. 261.
34 Berry, 'Objections to Rhondda Forest Recreation Project', p. 6.
35 Berry, 'Objections to Rhondda Forest Recreation Project', pp. 2–3.
36 Berry, 'Objections to Rhondda Forest Recreation Project', pp. 2–3.
37 Ron Berry, draft of letter of 24 June 1975, to John W. L. Zehetmayr, Forestry Commission Conservator in South Wales, Richard Burton Archives, Swansea University, Ron Berry Papers, WWE/1/10/14.
38 'Working Party Report', Richard Burton Archives, Swansea University, Ron Berry Papers, WWE/1/10/14.
39 L. Kitchen et al., 'Forestry and Environmental Democracy: The Problematic Case of the South Wales Valleys', *Journal of Environmental Policy & Planning*, 4 (2002), 139–55 (p. 145).
40 Kitchen et al., 'Forestry and Environmental Democracy', p. 145.
41 Leo Marx, 'Pastoralism in America', in Sacvan Bercovitch, Myra Jehlen and Albert Gelpi (eds), *Ideology and Classic American Literature* (Cambridge: Cambridge University Press, 1986), pp. 35–69 (p. 66).
42 Ron Berry, undated typed draft document, Richard Burton Archives, Swansea University, Ron Berry Papers, WWE/1/10/14. This echoes a remark made in the *Forestry Commission Annual Report 1919/20* which stated: 'The afforestation of land [. . .] is bound to cause inconvenience and even hardship to existing owners and occupiers: the cry of mutton versus trees will be raised'. William Linnard, *Welsh Woods and Forests: A History* (Llandysul: Gomer, 2000), p. 191.
43 See Kitchen et al., 'Forestry and Environmental Democracy', Kenneth O. Morgan, *Rebirth of a Nation: A History of Modern Wales 1880–1980* (Oxford: Oxford University Press, 2001 [1982]), and Michael Winter, *Rural Politics: Policies for Agriculture, Forestry and the Environment* (London: Routledge, 1996).
44 Kirsti Bohata, *Postcolonialism Revisited* (Cardiff: University of Wales Press, 2004), p. 81.
45 Bohata, *Postcolonialism Revisited*, p. 81.
46 Ron Berry, letter to Mr J. M. Evans, Planning Officer, Rhondda Borough Council, 14/16 June 1975, Richard Burton Archives, Swansea University, Ron Berry Papers, WWE1/10/14.
47 Berry, 'Below Lord's Head Mountain', p. 17.
48 Ron Berry, handwritten, undated draft document, Richard Burton Archives, Swansea University, Ron Berry Papers, WWE/1/10/14.
49 Ron Berry, undated typed draft, Richard Burton Archives, Swansea University, Ron Berry Papers, WWE/1/10/14.
50 Berry, 'Objections to Rhondda Forest Recreation Project', p. 5.
51 Coal Authority Environment Group, *The Environment*, 5 July 1999, 1.
52 See Linnard, *Welsh Woods and Forests*, for a detailed account of pitwood production. Although the text is very much a sympathetic record of the Forestry Commission in Wales, the data presented regarding timber use in heavy industry contextualises the perceived need for a nationalised woodland management/ timber production scheme.

53 R. A. Farmer, 'Forestry in South Wales', *Forestry*, 66/2 (1993), 124.
54 Sylvia Crowe, *Tomorrow's Landscape* (London: Architectural Press, 1956), p. 47.
55 Ron Berry, letter to the *Sunday Times*, 4 October 1976, Richard Burton Archives, Swansea University, Ron Berry Papers, WWE/1/10/14. A report considering the Commission's operations in the area noted that 'it is clear that the Forestry Commission was not, at the time of planting, particularly sensitive to local communities. In many situations, the forest is planted to the limits of the Forestry Commission land. The patterns of high-density, linear-edged planting reflect the productivist foundations of the Forestry Commission. Consequently dark block of conifers overshadow many houses and communities'. Kitchen et al., 'Forestry and Environmental Democracy', p. 146.
56 Bohata, *Postcolonialism Revisited*, p. 81.
57 Berry, 'Below Lord's Head Mountain', p. 5.
58 Berry, 'Objections to Rhondda Forest Recreation Project', pp. 4–5.
59 Buell, *Writing for an Endangered World*, p. 31.
60 *The Times*, undated cutting, Richard Burton Archives, Swansea University, Ron Berry Papers, WWE/1/10/14.
61 Ron Berry, undated typed draft document, Richard Burton Archives, Swansea University, Ron Berry Papers, WWE/1/10/14.
62 Ron Berry, undated published letter, Richard Burton Archives, Swansea University, Ron Berry Papers, WWE/1/10/14.
63 Ron Berry, undated typed draft document, Richard Burton Archives, Swansea University, Ron Berry Papers, WWE/1/10/14.
64 Jean Baudrillard, *Simulacra and Simulation* (Ann Arbor, MI: University of Michigan Press, 1994).
65 Although the handwritten draft document is undated, the contents suggests that it was written during 1973 as part of his correspondence with the *Western Mail*. Richard Burton Archives, Swansea University, Ron Berry Papers, WWE/1/10/14. Berry's prediction is confirmed by the study by Lawrence Kitchen et al. of the Forestry Commission in south Wales, which observes that clear-felling 'leaves orange scars on the landscape', and 'stumps and small off-cuts are left to die on the ground, leaving areas that appear devastated'. Kitchen et al., 'Forestry and Environmental Democracy', p. 149.
66 Ron Berry marginalia, 'Working Party Report', Richard Burton Archives, Swansea University, Ron Berry Papers WWE/1/10/14.
67 Berry, 'Objections to Rhondda Forest Recreation Project', pp. 1–2.
68 Ron Berry, undated typed draft document, Richard Burton Archives, Swansea University, Ron Berry Papers, WWE/1/10/14.
69 Ron Berry, letter to A. K. Gillard, Borough Secretary, Rhondda Borough Council, 22 August 1975, Richard Burton Archives, Swansea University, Ron Berry Papers, WWE/1/10/14.
70 *Rhondda Leader* cutting, 22 August 1975, Richard Burton Archives, Swansea University, Ron Berry Papers, WWE/1/10/14.
71 Jean Baudrillard, 'The Precession of Simulacra', *Simulations*, trans. Paul Foss, Paul Patton and Philip Beitchman (New York: Semiotext(e), 1983) pp. 1–75 (p. 12).

8

LAND OF MY FEATHERS: RON BERRY AND NIALL GRIFFITHS ON THE WING

Tomos Owen

'Watching peregrines', for Ron Berry, 'becomes obsessional'.[1] Once glimpsed, avian life catches his eye: birds hover above and swoop across his work. If home, pub and workplace can seem cramped to the point of claustrophobia, with family, friends or co-workers being intimate to the point of incursion, then Berry's work also positions human life among the flora and fauna of a wider Welsh environment. If Berry is one of Wales's most distinctive writers of industry, he is a significant environmental writer too, demanding that his readers reconsider what it means to think about Welsh landscape, to think of landscape as Welsh.

Berry and Niall Griffiths are authors of troubled mental and environmental states. As Matthew Jarvis has brilliantly argued, the natural landscapes encountered in contemporary anglophone Welsh poetry are never natural, and can only be thought of as natural when discursively framed by a culture to which nature constitutes an opposite. For Jarvis, this entails a broadening of horizons in our definitions of 'nature' to include even those elements which are not 'natural': his focus 'is with buildings and streets, just as much as it is with rivers, valleys or the experience of sunlight'.[2] We might add to Jarvis's list the coal mines and factories of industrial south Wales in a consideration of Berry's work. His first novel *Hunters and Hunted* (1960) (hereafter *HH*) offers lively renderings of the cultures, societies and landscapes of industrial Wales, while *Peregrine Watching* (1987) (hereafter *PW*) is a remarkable piece of environmental writing in its consideration of those other tenants, the birds, alongside Berry, the spectator and interloper within their shared environment. In doing so, *Peregrine Watching* challenges anthropocentric conceptions of landscape even while acknowledging that landscape as a contested space. There are other occupants; these Welsh environments have always been tenanted by residents other than human. The birds look back and, in looking, knock Berry off his perch.

'We are all Ron's progeny', claims Niall Griffiths in his foreword to the Library of Wales edition of Berry's *So Long, Hector Bebb*.[3] Griffiths implies that Berry's writing is itself a begetting force for those authors like himself 'who feel driven to explore structure and voice, to barge the boundaries of the novel form'.[4] And more similarities could easily be enumerated: violence, trauma, a search for authenticity and a simultaneous collapse of social values. This essay selects another concern common to both writers, namely the representation of non-human life and the construction of wider Welsh textual environments. Griffiths's *Stump* (2003) and *Runt* (2007) bristle with animal life, and are populated by damaged individuals within damaged environments. Bringing together these shared aspects of Griffiths's and Berry's work, this essay thus argues non-human life in general, and avian life in particular, sharpens each author's interrogation of Welsh landscape in environmental, national, linguistic and literary terms. Birds and other animals peck and claw at Cambro- and anthropocentric conceptions of landscape and society even as they inhabit the same terrain as their human counterparts. Much is revealed by bird watching and by the birds, watching.

I: *Animals, fishes, birds, poetry, nonsense: Hunters and Hunted*

> 'Twp as a mule, off his head,' she said to Miskin. 'I've never seen a sillier boy. Pits, pits, you'll be killed in the pit like your father, like your uncle Joe, or thrown on the scrap-heap like my brother Evan. Dogs, animals, fishes, birds, *poetry*, *nonsense*. You're wasting your life; I shan't give you any sympathy.' (*HH*, 24)

So speaks the exasperated mother of the convalescent in *Hunters and Hunted*. Her son, the wordy and wisecracking Beynon, is incapacitated after an accident in the pit, which has fractured his toe but not stilled his tongue. Imploring that he use his convalescence to do some proper studying to become a teacher, Mrs Beynon despairs of her headstrong son and his errant ways. Though she might have added drink and women to her litany of grievances, she nevertheless enumerates a series of other errancies and wastings of time which have prevented him from following his brother to teacher training college, and which have instead kept him underground. Mrs Beynon's words, even in their exasperation at her feckless son, gesture towards the tensions and preoccupations of the novel as a whole. It opens, for instance, with three men hunting with their dogs across the landscape of Blaenddu, Berry's fictionalised Rhondda. But as Mrs Beynon implies, as well as being hunters they might easily be hunted and could all-too-readily fall victim to the predatory nature of underground work which has already maimed generations of Blaenddu menfolk. As far as she is concerned, both industrial work and natural hobbies are a waste of a life within this landscape; help will only come from lifting one's eyes beyond the encircling hills and breaking out of this environment. Perhaps unwittingly, however, Mrs Beynon's taxonomy of miscreant pastimes includes another entry against which her son should guard himself: poetry. In Beynon, *Hunters and Hunted* reveals a character whose bravado in the social realms of work, pub and hunt is underscored by a delight in language and a private interest in poetry.

Connecting poetry and animals has a distinct philosophical pedigree. Jacques Derrida, for instance, contends that 'thinking concerning the animal, if there is such a thing, derives from poetry [and] is what philosophy has, essentially, had to deprive itself of. It is the difference between philosophical knowledge and poetic thinking.'[5] Berry has animal metaphors constantly to hand: there is something metaphoric about his representation of animals that develops into a concern with non-human subjectivity across his writing. Beynon's wordplay may be dismissed as asinine nonsense, but it nonetheless grants him a unique perspective on his community. Responding to his girlfriend Louisa, he subverts Yeats's bee-loud glade at Innisfree and recasts it in a council house, 'a nest of draughts and shade' in 'old Blaenddu' (*HH*, 40). Beynon's tricksy language is an early indicator of the style Berry was to develop across his career, that which John Pikoulis admiringly describes as the 'impressive linguistic demonstration' of the valley 'subculture'.[6] Yet to describe Beynon as 'Twp' as a mule is also to insist, stubbornly, on the stubbornly Welsh terms of Berry's engagements with the literary question of the animal in his writing.

A conversation between Beynon and the local grandee Major Mainwaring reveals Berry's appreciation of the precariousness of the historical moment. Changes are afoot, as the Major says, offering Beynon the prospect of a more secure factory job, because 'Men who have devoted their lives to coal mining will find themselves in a very sorry position in the labour market' (*HH*, 70). Even here, however, the serious note sounded by the Major about a disruptive shift in the means of production in the south Wales coalfield is undercut by the bathetic reminder that throughout the conversation Beynon has been carrying an enormous trout, caught and soon to be gifted to a girlfriend. Stephen Knight has identified in Berry's male protagonists a misdirected energy, often set against a 'dying industrial world'; in Berry's second novel, *The Full-Time Amateur*, Knight finds in its protagonist a volatile temperament which 'relates to a lack of clear identity arising from the insecure and inherently worthless nature of the work available to him'.[7] While Beynon is not as violent an individual as Hughie Davies, the correlation between a declining and insecure industrial society and the kind of miscreant individuals who populate Berry's texts certainly holds for *Hunters and Hunted*. Indeed, for Beynon, Miskin and Williams life with their dogs hunting around Blaenddu is an alternative source of meaning and focus. Mastery over their dogs and command of a hunt might be read as a means of restoring control over a life within human communities where all is set unpredictably to change.

Hunters and Hunted precipitates an intriguing trend in Berry's writing in which industrial and rural Welsh landscapes intersect and overlap. Beynon, for instance, navigates his way towards the river 'across the railway line [. . .] down the bank to a hedge-sparrow haunted stretch of gorse above the river, where he assembled his rod' (*HH*, 66). From the built environment of the railway line to the natural world beyond, Beynon finds the landscape 'haunted' by the dunnocks in the gorse. This patch is a favoured haunt of the birds, but as becomes clear, animals and other non-human life haunt Berry's environments with more powerful and disquieting effects. Entering into one of his maudlin humours, Beynon, reciting a poem of his own creation, invokes another ghostly animal from the literary canon: 'Beynon hung his head. "Dilemma. To be or not to be? A human mole after the tradition of my predecessors, or a soldier of the Queen?"' (*HH*, 100). The mole which here tunnels its way into the novel is a remarkable creature. Caught between a return to work underground and conscription to the armed forces, Beynon confronts his existential doubt by echoing and also reappropriating Hamlet's most famous soliloquy. Is he to be – or not to be – a miner or a soldier? The sightless and subterranean mole figures here as a metaphor for a Welsh proletarian class yet, moreover (moleover?), Beynon identifies a patrilinear legacy: to become a human mole is to follow a 'tradition of my predecessors', including his own father, who died underground. The Prince of Denmark is also famously troubled by a subterranean patriarch:

HAMLET:	Swear by my sword
	Never to speak of this that you have heard.
GHOST (BENEATH):	Swear by his sword.
HAMLET:	Well said, old mole! Canst work i' the earth so fast?[8]

Hamlet's father's ghost, also hailed as a mole, troubles the ground beneath his son's feet. For Beynon too, the mountains around Blaenddu are also molehills, under which a ghostly, fossorial proletarian tradition lies buried but does not rest in peace. The allusive mole burrows into underground and intertextual networks which connect a specific history of industrial south Wales with the spectral literary figure of Hamlet's father who, like Beynon's, also works in the earth. Thus Beynon becomes aware that this is the land of his fathers because his fathers are in the land.

Later on, having avoided the draft but succumbed to a bout of tuberculosis, Beynon again turns to animal life for consolation: 'The cuckoos are flying in from Africa, and I'm in bed, spitting blood' (*HH*, 140–1). Consoling himself that his *hwyl* will return with the swallows (*HH*, 141), he begins writing poetry: 'Louisa came precisely when he arrived at a suitable title for his poem. Beynon hastily wrote it down: *The Eleventh Commandment*. The first line was ready manufactured: *Old gods turned crows who peck our heels*' (*HH*, 144). The mysterious and sinister image of the pecking crows in this strange poem, with its biblical invocation, emerges from Beynon's anxiety that 'This is a world of mechanical men. Crookbacks, honourable parasites and poets are dying out' (*HH*, 146–7). The pecking crows might also recall those at the Battle of Argoed Llwyfain described by Taliesin, reddened by the blood of the fallen combatants. Beynon's pecking crows gesture towards a Welsh poetic tradition, even as they signify a kind of otherness belonging to a different realm from that of the poet's human relationships.

This essay cannot provide a comprehensive inventory of all bird species in Berry's writing; suffice it to say that *Hunters and Hunted* is a textual aviary containing pipit, wheatear, yellowhammer, cornbunting, dipper, kestrel, peregrine, fieldfare, wren, woodcock, robin, thrush, blackbird, little owl, magpie, jay, grouse, raven, crow, cuckoo, gannet, stork, wren and harrier. Beynon and Louisa's argument is interrupted by the sight of a dipper, while Beynon's associative linguistic games figure her as both 'a little goose' and a marsh harrier/harsh marrier (*HH*, 197).

Falcons, however, seem particularly precious. A specific point of contention in the novel arrives when Miskin accepts a commission from Tommy Wills, the pub landlord and pigeon fancier, to shoot a peregrine nesting in a quarry above the village. 'You stupid bastard', exclaims Beynon upon learning of Miskin's actions. 'What happens when there are no more falcons to shoot?' (*HH*, 84, 85). Beynon berates his trigger-happy friend by citing the 1954 Protection of Birds Act; Miskin counters that the five pounds he received for the job 'Sounds like simple arithmetic' (*HH*, 85). Elsewhere Beynon, on his way home from the factory, is struck by the sight of 'four squawking young kestrels flitting around' (*HH*, 181). His poetic description draws him immediately to compare the hovering bird to the '*daughin*' of Gerard Manley Hopkins's 'The Windhover'. 'How the hell did Hopkins cook up so much from so little?', he asks: 'God's mouthpiece, God's megaphone, God's . . . just God's' (*HH*, 181). For Hopkins and Beynon, there is something sacred about the sight of a kestrel – 'just God's' – hovering in the air: the hovering bird figures a supra-human state of being.[9] Hopkins coined 'inscape' as a term to conceptualise the specific individuality of what he beheld (a kestrel, in the case of 'The Windhover'). If for Hopkins the encounter with the hovering kestrel provokes an outpouring of literary style, for Beynon in *Hunters and Hunted* the bird produces a stupefying effect; it is 'God's . . . just God's'. For Jacques Derrida, meanwhile, the question of the animal is a matter of acknowledging the otherness of the animal, not in order to bolster the claims of man over beast, but rather to appreciate the unbridgeable difference of each creature and to mark its 'unsubstitutable singularity'. Thus poetry, or literature more generally, has a unique capacity to acknowledge such uniqueness.[10]

Miskin and Beynon reappear in a short story, 'November Kill', another work in which animal life stalks and is stalked. Chasing a fox to its den their dog becomes trapped underground and the story narrates the efforts to dig it out. Stephen Knight reads the story as 'an affectionate recreation, rather than cold parody, of a pit rescue' seen in other Welsh industrial fictions,[11] and there are certain parallels: intimacy emerges between Miskin (whose dog it is) and Beynon in the physically demanding and emotionally wrenching retrieval of the dog from the fox's den. The boys' determination to rescue the bitch – conspicuously named Lady – is also inflected by their shared experiences of being sons to 'runaway mothers' (*CS*, 119). In their breaks between rescue efforts the story shows the boys going 'On and on, the same unforgiving rancour, the same helpless groping for motive, a reason to shed guilt, absolve themselves and their mothers' (*CS*, 120). 'Groping' is a load-bearing word in that sentence, connecting the boys' efforts as they dig the earth for the lost dog with a search for explanations for the departure of their mothers and their own resultant feelings of guilt and responsibility. Above the action of the story, 'A buzzard hung like an emblem above the horizon, standing still in the updraught' (*CS*, 116). An avian perspective, a bird's-eye view, looks down on human affairs even as that bird is endowed with an emblematic signification by the humans beneath.

II: Falcon, man, falcon: Peregrine Watching

Before accepting the shooting commission in *Hunters and Hunted*, Miskin presents Wills with a set of pigeon rings recovered from the plucking post of a peregrine:

> 'Found them this afternoon, all nice and tidy scattered among enough feathers to stuff a pillow.'
> 'Bastarding hawk,' Wills said.
> 'Falcon, man, falcon. Lost any pigeons lately?' (*HH*, 72)

For Miskin it is important to be accurate: the loss of Wills's prized racing pigeons is attributable to a falcon, not a 'bastarding hawk'. Yet in correcting Wills's mis-identification, Miskin accurately identifies a pattern of encounter in Berry's writing – falcon, man, falcon – which raises questions about cohabitation within the same environment and of what happens when man looks at falcons to find his own gaze already returned.

High above crag and scree, against a backdrop of muted browns and greys, it is clear-cut and distinct. It sits, watching. The sharpness of its appearance is heightened by the hook of its bill and the grip of its talons on its rocky perch: the mastery of the thing! The peregrine falcon which sits on the cover of *Peregrine Watching* arrests its reader with its fixing, petrifying gaze. The bird on the cover looks back; indeed, this bird is already looking at us: it is in fact the reader – not the bird – who is returning the look. Above the bird, on that cover image, in bold white capitals, is the book's title and the author's name: '*Peregrine Watching* / Ron Berry'.

If ornithology is its subject, then *Peregrine Watching* is ambiguous about who is watching whom: the book is highly suspicious of any straightforward assumption that the human observer does the watching, while the perched bird is passively watched. Falcon. Man. Falcon. Is Berry '*Peregrine Watching*'? Or is this a book about a *Peregrine Watching* / Ron Berry? For all the accuracy and precision of Berry the birdwatcher, *Peregrine Watching* is a rare bird, a tricky text to classify and identify to species. It is, according to the blurb on the inside cover, 'the first book of its kind, a distinctly personal account of watching peregrines at eyries in South Wales'. If writing an environment is, as Jarvis argues, an invitation to enter a landscape constructed according to a particular interpretation of it, then *Peregrine Watching* is both an invitation and a warning. When entering Berry's textual environments, we must tread carefully: there are other occupants here. Other creatures reside in *Peregrine Watching*; we must always be aware that, soaring high above us, there may be a peregrine watching.

For Jacques Derrida the experience of being stared at by an animal – his own cat, in his own bedroom – produced a sufficiently disquieting effect to prompt the writing of a book. In *The Animal That Therefore I Am* Derrida investigates the origins of the embarrassment he feels standing naked before the cat:

> I often ask myself, just to see, *who I am* – and who I am (following) at the moment when, caught naked, in silence, by the gaze of an animal, for example, the eyes of a cat I have trouble, yes, a bad time, overcoming my embarrassment.
> Whence this malaise?[12]

'Embarrassment' and 'malaise' might conventionally be thought of as properties of humanity, so that the uncomfortable feeling of shame experienced by the philosopher standing under the gaze of his cat might be thought of as an essentially human response. As Neil Badmington summarises it in an elegant reading of the scene, 'Because I have knowledge of my nudity and am ashamed, the argument might run, I must be human. *I blush, therefore I am.*'[13] Awkward awareness of nudity serves as confirmation of humanity; animals, by contrast, are naked without knowing it. However, as the art critic John Berger puts it in an essay called 'Why Look at Animals?', the animal 'does not reserve a special look for man', and this fact has important implications for our thinking about the human. Scrutinised across the 'narrow abyss of non-comprehension', man 'becomes aware of himself returning the look'.[14] For Berger and Derrida alike, the look of the animal decentres the human subject and strips it, naked, of its sovereignty. Paying no heed to the dominion of man over beast, animals look without prejudice: 'And so, when he is *being seen* by the animal, he [man] is being seen as his surroundings are seen by him [the animal]'.[15] The animal which looks back – be it Derrida's cat or Berry's peregrine falcon – throws the dominance of the human into doubt; man is now a tenant of a landscape rather than its author or master.

Berry, like Derrida, does not shy away from the consequences of this revelation: gazing skywards, Berry sees that 'Ravens and peregrines shared Cerrig Fawr when Wales was a shanks' pony nation. Ravens know more about peregrines than we do' (*PW*, 48). Bird life pre-dates human occupancy of this terrain: not only does Berry's account make room for avian inhabitants within a Welsh polity, but it also emphasises that in fact the ravens and falcons are primary instigators in the conception of a Welsh landscape. Wales was a 'shanks' pony nation', underdeveloped in terms of infrastructure (and relying on bipedal before mechanised locomotion) and awaiting the arrival of the transformative effects of modernity. Yet the birds were already cohabiting; it is humans who are the late arrivals. Berry even ventures to suggest that epistemological mastery over this patch of land does not belong to a human at all. Man is after the animal – an idea developed by Derrida:

> In what sense of the neighbor [. . .] should I say that I am close to or *next to* the animal, and that I am (following) it [. . .]? Being-with it in the sense of being-close-to-it? Being-alongside-it? Being-after-it? *Being-after-it* in the sense of the hunt, training, or taming, or *being-after-it* in the sense of a succession or inheritance?[16]

From the domestic cat in Derrida's Parisian suburb to the peregrine falcons soaring above Ron Berry's Rhondda would seem like an enormous shift. Confronted by these respective creatures, however, both Derrida and Berry are startled by a shared appreciation of the unbridgeable difference between man and animal. As Derrida says, of his cat:

> It has its point of view regarding me. The point of view of the other, and nothing will have ever given me more food for thinking through this absolute alterity of the neighbor or of the next (-door) than these moments when I see myself naked under the gaze of a cat.[17]

Appreciation of absolute alterity despite physical proximity is the mark of a cat owner and a peregrine watcher. This is an epiphany intensified by the returned gaze of the creature, by those moments in these texts when French philosopher and Welsh novelist see themselves seen by the animal.

Keeping watch for peregrines, Berry hears 'the delirious tikk-tikking', then spots a pair of copulating kestrels 'on a ledge behind a slanting silver birch': 'The female went shrilling after a ring ouzel. She came back to her perch in the tree. We gazed at each other. Her face had the downcast look of a victim, sad spouse of a wife-beater. This is anthropomorphic fancy of course' (*PW*, 13). Of course: Berry is quick to guard against all-too-conveniently projecting human interactions on to avian neighbours. The kestrels have the perspective of the absolute other that Berry the birdwatcher knows he should not attempt to appropriate. Nonetheless, the metaphor of domestic violence is summoned even as it is dismissed: like the emblematic buzzard soaring above 'November Kill', the kestrels in *Peregrine Watching* enable Berry to comment on domestic relations between humans while still retaining their otherness.

Later, hunkered down and monitoring the eyrie, Berry interrupts his narrative with a question: 'How *twp* are peregrines, I wondered' (*PW*, 25). This single sentence appears among a detailed description of the birds' activity: times and length of arrivals and departures; direction and speed of flight; calls and movements. The abrupt interjection – How *twp* are peregrines? – is no more than a peck, a thought which abruptly lands in the birdwatcher's head during a long vigil, before taking off again out of sight. Part of the intrigue of *Peregrine Watching* is the challenge of relating to non-human life, of what Andrew Bennett and Nicholas Royle describe as

> the *impossibility* of finding the right words, of adequately describing, of putting in language what a specific animal is like, what is entailed by an encounter with this particular creature. [. . .] For how on earth do you, should you describe a non-human animal? How can you say what it is like to be one?[18]

How *twp* are peregrines? Berry's eye is caught once again by the falcon:

> It's rather maniacal to *imagine* the vision of peregrines. The finest Leica camera is a Luddite contraption by comparison, consequently photography is for photographers. Image-addicts. Flick-worshippers.
> The Cerrig Fach tiercel of 1980 remains memorable. Perched on a spur above the nest, he hekked angrily (even *angrily* falsifies, because the sounding-board of evolution had registered peregrine vernacular before we unscrambled the yowls and yammering which resulted in Genesis 1.28)[.] (*PW*, 56)

Angry with himself for attributing anger, Berry chastises himself for failing to maintain a respectful distance. To attempt to conceptualise in human terms the adaptation of the birds to their environment (their eyesight), or to interpret their interactions in terms of human social relations (their anger), is a sign of madness. Specifying the seven 'map miles' covered by the Cerrig Fawr bird allows for a different way of conceiving of this Welsh environment. The science of cartography is limited not only, as the Irish poet Eavan Boland has it, because it cannot tell of trauma and hunger within a landscape, but also for the more radical reason that maps only reveal and conceal within a human framework.[19] Though he makes no attempt to claim it for himself (such a gesture would be maniacal), Berry allows instead for what is literally a bird's-eye view. Moreover there is something obscene – profane, even – in the biblical injunction, delivered by God to Adam and Eve in Genesis, to 'Be fruitful, and multiply, and replenish the earth, and subdue it: and have dominion over the fish of the sea, and over the fowl of the air, and over every living thing that moveth upon the earth.'[20]

Since the 1980s Donna Haraway has sought to think beyond the human and de-centre anthropocentric ways of conceptualising our world. Her 'Companion Species Manifesto', for instance, emphasises the tangled intricacies of our environments: 'In layers of history, layers of biology, layers of naturecultures, complexity is the name of our game.'²¹ Haraway's immediate point of departure is the relationship she experiences with her own pet – her dog. Like Derrida's *The Animal That Therefore I Am*, Haraway's 'Companion Species Manifesto' is sparked by an autobiographical history: two pets, Derrida's cat and Haraway's dog, give their respective philosopher-owners paws for thought. Haraway's emphasis is on those complex moments of entanglement when 'We make each other up, in the flesh'.²² *Peregrine Watching* shows little appetite to domesticate the 'quenchless ferocity and primordial patience' of the falcons (*PW*, 16), but peregrine and peregrine-watcher 'make each other up'. The shared gaze figures as what Haraway describes as '"prehensions" or groupings [by which] beings constitute each other and themselves. Beings do not pre-exist their relations'.²³ And there are consequences: 'The world is a knot in motion [. . .] There are no preconstituted subjects and objects, and no single sources, unitary actors, or final ends.'²⁴ Such grippings and graspings signify for Haraway a transformative means of interspecies interaction within an environment.

From its title and cover image, *Peregrine Watching* explores such mutually implied, mutually constitutive interactions: 'This immemorial land of my fathers seemed to be rife with peregrines', says Berry, in a gesture which incorporates avian life within the history of this environment. That history is marked by specifically Welsh coordinates, with what Berry describes as the '[e]ngineered aesthetics for industrial Wales' (*PW*, 10) when referring to the greened tips and slag heaps and the planted conifers over which the falcons have nested. The opening tracking shot of the book encompasses both a reservoir and the sitka plantations 'as far as the eye can see [. . .] Here in Wales, the Forestry Commission has effected a land-grab greater than any since the Roman invasions. Horizons have been degraded, watersheds obliterated, deciduous copses overwhelmed' (*PW*, 7). Another of Wales's literary ornithologists, R. S. Thomas, famously conceived of both reservoirs and coniferous plantations in colonial terms, and both Jarvis and Kirsti Bohata have written on the politics and poetics of afforestation in relation to Thomas's work. Bohata reads the coniferous plantations of Thomas's 'Afforestation' as an erasure of place, while Jarvis argues that 'Thomas's Welsh environment is a crucially cultural and political event to which the poem is a deeply felt and deeply critical response'.²⁵ Berry too is attuned to a colonial interpretation of such a 'land grab', likening the Forestry Commission's administration of a policy of afforestation to an invading Roman army. It takes a keen observer to see the birds within such a landscape, within Haraway's layers of history, biology and nature cultures:

> Blind to the flight of sparrows, we catch our breath at the sight of a humming-bird. Between archaeopteryx and the firecrest, contrasting shades by the countless million [. . .] Aeons of babel separate us from lost time out of mind in Rhode Island Reds and Yorkshire Rollers. We have shambled from the primeval slurry like sleep-walkers. (*PW*, 38)

Prehensile, the claws of the birds in Berry's landscape nonetheless grasp very firmly. The flitting firecrest is connected to the oldest known bird, the archaeopteryx of the late Jurassic period. Despite the scattering of species and confusion of tongues since the 'aeons of babel', Berry acknowledges the still living, still active connections of history, biology and nature-culture within his physical and textual environments. Moreover, *Peregrine Watching* figures man as only one among the many forms of life within this space: 'Prudently speaking, I become a fragmentary part of their [the peregrines'] lives' (*PW*, 64). It is for this reason that Berry emphasises that 'conservation does not mean "management". It means leaving be, stepping out of the skin of monomania, shedding nationhood and dogmas from on high, the huffs and puffs of consciousness buggered by realities' (*PW*, 87). Letting be as leaving alone and allowing to exist: this is conservation in a non-anthropocentric form as opposed to those huffs and puffs of consciousness. At these moments Berry's peregrines knock the human off its perch. Now a land of my fathers, it has also always been a land of my feathers.

III: Niall Griffiths in the Chthulucene

> Listen to the crows, he said. – What d'you think they're saying?
> One of Them Questions again. Always Them Questions of No Answers even if an answer was asked for which it never flippin is.
> Well, whatever you think it is . . . you're wrong.
> Flippin cheek I thought cos I *knew* what the crows were saying to each other even if I couldn't've said it in Person's Words. I've known what the crows and in fact *all* the birds say to each other since I was a pram-babby but I've never told any other human person about that cos they wouldn't know what I was talking about if I did and anyway it is a Secret between me and the birds.[26]

Crows can be grouped by several collective nouns. We might speak of a horde or murder of crows; we can talk of an unkindness of ravens, or a clattering of jackdaws. Magpies can come in a gulp or by the charm; choughs, grouped together, are a chattering. Niall Griffiths does not specify which member of the corvid clan is encountered in this passage from his 2007 novel, *Runt*. This is not because he does not know the difference: a reading of his work will show that he is a keen observer of avian life who knows the ravens from the carrion crows, the terns from the gulls, the harriers from the kites. But this exchange between the boy-narrator of the novel and his drunken uncle – Drunkle, as he is known – suggests another corvid collective, used for rooks (though also commonly for owls): this is a *parliament*. And in parliament, the crows speak.

As far as Drunkle is concerned, this is a parliament to which humans are not elected. The corvid conversation continues but, as Drunkle later claims, 'their calls are not for us. They don't care about us. Whether we live or die, as an entire species, I mean, is of no importance to them whatsoever'.[27] This clatter and chatter is bound up with issues of language. The croaking crows prompt a rhetorical 'Question of No Answers' while Drunkle broods on the possibilities of speaking the language of the crows only to conclude that this would be, so to speak, a wild goose chase: '[W]hatever you think it is . . . you're wrong.' Even as they are brought into contact with each other the avian and human realms are kept firmly apart, each separate from the other.

Things are different for his nephew, the sixteen-year-old narrator of the novel. While the question of actually translating the crows' cackling into 'Person's Words' might be beyond the ability of his tongue to speak, the boy nonetheless regards it as a 'Flippin cheek' to assume that crowspeak remains an unknown territory to human thought. Indeed, as we see here, the boy is versed in the language of the crows 'and in fact *all* the birds'. By this stage in the novel we are aware of the boy's extraordinary affinity with the flora and fauna within the environment; we are also aware that he suffers from a mental health condition, likely epilepsy or bipolar disorder (based on the various anti-convulsants and tranquillisers mentioned in passing). From the boy's own perspective we hear about episodes of mania or seizures which he describes as 'My Times'. Remarkably, as the boy communes with avian and other non-human life, the novel – because of its narrative perspective – is able to keep in the balance competing interpretations of his actions: on the one hand that he is hallucinating or going through heightened sensory experiences associated with his condition, on the other that the boy is a kind of savant with access to realms of knowledge extending beyond – beyond the human, beyond the present time, and beyond his present environment.

For Griffiths, Berry is a pioneer in his use of voice and structure to 'barge' the form of the novel. Animal life barges into Griffiths's novels, and the argy-bargy between human and non-human perspectives in *Stump* (2003) and *Runt* (2007) is the focus of what remains of this essay. Like Berry's, Griffiths's writing too is caught in the 'prehensions' of animal life; grasping non-human tentacles extend into the family of man. In this regard, Niall Griffiths and Ron Berry are birds of a feather.

Berry's insistence on shedding the 'skin of monomania' chimes, as we have seen, with Haraway's claim that humans and animals 'make each other up'. Haraway's most recent book develops this idea in relation not only to our pets and companion species but to our attitudes towards the environment. In *Staying with the Trouble* she invites her readers to make trouble – in the word's etymological sense of 'stirring up', 'to disturb', 'to make cloudy' – as a way of responding to ecological emergency. As she puts it, 'staying with the trouble requires learning to be truly present, not as a vanishing pivot between awful or edenic pasts and apocalyptic or salvific futures, but as mortal critters entwined in myriad unfinished configurations of places, times, matters, meanings'.[28] Niall Griffiths spells trouble. He is a troublesome, troubling writer, red in tooth and claw. Part of the 'trouble' stirred up by Griffiths and Haraway involves reconfiguring our relations to the earth and its inhabitants – its flora and fauna, animal, vegetable and mineral. Implied in these configurations is an endlessly complex set of relationships and entanglements, a sense that all life on earth – past, present and future – is mutually implied and connected. There is, however, a parallel sense that these relationships are unfinished, open-ended, unpredictable. Staying with the trouble means keeping a close watch over both sides of this bargain.

'Chthulucene' is Haraway's monstrous term for the 'elsewhere and elsewhen that was, still is and might yet be'.[29] In attempting to move beyond the human-centredness of the term 'Anthropocene', Haraway proposes that

> the Chthulucene is made up of the ongoing multispecies stories and practices of becoming-with in times which remain at stake, in precarious

times, in which the world has not finished and the sky has not fallen – yet. We are at stake to each other. [. . .] [H]uman beings are not the only important actors in the Chthulucene, with all other beings able simply to react. The order is reknitted: human beings are with and of the earth, and the biotic and abiotic powers of this earth are part of the story.[30]

Haraway's coinage derives in part from reference to the monstrous octopus-like deity, Cthulu, encountered in the works of H. P. Lovecraft. But Haraway also gets her teeth into the Chthulucene because a particular species of spider – *pimoa cthulu* – got its teeth into her while walking in the woods near her home in California. The modified spelling of 'Cthulu' to her own 'Chthulu' foregrounds the underground: this is the realm of the chthonic, the underworld. A certain mood or tone pertains here which is shared in the textual environments constructed by Berry and Griffiths: inter-species relations are open-ended and unfinished, 'ongoing' and still at stake. And narratives are crucial here too: these are 'multispecies stories' which demand that we reconsider our relations to space and to time, to the elsewhere and the elsewhen.

Although he is not bitten by it, the boy-narrator of Niall Griffiths's 2007 novel *Runt* is nonetheless caught in, or caught by, a spider's web. The moment comes when he is taken by Drunkle to the local pub, where they see Arthur, the violent and abusive local farmer enraged at the loss of his sheep to an unknown predator (though Drunkle's dog Arrn is suspected). Jumping atop the pool table, the boy

> got of a sudden a big distractment [. . .] way up there in the beamy ceilingness [. . .] and I saw a web right by my two eyes with no spider in it but some dead flies in it and one still alive [. . .] [A]nd I went into a long spiderness in my head and I could see everything with my eight eyes cos that's how many eyes spiders have and they must be able to see Everything with their eight eyes.[31]

Therianthropy is the name given to the mythical form of shapeshifting whereby human beings are able to metamorphose into other animals. Here, arachnid perspectives enter which connect times, matters and bodies: the smell of tobacco from smokers of the past, the spider, and the flies. *Runt*'s narrator is able to see these patterns of connectivity between species and times here partly on account of his mental condition. Indeed, a striking feature of the novel is that its exploration of the environment is most fully conducted by the character bearing social and neural dysfunction.

There are no spiders in Griffiths's 2003 novel *Stump*; nonetheless, the text bites. Driving from Liverpool to Aberystwyth, Alastair and Darren observe the horsefly which is accompanying them in the car on their journey. It has fallen to them to pursue and apprehend the narrator of the other strand of the novel, the recovering addict amputee now hiding out on the west Wales coast. Having just crossed the border into Wales, the horsefly bites. Pricking the skin and crossing the border are two images of penetration; to enter into Wales is also to enter, bodily, into a relationship with the critters and creepy-crawlies of the Welsh environment. Darren is heedless to the fly and thinks nothing of crushing it, but it is telling that his co-traveller Alastair, who urges him not to crush, has a stronger connection to Wales stemming from childhood holidays: he is able to sound Welsh spellings on road signs and shops, even if he is not able to understand them fully. Many of his recollections are situated within Welsh environments, particularly around Llyn Tegid. Alastair recalls time spent with his grandfather, catching a perch with 'tiger stripes on its muscled flanks [. . .] and the sharp spines of its fins that punctured his palms when he tried to hold it tightly'; though not bitten by it, the face and flickering tongue of a viper before it 'thrashed and whipped into the water to flee' continues to visit his dreams.[32] He is struck by the existence of the gwyniad, the fish species native only to Llyn Tegid, and also by the myth of Tegi, the mythical monster of the lake. These sub-aquatic creatures (with the exception of the mythical monster) might be thought of as specimens of Haraway's 'chthonic ones', those 'monsters in the best sense' which are 'both ancient and up-to-the-minute'.[33] Advancing 'tentacular thinking' as a mode of how we might 'make kin in the Chthulucene', Haraway argues that '[t]entacularity is wound in abyssal and dreadful graspings, frayings, and weavings, passing relays again and again, in the generative recursions that make up living and dying'.[34]

In the damaged, amputated pastoral of Griffiths's novels there are monsters of the worst sense, too. From their car Darren and Alastair mistake an approaching fog for what is in fact an enormous cloud of smoke:

> Tongues, tendrils of sticky smoke busy with motes ash grey and pink-frilled, lap at the windscreen. Splots of wet ash adhere, shunted by the wipers, leaving trails of sticky grease.

> – It's the fuckin, it's the fuckin foot n mouth thingio. Thee must be burning all the dead animals.
> [. . .]
> – Jesus fuckin Christ.
> Alastair says nothing, just stares. His head craning back over his shoulder as if joined to that burning, as if snagged by a tentacle of damp smoke.³⁵

Media coverage of the 2001 foot and mouth epidemic focused on the holocaustal images of burning sacrifice, and this harrowing sense of a ravaging inferno – alien but also material – is retained in Griffiths's rendering. It is the tentacle of smoke which grabs, which entwines and entangles Alastair in this strange animal slaughter, this immolation of the Welsh pastoral. As the car slows its pace to pass the fire and the two travellers are shocked beyond words, the text gives the strong sense that the drive into Wales is not merely a journey to another country, but is rather a voyage into an apocalyptic landscape or chthonic underworld belonging to another time and place: 'It's like the fuckin dark ages or summin'',³⁶ as Darren says. Inhalation of the smoke – in its greasy, abject materiality – brings to the nostrils the greasy, abject materiality of the incinerated cattle; it is a sign of trouble, a dreadful grasping between human and animal.

Such tentacularity takes on a more hopeful aspect elsewhere in the text. The narrator of the novel's other strand – who the Liverpool gangsters Alastair and Darren are tracking down – bears significant physical and psychological scars. A recovering alcoholic and drug addict, his narration is often tinged with the trauma of his past (including the loss of a partner and a limb), but also with the nervous anxiety of life in the present. Having settled in Aberystwyth, he attempts to rebuild his life, and in that attempt calls upon companion species. *Stump* opens with the visit of 'the fox, the ahl fox with the one eye' to the narrator's garden:

> This wild animal here in my garden. This talented predator, here in my head.
>
> I gulped water an watched the mist tendril in to refill the hole made by his absence [. . .] I could feel me sanity, me hard-won fuckin sanity, me sanity gained at the cost of a fuckin *limb*, being painlessly restored [. . .] Bein visited by a wild thing.
>
> How I fucking love this.³⁷

There is love here, in this exchange between man and fox; but there is also pain. If Ron Berry's peregrines look their viewers foursquare in the face, Griffiths's fox sees through one eye only. While the tendril action of the mist might recall Haraway's 'tentacular thinking', the scene is also a kind of broken parody of another famous vulpine encounter in modern Welsh writing, namely R. Williams Parry's celebrated sonnet 'Y Llwynog' (The Fox). In each case the human speakers are left moved and changed by the fleeting fox vanishing, like a shooting star. The exhilaration described by Griffiths's narrator makes this a strangely affirmative experience whereby a damaged man and a damaged creature practise what Haraway calls 'the arts of living on a damaged planet'.[38]

One of the consequences of that addiction for the narrator of *Stump* is the psychosis that remains: 'Fuckin panic attacks. Legacy of the wreckage wrought by booze'.[39] Late on in the novel Griffiths narrates one of these panic attacks to powerful effect, and it is telling that the passages of anxiety and self-loathing are interwoven by references to bird life:

> all evil on its way already here the entire world is sinister an pure fuckin hates me
> I turn me head and look behind me at the sea as if there's any solace to be found there and see a sparrow hopping along the pavement common little house sparrow [. . .]
>
> be calm be still it is starting to pass the sparrow is gone but there is a black an vicious evil shape on its way
> no there is a
> vileness inside everything
> no there is a
> sickness in human life
> no there is a
> crow hopping up the slipway from the beach to peck at a scrunched-up chip wrapper.[40]

The knowledge of the birds which intersperses the fragmented utterances of foreboding and panic comes from the bird guides which the protagonist has been reading as he recovers. Laura Salisbury has noted how several twenty-first-century 'neuronovels' or fictions of the brain – novels like Ian McEwan's *Saturday* and Sebastian Faulks's

Human Traces – 'rarely mime the disintegrated psychic fabric of neurological disturbance, either through a sustained or explicit use of the disruptive formal resources of modernism or by reconfiguring the shape of the human according to unrecognizably new, scientized topographies'.[41] By contrast, as these examples show, Griffiths insists on the first-person narration to insert the reader into the protagonist's stream of consciousness in modernist style. Connecting the narrator's internal trauma (the 'vileness inside everything' and 'sickness in human life') with the external stimuli of the seafront, birds hop in and among the fragments of narration. As with the birds in Berry's writing, the crow here figures as a macabre portent of the narrator's anxiety, but also as a creature of absolute alterity.

The formal experimentation of the depiction of the panic attack in *Stump* is further extended in *Runt*, which is narrated entirely by a protagonist suffering from a mental dysfunction. Such a gesture might well be read in light of Griffiths's praise of Berry's barging at the conventions of structure and voice. Using a reduced vocabulary and an idiosyncratic, associative style, *Runt* endeavours to give voice to a subjectivity conditioned by a neurological disorder, reaching its most intense pitch when the boy-narrator experiences moments of seizure which he describes as 'My Times'. These episodes are referred to on several occasions during the novel, but occur twice.

The first takes place on the hillside – the High Parts, as the boy describes it – during a thunderstorm:

> Drum drumdrum. All Times meeting coming together everything *in* me everything *on* me just One Time and it is Mine it is My Times.[42]

This remarkable episode continues for several pages, though this extract is enough to show the untimeliness – the sense of all times, places and points of view intersecting – which pervades Griffiths's writing. Such elsewheres and elsewhens come together in a spectacular, tentacular textual cluster. Conversant as he is with the crows, the boy narrates the sensation of communion with all life across all times. The singularity of 'his times' is in tension with the universality of the experience: he describes crows 'holding up my arms and legs and they flipped and lifted me into the blackness into the highness into the very-far-away-ness so the town and the High Parts and the planet they stood on turned into a pea blue and green, so very far away all in a belowness to me'.⁴³ Though uplifted by the crows, the boy's ascent is one which puts all times and places into a wider (including cosmic) context.

IV: Conclusion: Everything going into Owl

'My Times' return to *Runt* at the violent and dramatic conclusion of the novel, launching the boy once again beyond a singly human subjectivity into other realms of knowledge. The episode – 'the Bad Thing'⁴⁴ – comes when the boy, Drunkle, Arrn the dog and Rhiannon, abused wife of the tyrannical farmer-giant Arthur, are on the hillside during a thunderstorm. Exhilarated by the power of the storm, the group drive across the landscape 'towards the Hole and the Fountain and the Standing Stones' (p. 139), an area with preternatural power in its association for the boy and Drunkle with ancient inhabitation of this patch of land. Everything goes together:

> Yes
> Everything going into
> Owl: white ghost barn owl skimming through the rain and I watched him and he flew past close and watched me and I couldn't see his eyes cos of the rain and the coming darkness but still I felt myself going into those eyes and then the body of that bird and then I was looking out through Owl's eyes high above it all[.]⁴⁵

If for Ron Berry the gaze of the raptor put the human birdwatcher on his guard, the eyes of the owl draw Griffiths's boy-narrator into strigine ways of seeing. As with the eight eyes of the spider earlier in the novel, the proximity to the animal transmutes Griffiths's boy outside of his human frame. It is said that the owl of Minerva takes to the wing only with the falling of the dusk: knowledge comes only at the close of a historical epoch. Griffiths's spectral owl indeed does bring with it new knowledge as exhilaration turns to horror: in the flashes of lightning the boy-owl-narrator sees Arthur 'creeping towards them and in his hand an axe', intent on violent revenge for the blossoming relationship between Drunkle and his wife Rhiannon. 'UNCLE! RHIANNON!' shouts the boy 'in Owl's voice which they didn't know', as a warning.⁴⁶ Shortly following this, the 'No-Word Noise' made by the boy in his screaming is an attempt to enunciate 'the Name of The

World':[47] all creatures, all weathers, all times. The boy's emergency is a problem of voice; for the novel, it is a problem of form. Griffiths's *Runt* powerfully stages the challenge of writing about or speaking for non-human life within an environment while simultaneously connecting and communing with it in non-anthropocentric ways.

For Ron Berry, the ravens kept at the Tower of London are a 'daft shibboleth', one of the 'odious [. . .] trappings of Britannia'; clipping the wings of the ravens, or flaunting a captive peregrine on the wrist, should be a source of shame (*PW*, 45–6, 78). For Drunkle in Griffiths's *Runt*, ravens 'can do everything the culture forbids'. Drunkle knows that in 'the language of this place'[48] Bran is the name for a crow and a dead king. Meanwhile, however, his nephew acknowledges that the 'different words that came from the crows' are not readily translatable to the affairs of man. In Welsh, the native peregrine is also foreign (*hebog tramor*, literally 'overseas falcon'), having also something of the pilgrimage or peregrination about it. Retaining and respecting the 'significant otherness' of the birdlife which populates these works by Berry and Griffiths is thus both the challenge and the remarkable achievement of their writing on the wing.

Notes

[1] Ron Berry, *Peregrine Watching* (Llandysul: Gomer, 1987), p. 7.
[2] Matthew Jarvis, *Welsh Environments in Contemporary Poetry* (Cardiff: University of Wales Press, 2008), p. 12.
[3] Niall Griffiths, 'Foreword', Ron Berry, *So Long, Hector Bebb* (Cardigan: Parthian, Library of Wales, 2005), pp. ix–xiii (p. xii).
[4] Griffiths, 'Foreword', p. xii.
[5] Jacques Derrida, *The Animal That Therefore I Am*, ed. Marie-Louise Mallet, trans. David Wills (New York: Fordham University Press, 2008), p. 7.
[6] John Pikoulis, 'Word-of-mouth cultures cease in cemeteries', *New Welsh Review*, 34 (1996), 9–15.
[7] Stephen Knight, *A Hundred Years of Fiction* (Cardiff: University of Wales Press, 2004), p. 177.
[8] William Shakespeare, *Hamlet*, I. v. 159–62 (London and Glasgow: Collins, 1951).
[9] Niall Griffiths is also captivated by the kestrel as 'paragon of patience and plummet and rend and survive' in *Sheepshagger* (London: Vintage, 2002), p. 37.
[10] Derrida, *The Animal That Therefore I Am*, p. 9.
[11] Stephen Knight, *A Hundred Years of Fiction* (Cardiff: University of Wales Press, 2004), p. 178.

[12] Derrida, *The Animal That Therefore I Am*, pp. 3–4. Derrida's translator, David Wills, explains the play on the French *je suis* in Derrida's text, noting that it is the 'shared first person singular present form of *être* ("to be") and *suivre* ("to follow") [. . .] Throughout the book, especially its first two chapters, "I am" has, very often, to be read also as "I follow", and vice versa.' Derrida, *The Animal That Therefore I Am*, p. 162, translator's note.
[13] Neil Badmington, *Hitchcock's Magic* (Cardiff: University of Wales Press, 2011), p. 125. Italics in original.
[14] John Berger, 'Why Look at Animals?', in *About Looking* (London: Bloomsbury, 2009), pp. 3–28 (p. 5).
[15] Berger, 'Why Look at Animals?', p. 5. Italics in original.
[16] Derrida, *The Animal That Therefore I Am*, p. 10. Italics in original. American spelling retained.
[17] Derrida, *The Animal That Therefore I Am*, p. 11. American spelling retained.
[18] Andrew Bennett and Nicholas Royle, 'Animal', in Andrew Bennett and Nicholas Royle, *An Introduction to Literature, Criticism and Theory*, 4th edn (Harlow: Longman, 2009), pp. 151–9 (p. 154). Italics in original.
[19] See Eavan Boland, 'That the Science of Cartography is Limited', in *New Collected Poems* (Manchester: Carcanet, 2005), pp. 204–5.
[20] Genesis 1.28 (King James version).
[21] Donna J. Haraway, 'The Companion Species Manifesto', in *Manifestly Haraway* (Minneapolis and London: University of Minnesota Press, 2016), pp. 91–118 (p. 94).
[22] Haraway, 'The Companion Species Manifesto', p. 94.
[23] Haraway, 'The Companion Species Manifesto', p. 98.
[24] Haraway, 'The Companion Species Manifesto', p. 98.
[25] See Kirsti Bohata, *Postcolonialism Revisited* (Cardiff: University of Wales Press, 2004), and especially ch. 4, 'The Battle for the Hills: Politicized Landscapes and the Erasure of Place', pp. 80–103; Jarvis, *Welsh Environments in Contemporary Poetry*, p. 5. See R. S. Thomas, 'Afforestation', in *Collected Poems 1945–1990* (London: Phoenix, 2000), p. 130.
[26] Niall Griffiths, *Runt* (London: Jonathan Cape, 2007), p. 88.
[27] Griffiths, *Runt*, p. 88.
[28] Haraway, *Staying with the Trouble: Making Kin in the Chthulucene* (Durham, NC, and London: Duke University Press, 2016), p. 1.
[29] Haraway, *Staying with the Trouble*, p. 31.
[30] Haraway, *Staying with the Trouble*, p. 55.
[31] Griffiths, *Runt*, p. 101.
[32] Niall Griffiths, *Stump* (London: Vintage, 2006), p. 77.
[33] Haraway, *Staying with the Trouble*, p. 2.
[34] Haraway, *Staying with the Trouble*, p. 33.
[35] Griffiths, *Stump*, pp. 93–4.
[36] Griffiths, *Stump*, p. 95.
[37] Griffiths, *Stump*, p. 2.
[38] Haraway, *Staying with the Trouble*, p. 85.
[39] Griffiths, *Stump*, p. 115.

40 Griffiths, *Stump*, pp. 173, 174.
41 Laura Salisbury, 'Translating Neuroscience: Fictions of the Brain in the 2000s', in Nick Bentley, Nick Hubble and Leigh Wilson (eds), *The 2000s: A Decade of Contemporary British Fiction* (London: Bloomsbury, 2015), pp. 83–113 (p. 86).
42 Griffiths, *Runt*, p. 66.
43 Griffiths, *Runt*, p. 67.
44 Griffiths, *Runt*, p. 138.
45 Griffiths, *Runt*, pp. 140–1.
46 Griffiths, *Runt*, p. 141.
47 Griffiths, *Runt*, p. 142.
48 Griffiths, *Runt*, p. 91.

9

'WORD-OF-MOUTH CULTURES CEASE IN CEMETERIES'

John Pikoulis

'John Pikoulis profiles Ron Berry and his remarkable new novel, *This Bygone*' (essay reprinted, with revisions, from *New Welsh Review*, 9/1, 34 (Autumn 1996), 9–15)

I

He has just published his first novel in twenty-six years and his name is Ron Berry. Ron who? Twenty-six years is a long time and he has all but faded from the public eye, despite the stories he has published in the meantime. And yet he is a remarkable man. Now seventy-six, he is as candid and forceful as ever, though he and his family agree he has 'mellowed' over the years.

Barely five and a half feet tall, he is slender and balding with a fringe of fine grey hair. He is plagued by osteoarthritis and wears a neck collar; after two knee operations (one recent), he uses a walking stick and elbow stick.

Ron Berry was born in Blaenycwm, in the Rhondda, in 1920, the eldest in a family of five. His grandfather, an Englishman, was drawn from Blenheim by the coal Klondyke in Wales during the later years of the last century; his mother came from the Swansea valley. Though his parents were bilingual, he lost whatever Welsh he had when he went to school at the age of five. He was a restless boy – restlessness is one of the characteristics of his early life. He 'jibbed' or played truant at school, having falsified his father's signature confirming he had read his son's reports, and 'mitched' from Junior Tech, which he remembers as a 'mongrel institution'. Finally, he went down the pit (as his father had done before him) at the age of fourteen. What he experienced there forms the substance of *This Bygone*, his new novel, published by Gomer at £8.95.

As a young man, Berry was what he calls a 'Shoni Tarzan', one of the boys. A keen sportsman, he cycled and played rugby and, especially, football. He played for Swansea as an amateur. He also had a raging temper, derived, perhaps, from his mother, whom he calls a 'canny, long-headed' woman. His determination came from his father, a tough-minded, gentleman. From time to time, he would write love poems to the girls. On Sunday nights, he attended political meetings addressed by men like the Communist leader, Harry Pollitt. When he was fifteen, the (later) Speaker of the House of Commons, George Thomas, visited Treorchy Pavilion with a handkerchief up his cuff. It was the first cuffed handkerchief Berry had seen and he was impressed, though not sufficiently to make him want to vote for him. In fact, he has never voted in an election in his life. For him, all politicians are liars.

When France fell in 1940, most of the pits were shut or put into part time; no more export markets existed for them and there was no way of servicing them even if there were. Berry was drafted to Welbeck colliery village, near Mansfield, Nottinghamshire, under the Essential Works Order, and spent a few months working in the pit there. He never went underground as a miner again. After that he worked in the limestone tunnels dug near Portsmouth to serve as the Royal Navy's Headquarters during the conflict. He then became a fitter in an aircraft factory for about a year. After that, he joined the Merchant Navy – it was either that or the Army.

He completed only one journey, however, carrying supplies to the troops in North Africa. He lost two friends in a convoy attack and decided that the war was not for him. After much 'ducking-and-dodging', he gave the Merchant Navy the slip and returned to the Rhondda. Only if you had money could you vanish properly.

Back there, he suffered two misfortunes. The first was the result of an accident in a cup-tie match in 1943 in Porth when he collided with a full back, damaging his knee in the process; the cartilage was jammed in the joint. He never played football again. The knee was operated on once more a couple of years later. Before that, he was called up for Army service and sent with the Ordnance Corps first to Brecon and then to Sheffield. He was as unhappy there as he had been in the Merchant Navy. Within a year, he was reported missing AWOL. Fortunately, his knee was in such a poor state that he was discharged as medically unfit. That was the end of Berry's war.

Back in Blaenycwm, he attended a Training Centre and emerged as a carpenter. Towards the end of the war, he worked on the land and was drafted by the Labour Exchange first to Huntingdon and then to a spot deep in the country near Shrewsbury. The experience robbed him of the romance of nature. He also worked as a plate-layer during the building of the steelworks at Margam and in factories and building sites in London.

In 1948, he married Rene Jones and the two set up home in Blaenycwm in a house since demolished under slum-clearance. It was a hard life but not unusually so. Berry seemed to be searching for something and it led him into constant revolt against his circumstances. And yet he could not say what it was that he was searching for, only that he needed it as much as others need food and drink. But he has no regrets. He accepts the past with the shrewdness (and taciturnity) of the fated. He was living within the situation and trying to make what he could of it, as his hero in *This Bygone* does. Here is how he is introduced to the reader on the first page: 'Dewi Joshua had the self-contained style of youthful dream, feline eyes upslanted inside blunt cheekbones, his wedgy jaw pitted with a chin dimple. Dream dwelt in the light-flecked Tartar eyes' (*TB*, 5). Every phrase of that is arresting, taut and vivid. Here is the voice that Berry has made his own.

After marriage, he continued to move from job to job – or no job at all. As a result of his sporting injuries, osteoarthritis had set in and his mobility began to suffer as a result. He and Rene had five children: Lesley, Simone, Roderick, Maggie and Conrad. His friends included Mervyn Mathias, a clothing factory supervisor, who lent him books, Bob Thomas, the sculptor whose statue of Aneurin Bevan stands in Cardiff's Queen Street; he did a head of Berry, too, which remains in the family; and the artist, Jim 'Chunks' Lewis. At these meetings, words were flung from one to the other; he calls them 'aesthetic outings' run by amateurs without clout of any kind – they weren't even students. Even so, he was setting up as a writer of sorts, beginning with letters and progressing from there to poems and essays, some of which he submitted without success to the pre-eminent Welsh editors of the day, Keidrych Rhys and Gwyn Jones.

Sometime in the early 50s, he decided to go to Coleg Harlech, the residential college in north Wales which provided further education courses for mature students. However, he had no funds, so he wrote begging letters to the wealthy and famous, one of whom (another Berry) owned a Fleet Street newspaper; he responded. The result was a year at Coleg Harlech. Rene and the children stayed behind in the Rhondda. It was a bizarre experience but he enjoyed it. For once, he was dealing with an institution that was liberal and friendly.

After Harlech, he attended the Shoreditch Teachers' Training College but quit after only two terms. He calls it little better than a 'sausage factory' and he wanted no part of it. Besides which, he was devoting himself more to writing. While working as Assistant Manager in the swimming baths in Treherbert (where he and Rene now lived), he published essays in *John O'London's Weekly*. In 1960, his first novel, *Hunters and Hunted*, was published. In the following ten years, four more appeared – the last, *So Long, Hector Bebb*, in 1970. It took him eight years to write it, on and off; the style kept eluding him and he had to revise it until he found it. His other books came more easily. He was convinced that no-one had ever attempted anything like them before. *The Full-Time Amateur* attracted the attention of the film-maker, Bryan Forbes, but nothing came of it.

Then silence.

The silence was not of Berry's making; his novels were simply being rejected. The 1960s interest in 'regional novelists' had started to wane and the chill winds of mega publishing to blow. Let it stand as an indictment of the London publishing scene that he was silenced. Nothing daunted, he continued writing; as one novel was rejected, it was shelved and another begun. In this way, six novels were accumulated. He also wrote several plays for TV and radio, including 'Death of a Dog' for Yorkshire TV and 'Uncle Rollo' for BBC2, as well as a seventy-five-minute radio play, 'Everybody Loves Saturday Night' for Radio Wales. For a while in the early 1960s, he wrote interviews for the Pontardawe weekly *The Voice*, including one with a courteous but distant Vernon Watkins. He was also a reporter of Cardiff and Swansea home soccer games for the *Observer* for a season.

When he began to doubt his staying power as a novelist, he turned to a project he was to labour over for many hours – his autobiography. Three drafts of it emerged but it remains unpublished. The (Welsh) publisher who had agreed to bring it out decamped with the final draft when his empire collapsed and Berry is disinclined to revise it again.

When his children read it, he says, they discovered a very different father from the one they had known.

Berry calls himself a hopeless salesman of his work. If the novels don't fit, that is not his fault – he has done his best. Nowadays, he lives in an end-of-terrace house in Treherbert, near the top of the Rhondda, and does not mix much in literary circles. He has some supporters, notably Alun Richards and Dai Smith, and, in their time, Aled Vaughan and John Ormond, but no one has been able to reverse the tide of neglect he has suffered from. For a while, it seemed he would give up novel-writing altogether. In 1987, he brought out a book about peregrine falcons with Gomer. It was a throwback to his boyhood and, for ten years, he revelled in watching the birds, which had been shot to extinction in the 1930s but had returned to the Rhondda in the 1970s. It is as if R. S. Thomas had started writing about the birds of the Llŷn peninsula instead of poems.

And then he wrote a book about the mining life called *This Bygone*. For a century and more, coal mining was the supervening reality in south Wales but now it has vanished – no more astonishing turnaround could be imagined. Berry wished to record that milieu before it became the province of the historian. The title announces his memorial mission in recognition of a culture that disappeared only the day before yesterday. It took two years to write and he was in great good humour all that time, raking his youthful memories for material he could use, though the novel is neither autobiographical nor based on real-life characters.

The need to write it grew from the simple realisation that – as he puts it – 'word-of-mouth cultures cease in cemeteries'. Berry employs epigrammatic rhythms quite naturally and they have the effect of dignifying his thought with incisive reflection. 'Word-of-mouth culture' is what everyone lives (save, perhaps, those whom London *will* publish) but Berry's notion is lent additional authority by the Welsh writer's self-imposed obligation to give voice to the experiences of his people through a mixture of love, guilt and pity in a line that stretches back to the time of the bards. As Berry wrote, he stayed faithful to the language of the Rhondda, so much so that one of the ideal audiences for the novel will be the makers of dictionaries. Rarely has the sub-culture of the Rhondda received such impressive linguistic demonstration. For Berry, this is a badge of pride (or, as he would put it, necessity). It is what he knows better than anyone else. However, the issue is not simply one of fidelity to the subject for, in the tradition of the realistic novel from Gaskell and Dickens to Grassic Gibbon, Mark Twain to Faulkner, Berry is extending the boundaries of the realistic novel.

Though his initial doubt about whether he could sustain a novel of such scope and seriousness was dispelled by the need to bear witness to his own society, what he wrote turned into a challenging act of self-inquiry indistinguishable from his larger purpose. The novel bears a double focus: the individual and his society, the one folded into the other. Nothing illustrates this better than Berry's way of introducing characters (some quite minor) by noting their status, employment or marital or other relations in condensed histories that reflect a community's values. His lonely eye feeds on what it sees. Long ago, he realised that the price a man like him would have to pay for being a writer was loneliness and poverty. He could never write only on Sundays. Writing has been his passion and he comments on it with matter-of-factness that masks his dedication. He does not like inflating himself or indulging in self-pity and recrimination.

The author's photograph on the dust jacket of *Hunters and Hunted* shows a man who is far younger than Berry's forty years. He is handsome, full and fleshy in a polo-necked jersey – Richard Harris out of Laurence Harvey out of Richard Burton. He looks hopeful, 'butcher-y', and somehow already defeated. Upon the table at which he sits lies the object of his quizzical exasperation. Today, Berry is still handsome, with a spare, bird-like appearance and a confident, not to say challenging, humorous look. He has survived, and has now produced a work which invites comparison with earlier novelists of the coalfield like Lewis Jones and Gwyn Thomas. Berry hasn't read the former but admires Thomas, with qualifications. His novels, he says, will 'creak your head off' though he 'never sampled the muck and mire – he was an Oxford scholar. His slant on life was not mine.' Berry has seen his subject from the bottom up.

Fine as a documentary record *This Bygone* is, it is even more memorable as a stylistic achievement, elaborately artificial, as all fiction must be. 'The alternative to dissolution', Berry says, 'is to crystallise something as evidence. The books are a form of crystallisation' – or, in his case, carbonisation, for his prose is as sharp and gleaming as a lump of coal. 'You want the novel to be mint from yourself,' he says. That is what *This Bygone* is.

II

The novel tells the story of Dewi Saul Joshua. It opens in 1936, when he is eighteen, and takes him from collier in Pencaer pit to colliery owner (albeit on a small scale) during the war. It is also the story of Dewi, only son of Theo and Zena Joshua, becoming his own man. In a sense, the journey he makes is one from lack of definition (a remarkable result of his detachment from the Welsh tradition) to fulfilment. In another, it is the circle upon which he and Blaencwm tread, one over which they have little control. 'Everybody makes out as best they can', he declares near the end of the novel (*TB*, 179), and it is this minimalist philosophy that is pressed upon us.

Berry's portrait of the miners' life is unvarnished, spare, funny, biting and truthful. The words on the page, however, do not simply point to the subjects they describe – they possess a life of their own and attract as much attention as anything else. As they pile up, they flare into epiphanies, one true stroke leading to another.

In this scene, Dewi takes a dip in the Cwmffrwd colliery feeder dam before joining his 'butty', Irfon, and his wife, Hetty, for a picnic.

> Hetty Francis turned potatoes baking in the embers. 'Dewi! Try one of these.'
> He juggled the blackened potato from hand to hand.
> 'Pass the bloke some salt,' Irfon said.
> 'Reach it for himself, can't he!' She leered private triumph at Dewi. 'Shows what I got to put up with. This fella won't lift a finger.'
> He took a pinch of salt from a screw of greaseproof.
> [They then discuss the death of Dewi's previous butty.]
> Irfon blew, 'Phoo-phoo-phooph,' around a steaming bolus of potato. 'Us two'll be stretched out next to each other in Brynrhedyn [cemetery].'
> His wife gritted, 'That morbid mind of yours.'
> 'Me morbid?'
> 'Out of order,' smirked Hetty.
> Irfon thumbed his nose. 'Objection over-ruled. Address the bloody chair,' then, 'Scoot, you little bugger,' as his seven year old son flopped wetly on his lap. The child creamed angelic smiles at Hetty, writhing around to embrace his father's neck.
> 'Where to tonight, Ive?'
> 'Comrades' Club. You?'
> 'Do some pub crawling,' he said.

> Irfon lifted the boy, held him balanced, sitting on his head. 'I'll tan that arse for you,' and set him into skelping free, into the reaching arms of their eldest son.
>
> Hetty forked a chunk of potato to her mouth. 'Lovely kids they are.' Irfon chested pride. 'Eye-girl, you can say that agen.'
>
> Clear through a babble of children and water rose the desolate voice of the young tubercular wife of a Pencaer mains rider, I'm alone because I love you. The others left her soloist for a while, her twangy soprano out-pouring. Then soft humming finally released full-throated concord and running children held still, entranced, watching faces, grown-up brothers, sisters, mothers and fathers. (TB, 50–1)

What is interesting about this passage – and what prevents it lapsing into sentimentality – is its rarity value for Dewi, whose father died of 'the dust' when he was young and whose mother, Zena, 'changed to vinegar' (*TB*, 100) as a result, to the point where she lost her faith. Dewi cannot remember receiving kisses or smiles from her ever. All she does is idolise her dead husband and hold him up as a pattern for him to follow. Naturally enough, he revolts against them both and makes his own way in the world in the company of the formidable Elsie Kitchener, widow of his first butty, twenty-four years older than himself.

Elsie is probably the finest creation in the novel, a hard-bitten, capable, sensual woman, as Berry memorably puts it, an 'archetypal Venus, plaid dressing gown roped round her middle' (*TB*, 83).

> 'Realise this, [Dewi,] I'll be accused. My name'll be dirt.'
>
> 'Difference in our ages, you mean?
>
> 'Good looking fella you are, Dewi, but I'm old enough to be your . . .'
>
> 'Wait a minute,' he said. 'Leave the stupid buggers talk.'
>
> Delight enveloped her, teetering plumply summer-frocked on the pavement. [She thinks to herself.]
>
> 'I'm still a Dewinton Sixth Form girl at heart, but he's never been the boy to match the kind of girl I was. I can *bring him out*, look after him for years. Years. (*TB*, 54)

And bring him out – educate him – she does. She is the substitute mother he can love: 'Lovely boy you are,' she croons, 'my lovely boy' (*TB*, 23). Elsie is the triple goddess, 'helpmeet, earth mother and layer-out' (*TB*, 61), and her untimely death in the war robs Dewi of the love of his life. After that, he turns from his 'Ghost, eidolon, icon' (*TB*, 173) to his first girlfriend, Greta (a younger version of Elsie), a tough, sexually provocative businesswoman.

Accompanying this private history is a record of life in the Rhondda both beneath and above ground. Berry's authority is complete, especially when he employs the characters' vernacular idiom, technical talk and pithy humour.

> Chris fingered the teeth of his pit-saw. 'Ne'-mind, it's a steady job. I'll cut some lagging timbers.'
> 'Where you been working, Chris?'
> 'Four of us unloading duff in Aberselsig power station.'
> 'On bonus?'
> 'Not a red meg.'
> 'Donkey work, ah?'
> 'Long way there and back home was the trouble.' He tested the ring for movement. [He is tightening fishplate bolts.]
> 'Wedge, Dewi?'
> 'Few,' he said, 'then she'll stay firm while we lag-up the sides.'
> 'Sledge?'
> 'Course I want the bloody sledge.'
> Chris threw the sledgehammer. 'Watch your feet and less fucken lip.'
> '*Manno manno* fucken *shenko!*'
> Chris appealed, 'Keep your moss on for Chrissake.' (*TB*, 94)

Only Lewis Jones's 'Cwmardy' has realised pit life so authentically, but whereas Jones presents everything in order to rouse the reader's sympathetic anger, Berry maintains a scrupulous detachment. Here is Rhondda life, no more, no less.

His clipped dialogue is embedded in a narrative that resembles a cinema reel, now rolling fluently, now flicking from one briefly etched scene to another with the minimum of explanation. Throughout, his fidelity to his subject is apparent: 'Monday morning, the cage grounded like velvet at pit bottom' (*TB*, 24) – the omission of the definite article is typical of the style and lends it a telegraphic quality. 'Imperious Ossie', the checkweigher, is said to have 'deep sunken eyes glinty above the meaty snout of his nose, his scooped jawbone jowly from well-being' (*TB*, 31); a train in Gaer cutting sends up a 'windy gut-rumble' (*TB*, 30). When Irfon commiserates with Dewi on Elsie's death, 'They exchanged gently repetitive, fatalistic shoulder punches'

(*TB*, 127). On his first day as fireman, Dewi is greeted with the pluperfectly south Walian 'You-are, Dewi, sit over by there'. To which, one of the men choruses, 'Another fucken dot and carry on the books' (*TB*, 99).

Such native poetry is enhanced by Berry's habit of introducing dialogue with participial phrases, as if they were contemporary with his narration rather than being recalled, and the strongly transitive feel of sentences like this (explosives have been lit at the mouth of an old airway): 'earth and pulverised stones whined and hissed the frosted night' (*TB*, 83). Or take this typical passage: 'Cool wafts sliding down the tiered moraine whiffled abstract symmetries on Pwllmelyn pond. Fattening tadpoles writhed the shallows' (*TB*, 142–3). Rarely has English prose sounded so physical; the effect, though sometimes cramped, has a purchase on its subject like no other.

All this compression and angularity creates an extraordinary sharpness, the precision locking in the author's perceptions. When timbers creak and whine down the pit, they emit 'thin seeps faint as batsquealing' (*TB*, 57); when Dewi thinks of his life with Elsie, he 'waives[s] this review to zero' (*TB*, 82); when he apologises for bantering with Mrs Prudence Mackie, 'Bafflement whimsied her smile . . . She stepped away from him at the buffet table, murmur garbling from her like a troubled teenager. For no reason, Llew Kitchener silenced into Dewi's mind' (*TB*, 90–1). An inspector has 'the wary bonhomie of a guard dog' (*TB*, 147).

The flinty mosaic of Berry's style is at its most impressive in passages like this:

> He filled a rickety bucket with sump water, unscrewed the little filler cap, primed the pump, replaced the cap and triggered the switch down. Normally this was a labourer's job. Water hissing from a leaking manifold died to glassy wreathing. Rhythmic glugging sang inside the 2 inch pipeline. He studied the brattice nailed to a heavy wooden frame. The stiff sheets wafted ghostly, controlling airflow back to the main. He ran his fingertips over nail heads around the frame. Slowly walking away, he held high the Davy oil lamp. No gas. Safe. (*TB*, 100)

Such enthralling attentiveness! The poet laureate of the south Wales that was speaks.

Berry's perceptions act like small detonations or sharp prickles. After Elsie's death, Dewi experiences 'A sudden sense of wastage cold as sand' (*TB*, 132). There speaks the laureate of the human. And here is the laureate of nature:

> Two cock song thrushes vied for territories in Brynrhedyn, phrases repeated, inexplicably varied, repeated from bulging elms, distinct and vibrant above torpid dulciloquies of woodpigeons, above the oblivious (other than to raptors and chiffchaffs) onomatopoeia of chiffchaffs skulking, flick-flick-flick. Yellowhammers wheezed monotonous on gorsed slopes outside the cemetery wall, and from a shiver-throated starling on the chapel belltower, cutshort blackbird fluting and wheel-squeal mimicry. (*TB*, 177)

If the arc of Dewi's progress is towards fulfilment, there is still something missing in him. At one point, he declares: 'That's my answer. Action. Keep busy. Do, aye, DO' (*TB*, 141). Though his independence of mind and sense of responsibility are admirable, his minimalist philosophy seems to be a defence against any deeper involvement with others. It is as if the emotional scar of his parents goes too deep for healing. For Dewi, nothing exists but the moment – no larger aims, no aspirations, no political or trade union involvement. Despite the novel's crowding particulars, he exists in a vacuum.

He himself protests otherwise: 'He felt invulnerable, freed from his mother's depriving herself to rear him, delivered from the legacy of his father. Safe, his cap lamp softly whuffing. Secure and steadfast. Whole among men. And the other life with Elsie' (*TB*, 173). Is he, as he thinks, liberated by his passage through the novel or stunted by it? Even with Elsie, the source of his greatest happiness, a sense of unease persists, as if the great Earth Mother, with her greater grasp of life, enfeebles part of him, leaving him at odds with himself. By choice, they have no children. Eventually, his reticence seeps into the narrative, lending it a bleaker edge. When he becomes a mine owner himself, his mother congratulates him with: 'Yes, well, one thing for certain, your father would never have been his own boss, not in a hundred years.' That is the only time she prefers the live Dewi to the dead Theo, yet all he can respond with is: 'Makes a change' (*TB*, 156).

Dewi has certainly made the most of his opportunities but nothing has fundamentally changed. He works as hard as a pit owner as he did as a miner and at many of the same tasks. The level he owns is small and employs few. He may earn more money, but money never really mattered to him anyway. So what does Dewi want?

The truth may be: nothing at all. He aspires after a full and honourable life and achieves security but he remains the victim of the stunted 'bygone' the novel transcribes. When he declares, 'Everybody makes out as best they can', he does so 'cold as a robot'. When Greta becomes pregnant, he tells his butties. 'I'm supposed to feel excited, he thought. Supposed to be normal. Aye, normal. Here goes then, "We're having a kid, Ive. Nobody knows except Greta and me"' (*TB*, 201). When his mother hears the news, she is, as usual, digging and singing in the backyard (the novel makes as much play with popular song as a Dennis Potter play), 'her unconscious undertone hymnal [is] sweetly wailing, "*We're here because we're here because we're here because we're here, We're here because we're here we're here because we're here...*"' (*TB*, 202). The novel ends on that note, stoicism and meaningless endeavour being thrown into the balance.

Berry has little nostalgia for the 'bygone'. It existed, and he tells the reader about it, 'Boy inseparable from man in his time, in his place' (*TB*, 202). The boy continues to lurk in the adult, father to the man. There was undoubtedly a price to pay for subduing his life to the ethic of work, whatever other admirable attributes it produced, and Berry's remarkable novel counts the cost.

Afterword,
by Ron Berry's Children

Lesley: Ron – who never tried to teach me anything, but from whom I learned the most.

Simone: Ron – he could be no other way. He gave only his own example, and expected little.

Rod: My father – he was a wonderful grandfather to my children, I wish he had been more like that with his own children.

Maggie: My father – the writer. Not always there for me, but always for my son. He helped form him into the man he is today.

Conrad: Ron the cook – I learned never to ask what I was eating, his cooking habits were eclectic.

It is with some trepidation that we try to give an account of our family life. Among the multitude of maxims written by him, Ron said 'beware those who communicate easily', and 'it's hard to make a good sentence'. What can we say?

Well, we can write an affectionate story of life in our Ael y Bryn home, but its integrity will hold only with acknowledgement of Ron's complexities, his rogue personality. He had ferocious physicality, a passion for the natural world, and a singular perspective on the human condition. Ron also had – always – a belief in his literary worth. It is to be wondered how he somehow/sometimes held all this together in the chaos of a five-child family living in near absolute poverty. And to signify, to one and all, that writing came first, he raged at domestic distractions.

There always was evidence of difference. Simone recalls a teacher at primary school announcing to the class that her father, Ron Berry, was a writer who had a book published – a real book.

Lesley remembers her English teacher asking that Ron judge the competition stories by twelve-year-old girls. He did, and got payment in A1 tobacco.

Simone has many memories. Some early ones: 'Daddy' coming home from fishing with a khaki bag of rainbow trout from mountain streams. She remembers Ron teaching us which leaves and berries we could eat, what was poisonous, and naming the birds as they came into view or as we heard them sing.

Ron played harmonica at family gatherings. He talked to kids as if they were grown, yet we were all often addressed as 'boy/girl'.

We lived with the all-night tap-tap-tap of his portable typewriter. Daytime, we never missed Ron, never asked where he was. He would package up his doorstep cheese sandwiches, his flask of coffee and disappear, fishing, walking the hills, birdwatching, day after day, never forgetting his A1 tobacco. He was always jotting on scraps of paper. Language, language obsessed him.

As a child, Rod most remembers Ron's frustrations with lack of acknowledgement of his work, always waiting-waiting-waiting for something to happen. He was an unhappy man, a tortured writer who became a mellowed grandfather. Rod can recall his daughter, Bianca, play-acting with Ron's Dai cap and walking stick, joking with him, something we could never do as children. Ron was affectionate to all his grandchildren. Ron maintained a correspondence with Simone's daughter, whom he called Lizzie Fach, while she was studying dance at the Laban Centre in London. Lizzie was pleased to find that she could communicate with her grandfather about her studies, as he revealed a previously unknown interest in and knowledge of modern contemporary dance.

In Blaencwm, Ron kept pigs, sold vegetables, did odd jobs, carpentry, picked coal, and took us into the hills every Sunday. Simone has wonderful memories of winter mountain walks, single file in deep snowdrifts to the silent, high and frozen waterfall. At Ael y Bryn, he grew vegetables and fruit in the garden, cooked peasant stews with butchers' cast-off bones, fried trout, made blackcurrant wine. He repaired our worn-out shoes with scraps of leather, sought paper, typewriter reels, enough money to buy tobacco and a nightly drink in the Castle pub.

Somehow Ron acquired a motorbike, and later, a three-wheeled car. He was once again mobile and able to fulfil his imperative to be away, outside of society. From the cycling days of his youth, he knew Wales, and from his years as wanderer or itinerant labourer, he knew much of England, too.

For the most part, we necessarily became independent when quite young. Lesley stamped on piles of washing in the bath, there being no machine; she nursed the little ones to keep them quiet for Ron to write, and we all managed Rene's frustrations and breakdowns with some loyalty. From the age of eleven Lesley did the weekly shop, seeking out the cheapest basics in all the Treorchy shops. Ron thought her dependable enough to volunteer her to look after Alun Richards's four children when his wife had to have surgery!

Conrad remembers that his nine-year-old self was told to 'hold on' whilst on the back of Ron's motorbike going to Alun Richards's home in Swansea. They went sea-fishing on Alun's boat, and Conrad was told to swim back to shore with Alun's kids. Later, the children played while Ron and Alun talked (and drank) in the study all through the night. Nearly forty miles each way was quite the adventure in 1969; but they stayed for a good few days, so at least Ron was sober biking them home.

To us, it was normal family life. In fact, our upbringing was anything but normal. Rather, a weird mix of bohemia, disordered anarchy splattered with highly charged outbursts, from both parents. We knew for sure that we were poor, but other large families were also. It is surprising to realise that we rarely asked for anything.

Ron locked books away from us – Miller, Lawrence, Faulkner – we always found them, of course. His own work, we could read, or try to read. He said 'it takes an era of ego to navigate autobiography'. He handed out the manuscript with a 'read about the father you never knew you had'. But we did know. We had to know. Ageing changed him little. Yet as a single mother, Maggie was surprised at his empathy for her son. 'He'll call me Dad, so that he's got a Dad to talk about with his friends when he goes to school'. We called him Ron, as did all his grandchildren – except Tony.

What we can say, with integrity, his and ours, is that Ron knew himself – it was his grace and his gravity. He knew himself, and could only but *live* himself. Family sometimes had to be outside of that – his life. Ron was complicated, driven, passionate, honest and ultimately true to himself and his work.

Before the surgery that he never recovered from, Maggie asked Ron 'is there anything you want to do or anywhere you want to go, just in case . . .?' 'I've done everything I've ever wanted to do, girl', was his reply. He knew then that he was failing physically: 'I miss walking on grass.' He didn't mean the grass in the garden.

Ron wrote, 'a man can't renege on the way he's made', and 'inside my arrogance there is a core of humility'.

Bibliography

Austin, Craig, 'Great Welsh Novels Revisited: *So Long, Hector Bebb*', in *Wales Arts Review* (10 November 2016). Available at *www.walesartsreview.org/greatest-welsh-novel-6-so-long-hector-bebb-by-ron-berry*. Accessed 18 November 2016.

Badmington, Neil, *Hitchcock's Magic* (Cardiff: University of Wales Press, 2011).

Baker, Simon, 'Introduction', in Simon Baker (ed.), *Ron Berry: Collected Stories* (Llandysul: Gomer Press, 2000), pp. xii–xiii.

Bartra, Roger, *The Artificial Savage: Modern Myths of the Wild Man*, trans. Christopher Follett (Ann Arbor, MI: University of Michigan Press, 1997).

Bartra, Roger, *Wild Men in the Looking Glass*, trans. Carl T. Berrisford (Ann Arbor, MI: University of Michigan Press, 1994).

Baudrillard, Jean, *Simulacra and Simulation* (Ann Arbor, MI: University of Michigan Press, 1994).

Baudrillard, Jean, 'The Precession of Simulacra', *Simulations*, trans. Paul Foss, Paul Patton and Philip Beitchman (New York: Semiotext(e), 1983), pp. 1–75.

Bennett, Andrew, and Nicholas Royle, 'Animal', in Andrew Bennett and Nicholas Royle, *An Introduction to Literature, Criticism and Theory*, 4th edn (Harlow: Longman, 2009), pp. 151–9.

Berg, Peter, and R. Dasmann, 'Reinhabiting California', *The Ecologist*, 7 (10), 399–401.

Berger, John, 'Why Look at Animals?', in *About Looking* (London: Bloomsbury, 2009), pp. 3–28.

Berry, Ron, *Hunters and Hunted* (London: Hutchinson, 1960).

Berry, Ron, *Flame and Slag* (London: W. H. Allen, 1968).

Berry, Ron, *This Bygone* (Llandysul: Gomer Press, 1996).

Berry, Ron, *History Is What You Live* (Llandysul: Gomer Press, 1998).

Berry, Ron, *Ron Berry: Collected Stories*, ed. Simon Baker (Llandysul: Gomer Press, 2000).

Berry, Ron, *So Long, Hector Bebb* (Cardigan: Parthian, Library of Wales Series, 2006).

Berry, Ron, 'A Necessary Kind of Love', unpublished essay; copy given to John Perrott Jenkins by Berry's daughter, Lesley Berry.

Berry, Ron, 'The Disabled', unpublished short story; held amongst the other Berry Papers at the Richard Burton Archives, Swansea University, MSS 1, 2 and 3.

Beynon, H., and R. Hudson, *Coalfields Regeneration: Dealing with the Consequences of Industrial Decline* (Abingdon: Joseph Rowntree Foundation, Policy Press, 2000).

Boddy, Kasia, *Boxing: A Cultural History* (London: Reaktion, 2009).

Bohata, Kirsti, *Postcolonialism Revisited* (Cardiff: University of Wales Press, 2004).

Borsay, Anne, *Disability and Social Policy in Britain since 1750* (Hampshire: Palgrave Macmillan, 2005).

Bourdieu, Pierre, *Acts of Resistance* (Cambridge: Polity, 1998).

Bourdieu, Pierre, and Loïc Wacquant, *An Invitation to Reflexive Sociology* (Cambridge: Polity Press, 1992).

Buell, Lawrence, *The Environmental Imagination: Thoreau, Nature Writing and the Formation of American Culture* (Cambridge, MA: Belknap Press of Harvard University Press, 1995).

Buell, Lawrence, *Writing for an Endangered World* (Cambridge, MA: Belknap Press of Harvard University Press, 2001).

Burstyn, Varda, *The Rites of Men: Manhood, Politics and the Culture of Sport* (Toronto and London: University of Toronto Press, 1999).

Coleg Harlech, *Twenty-Eighth Annual Report, 1954–5* (Harlech, 1955).

Connell, R. W., 'An Iron Man: The Body and Some Contradictions of Hegemonic Masculinity', in Michael A. Messner and Donald F. Sabo (eds), *Sport, Men and the Gender Order* (Champaign, IL: Human Kinetic Books, 1990), pp. 83–95.

Crowe, Sylvia, *Tomorrow's Landscape* (London: Architectural Press, 1956).

Davies, Emma, '"Manufacturing Men": Literary Masculinities in Industrial Welsh Writing in English' (unpublished MA thesis, University of Swansea, 2001).

Defoe, Daniel, *Robinson Crusoe* [1729] (London: Penguin, 2012).

Derrida, Jacques, *The Animal That Therefore I Am*, ed. Marie-Louise Mallet, trans. David Wills (New York: Fordham University Press, 2008).

Dunk, Thomas W., *It's a Working Man's Town: Male Working-Class Culture* (Kingston and Montreal: McGill-Queens University Press, 2003 edn).

Eakin, Paul John, *Touching the World: Reference in Autobiography* (Princeton, NJ: Princeton University Press, 1992).

Farmer, R. A., 'Forestry in South Wales', *Forestry*, 66/2 (1993).

Forth, Christopher E., *Masculinity in the Modern West: Gender, Civilisation and the Body* (Basingstoke: Palgrave Macmillan, 2008).

Francis, Hywel, and Dai Smith, *The Fed: A History of the South Wales Miners*, 2nd edn (Cardiff: University of Wales Press, 1998).

Freud, Sigmund, 'Beyond the Pleasure Principle', in Angela Richards (ed.), *Penguin Freud Library*, trans. James Strachey (London: Penguin, 1984), vol. 11, pp. 275–338.

Geertz, Clifford, 'Deep Play: Notes on the Balinese Cockfight', *Daedalus*, 101/1 (1972), 1–37.

Gifford, Terry, *Pastoral* (London: Routledge, 1999).

Glancy, Mark, *Hollywood and the Americanisation of Britain: From the 1920s to the Present* (London: I. B. Taurus, 2014).

Griffiths, Niall, 'Foreword', Ron Berry, *So Long, Hector Bebb* (Cardigan: Parthian, 2006), pp. ix–xiii.

Griffiths, Niall, 'Book of a lifetime: Ron Berry, *So Long, Hector Bebb*', *Independent*, 17 December 2010. Available at: *https://www.independent.co.uk/arts-entertainment/books/reviews/book-of-a-lifetime-so-long-hector-bebb-by-ron-berry-2162262.html*. Accessed 12 November 2013.

Griffiths, Niall, *Runt* (London: Jonathan Cape, 2007).

Griffiths, Niall, *Stump* (London: Jonathan Cape, 2003).

Gullason, Thomas H., 'The Short Story: An Underrated Art', in *Studies in Short Fiction*, 2 (1964), 13–31.

Guttmann, Allen, *From Ritual to Record: The Nature of Modern Sports* (New York: Columbia University Press, 1978).

Haraway, Donna J., *Staying with the Trouble: Making Kin in the Chthulucene* (Durham, NC, and London: Duke University Press, 2016).

Haraway, Donna J., 'The Companion Species Manifesto', in *Manifestly Haraway* (Minneapolis and London: University of Minnesota Press, 2016), pp. 91–118.

Harsent, David A., 'Other New Novels', *Times Literary Supplement*, 3592 (1 January 1971), 5.

Hanson, Clare (ed.), *Re-Reading the Short Story* (London: Macmillan, 1989).

Hemingway, Ernest, 'Fifty Grand', in *Men Without Women* (London: Jonathan Cape, 1975), pp. 114–56.

Holt, Richard (ed.), *Sport and the Working Class in Modern Britain* (Manchester: Manchester University Press, 1990).

Jarman, T. Francis, 'Industrial Dust Disease: By the South Wales Medical Correspondent of *Medicine Today & Tomorrow*' (1939). Available at the SWCC pamphlet collection, South Wales Miners' Library, Swansea University.

Jarvis, Matthew, *Environments in Contemporary Welsh Poetry* (Cardiff: University of Wales Press, 2008).

Johnes, Martin, *Wales Since 1939* (Manchester: Manchester University Press, 2012).
Jones, Glyn, *The Dragon Has Two Tongues: Essays on Anglo-Welsh Writers and Writing*, ed. Tony Brown (Cardiff: University of Wales Press, 2001).
Kitchen, L., et al., 'Forestry and Environmental Democracy: The Problematic Case of the South Wales Valleys', *Journal of Environmental Policy & Planning*, 4 (2002), 139–55.
Knight, Stephen, *A Hundred Years of Fiction* (Cardiff: University of Wales Press, 2004).
Larkin, Philip, 'Aubade', in Philip Larkin, *Collected Poems* (London: Faber and Faber, 2003), pp. 171–2.
Leeworthy, Daryl, *A Little Gay History of Wales* (Cardiff: University of Wales Press, 2019).
Leeworthy, Daryl, *Labour Country: Political Radicalism and Social Democracy in South Wales, 1831–1985* (Cardigan: Parthian, 2018).
Leeworthy, Daryl, 'Partisan Players: Sport, Working-Class Culture and the Labour Movement in South Wales, 1918–1939', *Labor History*, 55/5 (2014), 580–93.
Linnard, William, *Welsh Woods and Forests: A History* (Llandysul: Gomer Press, 2000).
Lord Raglan, *The Hero: A Study in Tradition, Myth and Drama* (London: Methuen, 1936).
Malamud, Bernard, *The Natural* (New York: Harcourt Brace and Company, 1952).
Marx, Leo, 'Pastoralism in America', in Sacvan Bercovitch, Myra Jehlen and Albert Gelpi (eds), *Ideology and Classic American Literature* (Cambridge: Cambridge University Press, 1986), pp. 35–69.
McIvor, Arthur, and Ronald Johnston, *Miners' Lung: A History of Dust Disease in British Coal Mining* (Hampshire: Ashgate, 2007).
Mee, Bob, 'On This Day: Harry Greb dishes out one of boxing history's most savage beatings', in *Boxing News* (23 May 2019), n.p. Available at *boxingnewsonline.net*. Accessed 23 May 2019.
Minhinnick, Robert, 'A Rune Against Mendacity: At the Cremation of Ron Berry 22.07.97', *New Welsh Review*, 38 (Autumn 1997), 15.
Morgan, Kenneth O., *Rebirth of a Nation: A History of Modern Wales 1880–1980* (Oxford: Oxford University Press, 2001 [1982]).
Morrell, David, *First Blood* (London: Barrie and Jenkins, 1972).
Morse, Sarah, '"Maimed Individuals": The Significance of the Body in *So Long, Hector Bebb*', in Katie Gramich (ed.), *Mapping the Territory: Critical Approaches to Welsh Fiction in English* (Cardigan: Parthian, 2010), pp. 271–88.
National Clarion Cycling Club, *Handbook 1938*, pp. 157–61.

Oates, Joyce Carol, *On Boxing* (London: Bloomsbury, 1987).
Oates, Joyce Carol, *On Boxing* (New York: Ecco Press, 1995).
O'Brien, E. D., 'A Literary Lounger', *Illustrated London News*, 13 August 1960.
O'Connor, Frank, *The Lonely Voice: A Study of the Short Story* (London: Macmillan, 1963).
Office for National Statistics (ONS), Department for Work and Pensions (DWP), Department for Education and Skills (DfES) and National Assembly for Wales (2002), *Annual Local Area Labour Force Survey (LLFS) – Summary Publication 2001/02*.
Olney, James, *Metaphors of Self: The Meaning of Autobiography* (Princeton, NJ: Princeton University Press, 1972).
Osborne, Huw Edwin, *Rhys Davies* (Cardiff: University of Wales Press, 2009).
Pikoulis, John, 'Word-of-mouth cultures cease in cemeteries', *New Welsh Review*, 34 (Autumn 1996), 9–15.
Prys-Williams, Barbara, *Twentieth-Century Autobiography: Writing Wales in English* (Cardiff: University of Wales Press, 2004).
Richards, Alun, 'Letter to Ron Berry, 29 March 1963', in Dai Smith, *In the Frame* (Cardigan: Parthian, 2010), p. 192.
Richards, Alun, 'In Good Pasture: A memoir of Ron Berry and friends', *New Welsh Review*, 38 (Autumn 1997), 20. See Dai Smith, *In the Frame* (Cardigan: Parthian, 2010), p. 174.
Richards, Alun (ed.), *The Penguin Book of Welsh Short Stories* (Harmondsworth: Penguin, 1976).
Rimmon-Kenan, Shlomith, *Narrative Fiction: Contemporary Poetics* (London: Routledge, 1994).
Salisbury, Laura, 'Translating Neuroscience: Fictions of the Brain in the 2000s', in Nick Bentley, Nick Hubble and Leigh Wilson (eds), *The 2000s: A Decade of Contemporary British Fiction* (London: Bloomsbury, 2015), pp. 83–113.
Schama, Simon, *Landscape and Memory* (London: Fontana, 1996).
Sewel, John, *Colliery Closure and Social Change: A Study of a South Wales Mining Valley* (Cardiff: University of Wales Press, 1975).
Smith, A., and B. Twomey, 'Labour Market Experience of People with Disabilities', *Labour Market Trends* (August 2002), 415–27.
Smith, Dai, *Aneurin Bevan and the World of South Wales* (Cardiff: University of Wales Press, 1993).
Smith, Dai, 'An interview with Ron Berry' (1992), filmed by the Polytechnic of Wales as part of the Writers of Wales series.
Smith, Dai, 'An interview with Ron Berry', audio cassette recording, undated. Held at the South Wales Miner's Library, Swansea University. Transcribed by Georgia Burdett.

Smith, Dai (executive producer), *Read All About Us: Ron Berry* (BBC Wales, 1996).
Smith, Dai, 'Focal Heroes: A Welsh Fighting Class', in Richard Holt (ed.), *Sport and the Working Class in Modern Britain* (Manchester: Manchester University Press, 1990), pp. 198–217.
Smith, Dai, *In the Frame* (Cardigan: Parthian, 2010).
Smith, Dai, 'Introduction', in Ron Berry, *History Is What You Live* (Llandysul: Gomer Press, 1998).
Smith, Emma, 'Masculinity in Welsh Writing in English: the cases of Lewis Jones, Glyn Jones, Gwyn Thomas, and Ron Berry' (unpublished PhD thesis, Swansea University, 2006).
Smith, Emma, *Masculinity in Welsh Writing in English: The Cases of Lewis Jones, Glyn Jones, Gwyn Thomas and Ron Berry* (Saarbrücken: Verlag Dr Müller, 2009).
Sontag, Susan, *Illness as Metaphor* (London: Penguin Books, 1983).
The Coal Authority Environment Group, *The Environment* (July 1999).
The Richard Burton Archives, Swansea University, Ron Berry Papers, WWE/1/1/1.
The Richard Burton Archives, Swansea University, Ron Berry Papers, WWE/1/1/3/1.
The Richard Burton Archives, Swansea University, Ron Berry Papers, WWE/1/1/3/4.
The Richard Burton Archives, Swansea University, Ron Berry Papers, WWE/1/2/1/3.
The Richard Burton Archives, Swansea University, Ron Berry Papers, WWE/1/2/1/2.
The Richard Burton Archives, Swansea University, Ron Berry Papers, WWE/1/2/7/1.
The Richard Burton Archives, Swansea University, Ron Berry Papers, WWE/1/4/20.
The Richard Burton Archives, Swansea University, Ron Berry Papers, WWE/1/7/1/1.
The Richard Burton Archives, Swansea University, Ron Berry Papers, WWE/1/7/1/3.
The Richard Burton Archives, Swansea University, Ron Berry Papers, WWE/1/7/3/8.
The Richard Burton Archives, Swansea University, Ron Berry Papers, WWE/1/7/3/8.
The Richard Burton Archives, Swansea University, Ron Berry Papers, WWE/1/7/3/12.
The Richard Burton Archives, Swansea University, Ron Berry Papers, WWE/1/10/14.

Thomas, D. J., *Report of the Medical Officer of Health for Rhondda Urban District for the Year 1950* (Ferndale: W. T. Maddock, 1950).
Thomas, Gwyn, *A Welsh Eye* (London: Hutchinson, 1964).
Thomas, Gwyn, 'One Pair of Eyes' (BBC TV, 1968).
Thomas, M. Wynn, 'The Relentlessness of Emyr Humphreys', in *New Welsh Review*, 13 (1991), 37–40.
Thomas, Robert, 'Make it true, make it new', *New Welsh Review*, 38 (Autumn 1997), 14.
Times Literary Supplement, 3592 (1 January 1971), 5. Cited by Sarah Morse, '"Maimed Individuals": The Significance of the Body in *So Long, Hector Bebb* (1970)', in Katie Gramich (ed.), *Mapping the Territory: Critical Approaches to Welsh Fiction in English* (Cardigan: Parthian, 2010), pp. 271–87.
Tompkins, Jane, *West of Everything* (Oxford: Oxford University Press, 1992).
Toperoff, Sam, *Sugar Ray Leonard and Other Noble Warriors* (New York: McGraw-Hill, 1987).
Treasure, J. A. P., 'A study of the efficiency of groups of ex-miners disabled by Pneumoconiosis employed in light labour industries in South Wales', *The British Journal of Medicine*, 3 (1949), 127–38.
Trimbur, Lucia, '"Tough Love": Mediation and Articulation in the Urban Boxing Gym', *Ethnography* , 12/3 (2011), 334–55.
Virgil, *The Aeneid*, Book V, trans. W. F. Jackson Knight (Harmondsworth: Penguin Classics, 1963).
Wacquant, Loïc, 'Protection, discipline et honneur: une salle de boxe dans le ghetto américain', *Sociologie et Sociétés*, 27/1 (1995).
Wacquant, Loïc, 'The Pugilistic Point of View: How Boxers Think and Feel About Their Trade', *Theory and Society*, 24/4 (1995), 489–535.
Watt, Ian, *The Rise of the Novel* (Harmondsworth: Penguin, 1963).
Whiston Spirn, Anne, *The Language of Landscape* (New Haven, CT: Yale University Press, 1998), cited in Jim Perrin, 'Land and Freedom', *New Welsh Review*, 74, 8–18.
Williams, Daniel G., *Wales Unchained: Literature, Politics and Identity in the American Century* (Cardiff: University of Wales Press, 2015).
Williams, Gareth, '"The Dramatic Turbulence of some Irrecoverable Football Game": Sport, Literature and Welsh Identity', in Grant Jarvie (ed.), *Sport in the Making of Celtic Cultures* (London: Leicester University Press, 1999), pp. 55–70.
Winnifrith, Tom, 'Funeral Games in Homer and Virgil', in Michael Mallett (ed.), *Leisure in Art and Literature* (Basingstoke: Macmillan, 1992), pp. 14–26.
Winter, Michael, *Rural Politics: Policies for Agriculture, Forestry and the Environment* (London: Routledge, 1996).

Yamamoto, Dorothy, *The Boundaries of the Human in Medieval English Literature* (Oxford: Oxford University Press, 2000).

INDEX

Aberfan disaster 7, 15, 122
Anthropocene 123, 155
  see also Chthulucene

Baker, Simon 5, 70, 71
Barry, Desmond 91
Baudrillard, Jean 136
BBC 5, 89, 168
Berger, John 149
Berry, Rene (née Jones) 167, 168
Berry, Ron
  and American influence 5, 54, 60, 67(n), 70, 93
  career 24, 25, 26, 27, 29–30, 32, 69, 70, 71, 74, 77, 83, 85(n), 93, 94, 109, 166, 167, 168
  and class 2, 7, 22, 36, 73, 78, 79, 80, 81, 102, 104, 145
  disablement 92, 94, 101, 166,
  education 18, 19, 20, 70, 72, 85(n), 168
  family and relationships 13, 15, 17, 18–19, 21, 22, 25, 36, 47(n), 76, 78, 84, 177–80
  as historical witness 2, 6, 7, 14, 21, 27, 31, 45, 70–1, 72, 73, 76, 77, 83, 101, 117, 123, 137, 169, 170, 173, 176
  landscape 15, 16–17, 34, 42, 59, 76, 77, 116–17, 120, 127, 130, 131, 133–4, 135, 136, 137, 143,
  language use 6–8, 27, 30, 120, 165, 169, 174
  and masculinity 16, 18, 33, 35, 39, 40, 43, 46, 50, 51, 58, 61, 64, 70, 74, 78–9, 83, 84, 85, 99, 101, 110, 144
  and physicality 16, 19, 22, 39, 40, 51, 56, 70, 74, 84, 91, 92–3, 98, 102, 110
  political activism and views 9, 39, 40, 41, 72, 75–6, 86(n), 95, 105, 106, 123–4, 130, 131
  as reader 5, 7, 54, 93, 107, 170, 179
  on religion 23, 24, 41, 42, 53
  on sex and sexuality 35–6, 37–8, 44–5, 57–8, 73, 80, 84, 86(n), 102
  temperament of 14, 18–20, 22, 23, 26, 84, 92, 165–6, 177, 179–80
  on Wales and Welshness 10–11, 22, 109, 165
  on women 43–5, 80, 98–9, 100, 101, 172
  as writer 2, 6, 7, 28, 30, 31, 70, 94, 115, 142, 167, 178
  interviews:
    Firsthand, Radio Wales (1990), 5
    Read All About Us, BBC Wales, 5, 138
    Ron Berry Reading His Work and Talking to Professor Dai Smith (1992) 60, 72, 92, 105

short stories:
  Ron Berry: Collected Stories 5, 6, 46, 86
  'A Hero of 1938' 32, 33
  'Before Forever After' 29, 32, 41, 45, 102
  'Ben, the T.V. Playwright and his wife, Lottie' 29
  'Blood Money' 100
  'Boy and Girl' 43, 46
  'Clarion Boys' 33, 86
  'Comrades in Arms' 35, 44
  'End of Season' 33
  'King of the Foc'sle' 32
  'Left Behind' 42, 120, 123
  'Lew's Old Man' 41, 47
  'July Saturday in 1940' 105
  'Max Thomas' 32
  'My Uncle Dan' 36
  'Natives' 40, 42, 45, 96, 106, 107, 120
  'Nice Clean Place' 31
  'November Kill' 34, 44, 146, 150
  'Protocol Spin-Off' 32, 41
  'Reaping the Sown' 37, 45
  'Reardon Jones, MM' 37
  'Rosebud Prosser' 32, 44
  'Summer's End: Snaketown' 36
  'The Foxhunters' 35, 44
  'The Old Black Pasture' 1, 2, 33, 38
  'Time Spent' 30, 33, 38, 44, 97, 100, 101, 117
  'Who Belonged Just Long Enough Ago' 46(n)
non–fiction:
  History Is What You Live, 5, 13–28, 30, 36, 39, 41, 42, 71, 73, 74–6, 77, 85, 86, 94, 115, 117, 118, 120, 121, 122, 123, 125, 132
  Peregrine Watching, 5, 115, 127, 132, 134, 121, 142, 147–53, 162
novels:
  Flame and Slag, 10, 11, 113, 119, 120, 122, 127, 137
  Hunters and Hunted, 2, 4, 70, 72, 85, 99, 116, 137, 141–7, 168, 170
  So Long Hector Bebb, 5, 8, 29, 49–68, 71, 73, 74, 79–83, 137, 142, 168
  The Full Time Amateur, 29, 71, 73, 77–8, 85, 99, 101, 116, 117, 120, 123, 124, 137, 144, 168
  This Bygone, 2, 3, 4, 29, 71, 78, 95, 100, 104, 116, 165, 166, 167, 169, 170, 171, 172
  Travelling Loaded, 71
unpublished non-fiction
  'Sing a Song of Ego, Boy' 83–4
unpublished novels:
  'Splinters Off A Square Peg', 69, 76
  'Below Lord's Head Mountain', 115, 116, 126, 129, 132
  'More Guts Than Sense', 74, 75
unpublished short story:
  'The Disabled' 99, 104, 106–7, 112(n)

Bevan, Aneurin, 41, 80, 167
Bevin, Ernest 24, 27, 95,
Bohata, Kirsti 129, 152
Borsay, Anne 95, 102
Bourdieu, Pierre 78
Boxing 8, 39, 49–59, 73, 74–83, 85
Brecon 75, 76, 167
Buell, Lawrence 115, 121, 132

Cardiff 9, 15, 17, 69, 118, 120, 126, 134
Chthulucene 153, 156, 157
Coal mining 4, 15, 16, 18, 23, 71, 72, 76, 80, 83, 91, 94–7, 99, 108, 115, 119, 122–3, 130, 136, 144, 169
Coleg Harlech 20, 72, 168
Collieries 15–19, 32, 62, 81, 82, 116, 117, 120, 122, 127, 166, 171
Cycling 7, 17, 25, 33–4, 73–6, 179

Index

Davies, Rhys 31, 71, 79
Derrida, Jacques 143, 146, 148, 149, 150, 152
Disability 8, 91–113, 122,
Disabled Persons Employment Act (1944) 95
Dust 15, 16, 23, 30, 38, 91, 93, 96–8, 100–1, 106, 122, 172

Edwards, Dorothy 31
Epilepsy, 106, 154
Evans, Caradoc 37
Evans, Margiad 31

Farr, Tommy
 Berry's intended biography 87(n)
First World War 31
Football 69,70, 73–4, 76–7, 79, 84, 93, 125, 166
 see also Soccer
Forbes, Bryan 29, 168
Forestry Commission 15, 115, 126–34, 152–3
Forth, Christopher E. 50, 56, 57, 59

Gifford, Terry 115, 121, 132
Griffiths, Niall 5, 49, 79, 91, 109, 141–64

Hanson, Clare 31, 38
Haraway, Donna 151–3, 155–7, 159
Hemingway, Ernest 5, 55, 56, 67, 79
Hines, Barry
 Kes (1968) 81
Hopkins, Gerard Manley
 'The Windhover' 146
Horner, Arthur 75

Injury 22, 41, 65, 70, 81, 85, 92, 92, 94–6, 98, 101–2, 104, 105, 106, 120, 122, 167

Jarvis, Matthew 116, 141, 142, 148, 152
Johnes, Martin 27

Jones, Glyn 11, 31, 72, 109
Jones, Gwyn 72, 167
Jones, Lewis 5, 93, 101, 170, 173
Jones, Lloyd 91
Jones, Jack 5, 79, 93
Larkin, Philip 16
Lawrence, D. H. 4, 5, 179
Lewis, Alun 31
Lewis, Jim 'Chunks' 6, 18, 167

Merchant Navy 19, 23, 25–7, 71, 166
Miller, Henry 5, 93, 179
Minhinnick, Robert 108

National Coal Board 122, 124, 132
New Welsh Review 4, 30, 47(n)

Oates, Joyce Carol 50, 53, 58, 79, 81
Observer 69, 70, 168
O'Connor, Frank 31, 32, 38

Penguin Book of Welsh Short Stories (1976) 29
Planet: The Welsh Internationalist 29–30
Pollitt, Harry 86(n)
Pneumoconiosis 85, 94–8, 100–1, 117
 see also Dust

Remploy 97
Reservoirs 131, 152
Rhondda 2, 6, 8, 9, 14–18, 243, 25, 27, 70–2, 79, 83, 84, 92, 95, 115–17
 Blaencwm 9, 14, 15, 22, 92, 116, 117, 118, 121, 122, 125, 127, 129, 131, 132, 135, 137, 178
 Blaen y cwm *see* Blaencwm 9, 23, 92, 118, 124, 125, 165, 167
 Pen Pych 9, 15, 26, 92, 116–20, 125, 129
 Porth 75, 76, 83, 96, 166

Rhondda Fawr 2, 116–18, 136, 137
Treherbert 21, 26, 71, 77, 129, 168, 169
Treorchy 9, 16, 25, 75, 83, 85, 116, 166, 179
Richards, Alun 5, 10, 29, 70, 84, 169, 179
Memories of Ron Berry 29, 46(n)
see also Penguin Book of Welsh Short Stories

Salisbury, Laura 159
Second World War, 4, 31, 71, 76, 92, 166–7
Sillitoe, Alan 2
Saturday Night, Sunday Morning (1951) 73, 74
Smith, Dai 27, 49, 57, 60, 70, 72, 92, 93, 105, 109, 117, 169
Smith, Emma 62, 82, 98
Soccer 7, 28, 73–4, 76–8, 82, 85, 168
see also Football
Socialist Medical Association 97
Sontag, Susan
Illness as Metaphor (1978) 108
Storey, David 2
This Sporting Life (1960) 73
Swansea Town 69, 70, 76, 78, 93, 166, 168

Thomas, Dylan 31
Thomas, Gwyn 6, 10, 11, 70, 71, 72, 83, 93, 119, 170
Thomas R. S., 152, 163, 169
Thomas, Robert (Bob) 22, 46, 167
Tompkins, Jane 60, 62

Williams, Daniel G. 50, 81
Williams Parry, R.
'Y Llwynog' 159

Yeats, W. B. 77, 143